AQA

GCSE

Religious Studies A
Sikhism

Cynthia Bartlett
Marianne Fleming
Peter Smith
David Worden

Series editor
Cynthia Bartlett

OXFORD
UNIVERSITY PRESS

OXFORD
UNIVERSITY PRESS

Great Clarendon Street, Oxford, OX2 6DP, United Kingdom

Oxford University Press is a department of the University of Oxford. It furthers the University's objective of excellence in research, scholarship, and education by publishing worldwide. Oxford is a registered trade mark of Oxford University Press in the UK and in certain other countries

British Library Cataloguing in Publication Data
Data available

978-1-38-207356-1

(Kerboodle Book: 978-0-19-837065-0)

10 9 8 7 6 5 4 3 2 1

Paper used in the production of this book is a natural, recyclable product made from wood grown in sustainable forests. The manufacturing process conforms to the environmental regulations of the country of origin.

Printed and bound by CPI Group (UK) Ltd, Croydon, CR0 4YY

Links to third party websites are provided by Oxford in good faith and for information only. Oxford disclaims any responsibility for the materials contained in any third party website referenced in this work.

The manufacturer's authorised representative in the EU for product safety is Oxford University Press España S.A. of El Parque Empresarial San Fernando de Henares, Avenida de Castilla, 2 – 28830 Madrid (www.oup.es/en or product.safety@oup.com). OUP España S.A. also acts as importer into Spain of products made by the manufacturer.

Approval message from AQA

This textbook has been approved by AQA for use with our qualification. This means that we have checked that it broadly covers the specification and we are satisfied with the overall quality. Full details of our approval process can be found on our website.

We approve textbooks because we know how important it is for teachers and students to have the right resources to support their teaching and learning. However, the publisher is ultimately responsible for the editorial control and quality of this book.

Please note that when teaching the AQA GCSE Religious Studies course, you must refer to AQA's specification as your definitive source of information. While this book has been written to match the specification, it cannot provide complete coverage of every aspect of the course.

A wide range of other useful resources can be found on the relevant subject pages of our website: www.aqa.org.uk.

Please note that the Practice Questions in this book allow students a genuine attempt at practising exam skills, but they are not intended to replicate examination papers.

Contents

PART TWO: THEMATIC STUDIES

Chapter 3: Relationships and families

Chapter 4: Religion and life

Chapter 5: The existence of God and revelation

Chapter 6: Religion, peace and conflict

Chapter 7: Religion, crime and punishment

Chapter 8: Religion, human rights and social justice

Introduction

This book is written specifically for GCSE students studying the AQA Religious Studies Specification A, 3.1.7 Sikhism and 3.2.1 Religious, philosophical and ethical studies.

Chapters 1 and 2 cover the beliefs, teachings and practices of Sikhism, including beliefs about God, reincarnation, liberation and equality, and the way Sikhs live out their faith, including worship and festivals.

Chapters 3 to 8 cover religious, philosophical and ethical issues, including Relationships and families, Religion and life, the Existence of God and revelation, Religion, peace and conflict, Religion, crime and punishment, and Religion, human rights and social justice.

For the full course you must study two world religions, and four out of six of the philosophical and ethical themes. There are two examination papers, one on the religions and the other on the issues.

Assessment guidance

Each chapter has an assessment guidance section that helps you to familiarise yourself with the AQA paper. There are multiple-choice questions worth 1 mark, short-answer questions worth 1 mark, and longer questions worth 4 and 6 marks that test your ability to retell and explain facts. There are longer evaluation questions worth 12 marks that test your ability to analyse and evaluate different viewpoints.

Examination questions will test two assessment objectives, each representing 50 per cent of the total marks:

AO1: Demonstrate knowledge and understanding of religion and beliefs including:

- beliefs, practices and sources of authority
- influence on individuals, communities and societies
- similarities and differences within and/or between religions and beliefs.

AO2: Analyse and evaluate aspects of religion and belief, including their significance and influence.

For AO1 questions, the grid below gives guidance on how marks will be allocated:

Marks	Question type	Criteria
1 mark	Multiple choice	The correct answer chosen from 4 options
1 mark	Short-answer	One mark for a correct point
4 marks	Asking for two ways in which beliefs influence Sikhs today OR two different ways in which religion is practised OR two similar or different beliefs about an issue studied in the themes, including one from Christianity and one from another religion or in the case of theme C, non-religious perspectives	For each of the **two** ways / beliefs: • one mark for a simple explanation of a relevant and accurate way / belief; • two marks for a detailed explanation of a relevant and accurate way / belief
6 marks	Asking for two Sikh beliefs or teachings OR two Sikh practices OR two religious beliefs about a philosophical or ethical issue PLUS reference to scripture or sacred writings	For each of the **two** beliefs / practices: • one mark for a simple explanation of a relevant and accurate belief / practice; • two marks for a detailed explanation of a relevant and accurate belief / practice; **PLUS** one mark for naming a relevant, accurate scripture or sacred writing, and one mark for applying it to the question

The grid below gives you some guidance on different levels for the 12 mark evaluation question (testing AO2).

Levels	Criteria	Marks
4	A well-argued response, reasoned consideration of different points of view Logical chains of reasoning leading to judgement(s) supported by knowledge and understanding of relevant evidence and information	10–12
3	Reasoned consideration of different points of view Logical chains of reasoning that draw on knowledge and understanding of relevant evidence and information	7–9
2	Reasoned consideration of a point of view A logical chain of reasoning drawing on knowledge and understanding of relevant evidence and information OR Recognition of different points of view, each supported by relevant reasons / evidence	4–6
1	Point of view with reason(s) stated in support	1–3
0	Nothing worthy of credit	0

For the latest mark schemes, please also refer to the AQA website.

In modern Britain Sikhs practise their religion alongside people from many different faiths. The AQA GCSE specification requires that students understand Christian beliefs on three issues in each of the ethical and philosophical themes and are able to compare these with other faith perspectives, including Sikhism (or between Christianity and non-religious viewpoints in the case of Theme C).

Theme	Students must be able to explain different beliefs on the following:
A: Relationships and families	• Contraception • Sexual relationships before marriage • Same-sex sexual relationships
B: Religion and life	• Abortion • Euthanasia • Animal experimentation
C: The existence of God and revelation	• Visions • Miracles • Nature as general revelation
D: Religion, peace and conflict	• Violence • Weapons of mass destruction • Pacifism
E: Religion, crime and punishment	• Corporal punishment • Death penalty • Forgiveness
F: Religion, human rights and social justice	• Status of women in religion • The uses of wealth • Freedom of religious expression

You should also bear in mind non-religious views such as atheism and humanism, and understand the influence of beliefs teachings and practices on individuals, communities and societies.

Spelling, punctuation and grammar (SPaG) is also important so it will be useful to practise the 12 mark extended writing questions. There are 3 marks available for SPaG: 1 mark for threshold performance, 2 marks for intermediate performance and 3 marks for high performance. You should aim to write correctly using a wide range of specialist religious terms.

Examination grades will be awarded on a scale of 9-1, with 9 representing the best performance.

Kerboodle book

An online version of this book is available for student access, with an added bank of tools for you to personalise the book.

Part 1: The study of religions

1 Beliefs and teachings

1.1 The nature of God

■ The origins of Sikhism

The Sikh way of life began more than 550 years ago in the Punjab, a part of South Asia in which Hindus and Muslims were living. The word **Sikh** means a learner or a disciple. Today, there are about 30 million Sikhs worldwide, of whom approximately 432,000 were recorded in 2011 as living in the UK.

Sikhs call their faith or religion 'Sikhi' (a way or path of learning) or the 'Sikh dharam' (a wise and responsible way of life, and the training to live such a life). 'Sikhism' is the western word used to describe this religious tradition. It was founded by ten consecutive **Gurus**, beginning with Guru Nanak. Today, Sikhs revere their sacred scripture, the **Guru Granth Sahib**, as a living Guru. It includes the verses of the early Sikh Gurus and saints from other faiths.

■ The nature of God

Sikhs believe that God is beyond human description and beyond gender. Sikhs do use 'he' and 'him' but only to be able to talk and write easily about God. They believe that any words used to describe God's greatness are inadequate, although the words of sacred teachings expand their awareness of God's greatness. Sikhs believe that God can be experienced because he reveals himself to individuals. For example, his presence is communicated through Naam (the eternal 'word' or vibration of God's presence that we can tune into by living with wisdom and virtues), by absorbing scripture and by remembering God with words such as Satnam ('True Name', meaning God's presence is life's constant truth), and by learning through the Guru (one who enlightens).

Sikhs believe that God has no limits. God is immanent and so is in everything. At the same time he is transcendent, above and beyond creation. Sikhs have many names for God but none can describe properly the nature of God. Waheguru (Wonderful Lord or Teacher) is one name which Sikhs use in meditation.

■ The Mool Mantra

The Guru Granth Sahib opens with words of the **Mool Mantra**, meaning 'root chant'. Sikhs believe that this was the first teaching revealed to Guru Nanak, after he had become enlightened. It summarises Sikh teachings on the nature of God and starts with 'Ik Onkar'.

Objectives

- Understand Sikh beliefs about the nature of God.
- Consider the importance of the Mool Mantra for Sikhs.

Key terms

- **Sikh:** a learner or a disciple; a believer in the religion of Sikhism
- **Guru:** a spiritual teacher of wisdom; there are ten Gurus in Sikh history, followed by the Guru Granth Sahib, 'the living Guru'
- **Guru Granth Sahib:** the holy scriptures of the Sikh faith, regarded as the ultimate authority
- **Mool Mantra:** the 'root chant', a statement of all the core beliefs at the beginning of the Guru Granth Sahib
- **gurdwara:** a Sikh place of worship; it literally means 'the door of the Guru'

Research activity

Use the internet to find out about other names Sikhs use for God. Start by looking up 'Akal Purakh'.

'God is One and All is God' (Ik Onkar): God is the one Creator, whose eternal presence vibrates within and beyond all creation. For Sikhs, to remember God's oneness is to recognise the oneness of creation and of the human family, and to live by values that help everyone flourish.

'The Name Is Truth (Satnam)': the word for truth is Sat and God is sometimes addressed as Satnam. God is eternal Truth and can be reached by humans if they reflect on truth.

'Creative Being Personified' (Karta Purakh): God is present in the creation that he made. He is present in the souls of human beings who can therefore understand what is right and what is wrong; so it is possible for humans to have a personal relationship with God.

'No Fear (Nirbhau). No Hatred (Nirvair)': there is no fear or hatred in God because God is One and there is nothing else. Fear and hatred can only arise if someone or something causes it and another is affected by it. God is not subject to any other being. He is One.

'Image Of The Undying (Akaal Moorat)': God is eternal, beyond time, and there has never been a time when God did not exist. God is changeless.

'Beyond Birth (Ajooni)': God is not born and cannot die. God is immortal, unlike humans who exist in a cycle of birth and death.

'Self-Existent (Saibhang)': nothing brought God into being. God was not caused by anything that came before God nor is he dependent on anything else.

'By Guru's Grace (Gur Prasad)': God makes himself known through his word. If Sikhs try to understand God's word, through worship and prayer and in the way they live, they will receive God's blessing.

Sikhs believe that this one God is the God of all religions, the God everyone worships. Therefore, different religions are all paths that humans take to reach the one God.

■ The importance of the Mool Mantra

The Mool Mantra is the most important statement for Sikhs and summarises Sikh beliefs. Sikhs say the Mool Mantra daily in their prayers. It is also recited in worship and in the ceremony of initiation at the gurdwara. The first words of the Mool Mantra, 'Ik Onkar', as written in Punjabi, are used as a symbol of the Sikh religion. They can be found in the gurdwaras or in Sikh homes.

> ❝ One Universal Creator God.
> The Name Is Truth.
> Creative Being Personified.
> No Fear. No Hatred.
> Image Of The Undying,
> Beyond Birth,
> Self-Existent.
> By Guru's Grace … ❞
> *Guru Granth Sahib 1*
> *(the Mool Mantra)*

▲ *The words which begin the Mool Mantra – a symbol of the Oneness of God*

> ❝ My Lord of the Universe is great, unapproachable, unfathomable, primal, immaculate and formless. His condition cannot be described; His Glorious Greatness is immeasurable. My Lord of the Universe is invisible and infinite. ❞
> *Guru Granth Sahib 448*

⭐ Study tip

Try to learn the different phrases of the Mool Mantra. They will help you remember Sikh beliefs about God.

Summary

You should now understand Sikh beliefs about the nature of God and the importance of the Mool Mantra.

Activities

1 What does the word 'Sikh' mean?
2 Explain the importance of the Ik Onkar symbol for Sikhs.
3 Why do Sikhs have many names for God?

■ God the Creator

Sikhs believe that God created everything: the world, the universe and any other universes that may exist. There are no creation stories in Sikhism. God brought into existence creation, including all universes, and has sustained it since then. Sikhs accept scientific views

▲ *'He created the sun and the moon; night and day, they move according to His Thought' (Guru Granth Sahib 580)*

about how life was created, such as the theory of evolution, but believe that all is done through God's will. God wills the universe to exist and gives order to everything. Sometimes the world is described as God's 'pastime' or his 'play'. This does not suggest that the world is a trivial thing that God does not take seriously, but rather indicates the greatness of God compared with the world in which humans live, and the fact that God created it.

■ God as unknowable, beyond time and space

Sikhs understand that God is beyond complete human understanding and beyond names. He is eternal (beyond time), infinite (beyond space), and formless (beyond the forms and limits of creation). The term 'nirgun' (meaning without material qualities or characteristics) describes this aspect of God. God was present before the creation when there was nothing else. While human language cannot express what God is like, sacred teachings help Sikhs to remember God's presence as a mystery that cannot be explored beyond their everyday lives.

> ❝ He is the Perfect Transcendent Lord, from the very beginning, and throughout the ages. ❞
>
> *Guru Granth Sahib 397*

■ Perceiving God's presence in the universe

Sikhs believe that every part of the universe reveals God's oneness. The energy of God's eternal presence vibrates everywhere, with a hidden wisdom and power that constantly creates, sustains and connects everything that exists. God's light is in all things and is present within every human being as the soul or divine spirit.

Objectives

- Understand Sikh beliefs about God as **Creator**.
- Consider how God may be shown in and through the universe, as well as being separate from the universe.

Key terms

- **Creator:** the one who makes things and brings things about
- **monotheistic:** believing in only one God

> ❝ He established the earth, the sky and the air, the water of the oceans, fire and food. He created the moon, the stars and the sun, night and day and mountains; he blessed the trees with flowers and fruits. He created the gods, human beings and the seven seas; He established the three worlds. ❞
>
> *Guru Granth Sahib 1399*

> ❝ Great is the Play of God! He Himself laughs, and He Himself thinks; He Himself illumines the sun and the moon. He Himself is the water, He Himself is the earth and its support. He Himself abides in each and every heart. ❞
>
> *Guru Granth Sahib 1404*

Sikhs use the word 'sargun' (meaning with material characteristics or qualities) to describe this aspect of God, which is revealed through creation. As a result, Sikhs understand there are ways in which God can be grasped by humans, through sacred teachings like the Mool Mantra, by observing nature, and by searching within. Uniquely within all of creation, humans have the ability to reason and make wise choices, instead of being completely controlled by impulses. This means humans have a unique potential to connect with God.

> 66 Sing the Praise of the One, the Immaculate Lord; He is contained within all … He pervades the continents, solar systems, nether worlds, islands and all worlds. 99
>
> *Guru Granth Sahib 706*

Stories from Sikh tradition

Guru Nanak made several long journeys during his lifetime, teaching about God. It is said that on one journey he visited Makkah. He was tired and lay down to rest. He went to sleep with his feet pointing towards the famous shrine there, the Ka'aba. A night watchman, doing his rounds, found the Guru and kicked him and asked him how he could dare to point his feet towards the holy shrine – it was a sign of lack of respect for God. Guru Nanak replied, 'Kindly turn my feet in the direction where God is not.'

Because Sikhism emphases one Creator, it is often described as **monotheistic**. However, while the Sikh Gurus recognised that God is beyond time and space, they observed how people dismissed the life around them by focusing on God as separate from this world, or reachable only in the afterlife. Hence the Gurus put great emphasis on God's presence within the universe, as a divine light in all beings or as harmony that humans can tune into, to live a good and fruitful life. All Sikh teachings, values and practices develop from this combined view of God, as beyond yet firmly within creation. Sikhs understand that to lovingly serve creation is to lovingly serve the Creator.

Activities

1 Explain the importance of the Sikh belief that God is the Creator.

2 Explain why it is important to Sikhs that in the beginning was God and nothing else. Consider the words of the Mool Mantra on page 9 to help answer this question.

3 In what ways do Sikhs understand that God reveals himself within the universe?

4 Explain why Sikhs believe that God is both separate from the universe and shown in and through the universe.

> 66 Forever and ever, **He is the One, the One Universal Creator.** Many millions are created in various forms. From God they emanate, and into God they merge once again. His limits are not known to anyone. Of Himself, and by Himself, O Nanak, God exists. 99
>
> *Guru Granth Sahib 276*

> 66 You are without colour or mark. The Lord is seen to be manifest and present. 99
>
> *Guru Granth Sahib 74*

Links

To find out more about Guru Nanak, look at pages 22–23.

Activity

Read the story from Sikh tradition. Suggest the reaction of Muslims and Sikhs to the teaching of Guru Nanak on this occasion.

Extension activity

Use the internet to find out more about Guru Nanak's visit to Makkah (Mecca).

⭐ Study tip

Try to learn short phrases from the quotations which show Sikh beliefs about the Creator.

Summary

You should now understand Sikh beliefs about God the Creator, and how he is both within and separate from the universe.

■ Union with God

Sikhs believe that God has given humans an opportunity to reunite with him. Life is seen as a cycle of birth, death and rebirth but the aim of life is to become one with God. This means being able to move from the cycle of life and death into an existence which God has planned, which he wills for humanity, and which is a blissful, perfect state. Humans can do much to achieve this through the kind of life they live, although God's grace and mercy need to be accepted as well, since human nature is not perfect. While Sikhs hope to make good spiritual progress during a lifetime, they accept that it may take several lifetimes before they can be liberated and reunited with God. Sikhs believe that there are five basic virtues and many others that can be developed during the life of any human.

■ The virtues

Truth and truthful living

God is truth and so to get close to God, Sikhs need to live a truthful life. Truth is involved in many aspects of daily life. **Truthful living** includes speaking the truth, being realistic, working honestly, acting fairly and treating all as equals. In fact, **justice** is another virtue that is part of truthful living because it recognises unfairness and seeks to put right the wrong. Justice recognises the rights of all people and works to protect them; it will respect all equally, and oppose exploitation.

Compassion and patience

Sikhs believe that **compassion** is a quality that God possesses. God is seen as merciful, looking with kindness and goodness on everything he has created. He wills the best for his creation and so human beings should do the same. In practical terms, this means being aware of the needs of others, their suffering and their vulnerability, being careful and kindly in speech, and serving others. In this way, compassion also involves **patience**. Sikhs should be tolerant of others, forgive their faults or weaknesses, and be prepared to make sacrifices for others. It needs determination and an ability to recognise God in others; patience is part of kindness.

Contentment

In remembering God, Sikhs try to live a life that is centred on him and not on desiring things they do not have or on gaining material possessions. Sikhs are encouraged to accept the life that has been given to them by God and to try to do God's will. They believe that **contentment** leads to happiness because it gets rid of worry for the future and fear of the unknown. This may seem to be good and sensible advice but in fact it is difficult to achieve and needs to be worked at. Sikhs can do this by focusing on God and not thinking about themselves.

Objectives

- Consider the Sikh belief that human life is an opportunity to unite with God.
- Know and understand why Sikhs are expected to develop virtues.

Key term

- **truthful living:** following God, who is Truth, in the way in which life is led; it includes spreading the truth, and honesty and fairness in dealings with others

Links

To learn more about rebirth and liberation, see pages 14–17.

> ❝ Truth is higher than everything; but higher still is truthful living. ❞
> *Guru Granth Sahib 62*

Humility and self-control

Humility is an attitude which Sikhs believe should be shown towards God and others. It is a recognition that before God, humans should not believe in their own importance because God is the ultimate reality. His greatness and power cannot be described and in comparison with God, humans must be humble. Equally they should not be self-important in their dealings with other people or believe that they have more to give or more important things to say than others. **Self-control** is therefore very important in developing and achieving the ability to be humble. Sikhs should engage in self-discipline, regular prayer and bringing God to mind. Another word for self-control is **temperance**, which means to act, think or speak in moderation, making sure that one is in control. By meditating on God's name and so eliminating evil thoughts, humility and self-control can be developed.

Love

Sikhs believe that God is a loving God and so in response to God, Sikhs must also be full of **love**. A loving attitude means that Sikhs accept everyone with whom they come into contact for the people they are, and they treat them with kindness and respect. Sikhs should not hate anyone and should forgive any wrong that is done to them. They believe that part of their loving response to God is to serve others and show love towards them.

Wisdom and courage

In a sense, to have **wisdom** means to understand the importance of all the Sikh virtues. Wisdom involves the knowledge and understanding of religious beliefs and principles, and an ability to put this knowledge to good effect in daily living. For Sikhs, wisdom will result in living a good life, with high moral standards and a desire to live a life as close to God as possible. No one expects to find this easy and so Sikhs believe that **courage** is another important virtue. There are many people in Sikh history, including the Ten Gurus, who have shown great courage in remaining true to their faith and to Sikh principles. Courage takes great spiritual strength, often in the face of suffering; some of the Gurus showed such courage in sacrificing their lives for their beliefs, and for the right of others to practise their faith.

> IF YOU HAVE EVER DONE A GOOD DEED FOR SOMEONE OR IF SOMEONE HAS DONE A BAD DEED UPON YOU, FORGET BOTH INSTANTLY.
>
> BACHAN SANT BABA ISHER SINGH JI (RARA SAHIB WALE)

▲ 'Be kind to all beings – this is more meritorious than bathing at the sixty-eight sacred shrines of pilgrimage and the giving of charity.' (Guru Granth Sahib 136)

> " My mind is imbued with the Lord's Love; it is dyed a deep crimson. Truth and charity are my white clothes. "
>
> *Guru Granth Sahib 16*

Discussion activity

Look at the poster to the left and discuss what it means. What virtues does the poster encourage?

Activities

1 Explain how Sikhs can reach union with God.

2 How do Sikhs try to achieve contentment?

3 Describe ways in which a person could achieve 'truthful living' in relation to their friends.

4 What difference would truthful living make to relationships?

Extension activity

Find out which of the Ten Gurus died because of their religious beliefs, and the reasons for their deaths.

⭐ Study tip

Write a list of the Sikh virtues and try to learn them so that you can refer to them when writing about Sikh life.

Summary

You should now understand the Sikh belief that human life provides an opportunity to unite with God and that to do so means developing Sikh virtues.

1.4 Karma, rebirth and mukti

■ Rebirth

Sikhs believe in **reincarnation**, which means that when a human being dies, their soul is reborn into another body. Such a **rebirth** is part of a cycle of being born, dying and being reborn. The cycle will keep repeating itself until the soul is liberated or freed from this pattern and becomes united with God.

> 6 Those who do not serve the True Guru [God], and who do not contemplate the Word of the Shabad – spiritual wisdom does not enter into their hearts; they are like dead bodies in the world. They go through the cycle of 8.4 million reincarnations, and they are ruined through death and rebirth. 9
>
> *Guru Granth Sahib 88*

Sikhs believe that all animals, including human beings, have souls, and at death the soul changes its form of life and will be reborn into a new stage of its existence. The goal is to achieve liberation from rebirth.

■ Karma

Karma is a term which Hindus and Buddhists use as well. It refers to the sum total of a person's actions and words, which determine what happens to that individual in the future. So, given that individuals may have many rebirths into this world, the actions they have done previously will affect both their future and the kind of existence they have. Sometimes karma is described as 'destiny' because it relates to what will happen in the future.

> 6 The body is the field of karma in this age; whatever you plant, you shall harvest. 9
>
> *Guru Granth Sahib 78*

The belief in karma means that for Sikhs, rebirth is not a random event but something that depends on what they have done previously. Sikhs believe that being born as a human being on Earth indicates that an individual has done good things in previous lives and that God's will has caused this to happen. Once born as a human, a person has the opportunity to make further progress towards liberation, and needs to make the most of what God has given. They can do this in two ways. First, they can build up good karma by doing good and behaving well towards others, and second, by receiving God's grace.

While karma may be used to explain suffering, Sikhs are taught not to judge, because God is a mystery and God's will cannot be explained. Remembering the Creator and serving his creation are ways to work through the negative burden of karma and grow through acceptance.

▲ *Sikhs believe that all living beings have souls*

> 6 By the karma of past actions, the robe of this physical body is obtained. By His Grace, the Gate of Liberation is found. 9
>
> *Guru Granth Sahib 2*

⭐ Study tip

Make sure you know how the key terms used on these pages are connected.

Stories from Sikh tradition

There is a traditional Sikh story about a man who is blind. One day, he reads the thoughts of a passing stranger. The stranger has assumed the man is blind because he is being punished for not seeing something important in a past life. The man who is blind chuckles, remarking that he too had been quick to unfairly judge others in a past life. This story helps us reflect on Sikh teachings about karma, the idea that whatever we think and do has ripple effects in our life and across lifetimes.

The concept of karma had long been established in the religious traditions of South Asia. On the one hand, the Sikh Gurus accepted that it helps people be more self-aware and accountable for what they do. But they also critiqued how people used it as an excuse to judge others, to justify suffering, to stay stuck where they were, or to perform actions and rituals in a calculating and self-centred way for personal spiritual gain. The Gurus taught that people need to base their actions on doing what is good and right, and lead a selfless, worthy and fruitful life.

So, instead of focusing too rigidly on cause and effect, the Gurus encourage Sikhs to think more about the overall mindset formed through accumulated thoughts and actions, which move us closer to, or further away from, God. They also emphasise the mystery of divine will and the active support of divine grace. This teaches Sikhs that we cannot always truly know the reasons for our circumstances. We have to balance acceptance, trust and patience with taking the initiative to do the right thing and rise to the best in us.

■ Mukti

The word **mukti** means 'liberation', 'freedom', 'release' and is also sometimes translated as 'salvation'. This is the point at which the mind is free from the hold of the ego, allowing the soul to connect and unite with God. The Gurus taught that a person cannot achieve mukti by selfishly seeking it. It comes about through a genuine commitment to developing a selfless state of spiritual awareness. This means that it is possible to achieve mukti when you are alive, and a person who has achieved mukti is called a jivan mukat.

To achieve mukti involves overcoming, disentangling and freeing the mind from thoughts, impulses and actions that move a person further away from God. This helps cleanse the soul of negative imprints from their present life or past lives. The focus here is what to detach from to achieve mukti. The path to mukti also involves taking positive steps. It involves a process, with Sikhs learning in stages to transform their inner selves through their way of life. Sikh teachings emphasise that mukti is enabled, not just by our efforts, but by divine grace. The experience of mukti cannot be described but Sikhs understand it as a state where ultimate bliss, happiness, contentment and peace are to be found.

Research activity

Use the internet to search for Sikh descriptions of mukti. Divide your notes into two columns headed 'Positive' and 'Negative', and decide where the descriptions you find best fit.

Discussion activity

With a partner, consider the events that have happened in your own lives during the past 24 hours. Discuss whether things might have been different if you had decided in advance to keep a list of the good and bad actions you had taken during that time.

Activities

1 **a** What did the Gurus observe about the concept of karma?
  b How did the Gurus develop the concept of karma as a result of their observations?

Summary
You should now understand the meaning of karma, rebirth and mukti, and be able to explain their importance to Sikhs.

1.5 The five stages of liberation

The stages of liberation

Sikhs believe that there are five stages (**khands**) through which a human being can pass and that will lead to God, the Ultimate Truth or Reality. These stages are like the stages of a journey and usually they will not all happen within one lifetime. As Sikhs move through these stages, there is no suggestion that they should withdraw from the world to concentrate on God. Sikhs believe that living in community is what God intends for human beings and that it is through daily life that God is revealed. These stages of **liberation** from the cycle of birth, death and rebirth can be passed through while living a normal life, provided that a person becomes God-centred.

The five khands

The five khands are piety, knowledge, effort, grace and truth.

All human beings are born into the stage of **piety**, which enables them to meet with God through commitment or devotion to him.

Knowledge is gained once an individual has begun to devote time to God and learn about him. With knowledge, they begin to be aware of how vast the universe is and how little they know about God or their own existence. The more a person knows, the more they realise how vast is the amount of knowledge to be gained and how little they know of it. This helps them to become humble, spiritually aware and open to God.

By devoting oneself totally to God, an individual develops their mind and their intelligence as far as it is possible for a human being to do. The person has made the **effort** to 'tune in' to God and develop their personality and gifts as far as they can.

Grace is only reached when God takes a part in the development of the individual. God, through his love, enables spiritual growth and strength. Grace is a blessing from God; it results in the person being at peace in themselves, knowing God.

> **❝** By the Grace of the Holy, let your mind be imbued with the Lord's love. **❞**
>
> *Guru Granth Sahib 866*

The final stage involves finding God in his completeness. God is **truth** and this stage cannot really be described at all, just experienced.

Barriers to mukti

Sikhs believe that if they understand what gets in the way of spiritual progress, or moving closer to God, they will be more able to avoid or control it. Sikhs believe that illusion, self-centredness and the five evils take people away from God. The five evils are regarded as opposites to the virtues that Sikhs need to develop.

Objectives

- Know and understand the five stages of liberation.
- Consider barriers to salvation, including illusion, self-centredness and the five evils.

Key terms

- **khand:** a stage or a part of human spiritual development
- **liberation:** freedom from the cycle of life, death and rebirth
- **piety (dharam khand):** the first stage of liberation; the opportunity for devotion to God
- **knowledge (gian khand):** the second stage of liberation; knowing God through experiencing him
- **effort (saram khand):** the third stage of liberation; the limit of development by human effort
- **grace (karam khand):** the fourth stage of liberation; spiritual blessing given by God
- **truth (sach khand):** the fifth stage of liberation; the realisation of God
- **illusion:** everything in the world which seems real, but is not; in Sikhism called maya

> **❝** Why do you take pride in trivial matters? Like an overnight guest, you shall arise and depart in the morning. Why are you so attached to your household? It is all like flowers in the garden. **❞**
>
> *Guru Granth Sahib 50*

Illusion and self-centredness

One of the difficulties that can prevent individuals from spiritual growth is the **illusion** that the things in life that will not last, which are brief and impermanent, are the things that are permanent and valuable. This illusion is like an addiction that prevents people from seeing the truth. It means they cannot escape the cycle of life, death and rebirth.

Self-centredness, sometimes called ego, prevents people from getting close to God and obeying his will. The development of the Sikh virtues, such as humility, contentment and the willingness to serve other people (sewa), helps Sikhs to turn away from self-centredness.

▲ For Sikhs, contributing to the community and taking part in sewa help to prevent self-centredness

The five evils

The five evils are anger (krodh), lust (kam), greed (lobdh), worldy attachment (moh) and pride (ahankar).

Anger results usually from a lack of self-control. This emotion causes someone to stop thinking and to act without balance. For Sikhs, hatred, which often leads to anger, is not acceptable when directed at a person whom God created.

Uncontrolled **lust** and sexual desire outside marriage is seen to result in weakness and lack of balance. It can lead people to further wrongdoing and may encourage untruthfulness and lack of reliability. Sikhs believe that sex within marriage is good and part of God's will, but sex outside marriage, or within marriage when it is against the partner's will, leads people further away from God.

Greed results in a desire to possess more than what one needs for daily life, and possibly leads to a wish to possess what belongs to someone else. It is selfish and self-centred. It results from a lack of self-control and from ignoring the principles of equality and justice. It centres life on material things, and spiritual life is neglected.

Worldly attachment is connected with greed because both place too great an emphasis on possessions and relationships within the world. As a result, they may remove the desire for spiritual growth and the development of the mind needed to recognise God. It moves a person's priorities away from God.

Sometimes the evil of **pride** is called 'false' pride because it involves being proud of things which are given, rather than achieved, or things that are not important, such as intelligence, talent or material wealth. Pride leads people away from humility and the basic belief in the equality of all, and makes them feel more important than others. It encourages unhelpful reactions in others, such as jealousy or rivalry, or simply makes people unhappy with their own situation.

Activity

Draw a diagram with a person in the centre. On one side place all the Sikh virtues and on the other the barriers to mukti, including the five evils. You can refer to this diagram when studying.

Activities

1 What do Sikhs mean by 'illusion'?

2 Explain why self-centredness prevents individuals from approaching God.

3 'For Sikhs, it is easier to avoid the five evils than to develop the Sikh virtues.' Evaluate this statement, giving two points of view and developed arguments to support them.

> ❝ **Those who are committed to the Nam, see the world as merely a temporary pasture.** Sexual desire and anger are broken, like a jar of poison. ❞
>
> *Guru Granth Sahib 153*

⭐ Study tip

You do not need to learn the Punjabi terms for the five stages or the five evils, but try to learn the English translations and what they mean.

Summary

You should now understand the five stages of liberation, and understand how illusion, self-centredness and the five evils act as barriers to mukti.

Gurmukh (God-centred)

Sikhs aim to have their mind centred on God at all times. A God-centred person (**gurmukh**) has turned towards God and is in this sense becoming a perfect person, as God intended. Such a person lives in accordance with Sikh teaching and meditates on the Name of God. He or she is free from attachment, pride and ego, and from the evils that can overwhelm a person, and instead does good because it is good, not for any other motive.

> ❝ The Gurmukh attains infinite spiritual wisdom and meditation. **The Gurmukh acts in harmony with God's Will; the Gurmukh finds perfection.** The mind of the Gurmukh turns away from the world … he merges in the True Lord. He truly practises Truth forever; true devotion is implanted within him. ❞
>
> *Guru Granth Sahib 1058*

Manmukh (man-centred)

Manmukh describes people who are centred on themselves and their own desires. They are attached to worldly wealth and things that will not last. They are not content with life because they always want more. They are not aware of the needs of others and so their way of life is selfish and self-centred. They constantly think about 'I', the ego, and act in the world in a way that will satisfy their own desires. Their words and actions and their lifestyle are controlled by the five evils and by the illusion that convinces them that temporary material things are permanent and important. This prevents them from being liberated and achieving mukti.

> ❝ The foolish self-willed manmukh does not remember the Lord, and shall regret and repent hereafter. Thus says Nanak: O mind, you are full of pride; loaded with pride, you shall depart. O mind, don't be so proud of yourself, as if you know it all … ❞
>
> *Guru Granth Sahib 144*

> ❝ The self-willed manmukh is blind in the world; his mind is lured away by sexual desire and anger … The Gurmukhs earn the wealth of the Lord, contemplating the Word of the Guru's Shabad. They receive the wealth of the Naam; their treasures are overflowing … they utter the Glorious Praises of the Lord … Within the Gurmukh is intuitive peace and poise … ❞
>
> *Guru Granth Sahib 1414*

Objectives

- Understand the importance for Sikhs of being God-centred rather than man-centred.
- Know and understand why Sikhs believe they should eliminate pride or ego.

Key terms

- **gurmukh:** God-centred; wisdom-centred
- **manmukh:** self-centred; ego-centred
- **haumai:** pride or self (ego); relying only on oneself, not God

Links

For more information on the barriers to mukti, see pages 16–17.

▲ *Meditating on the name of God helps Sikhs to become gurmukh*

■ Haumai

Haumai is difficult to translate exactly; it can mean 'pride', 'self-reliance' or 'egotism'. For many people, self-reliance would be seen as a good thing, a virtue, and of course in some ways it is. However, Guru Nanak taught that this quality often prevented individuals from understanding their dependence on God and from wanting to seek liberation. He wanted people to understand that while they try on their own to affect what happens in the present or in the future and do not listen to or obey God, there is no chance of release from rebirth. Haumai is sometimes described as a spiritual disease which those who are manmukh have. It produces confusion and brings suffering. It takes over a person's life and the only way to overcome it is to become gurmukh, to remember God and to forget self.

> **"** Living in ego, mortal beings are created. When one understands ego, then the Lord's gate is known. **"**
>
> *Guru Granth Sahib 466*

> **"** **Egotism [haumai] is opposed to the Name of the Lord;** the two do not dwell in the same place. In egotism, selfless service cannot be performed, and so the mind goes unfulfilled. **"**
>
> *Guru Granth Sahib 560*

Stories from Sikh tradition

The two villages

Guru Nanak and his disciple Mardana came to a village and wanted to rest for a while. They knocked on the door of a house and asked where the inn was. The man shut the door in their face with the words, 'Visitors are not welcome here'. They went to several other houses but people were rude, unhelpful and unwelcoming. 'Go away,' they said. 'There's nowhere like that around here; we don't like visitors.'

Guru Nanak decided to walk on to the next village. A man saw them coming. He said that he could see they were thirsty and hungry and he asked them if they would like a drink of water. Then he asked them whether they needed a place to stay and told them that he had a friend who would give them a meal and rooms for the night. As they talked, other people came past and were friendly. They had a good night's sleep and went on their way.

As they walked, Guru Nanak said, 'I hope that village is uprooted and scattered.' Mardana was amazed and suggested that surely it would be better if that happened to the first village. 'No,' said Guru Nanak, 'if the selfish people in the first village were scattered across the world, the whole world will become selfish. If the people in the last village were spread across the world, they would make it a better place.'

Sikhs believe that some people are able to live moral lives and sometimes do good things, but they do not understand that too great an attachment to worldly things causes suffering and prevents someone from seeking God, the eternal and ultimate reality. It may be that the 'happier' one is with life, the less likely one is to recognise the need for God.

> **"** Suffering is the medicine, and pleasure the disease, because where there is pleasure, there is no desire for God. **"**
>
> *Guru Granth Sahib 469*

⭐ Study tip

In Sikhism the word 'Guru' can refer to one of the Ten Gurus, to the Guru Granth Sahib or sometimes to God. This helps to explain words like gurdwara ('the door of the Guru') and gurmukh ('God-centred').

Summary

You should now know and understand the meaning of the key terms of gurmukh, manmukh and haumai, and be able to explain their importance for Sikhs.

Activities

1 Explain the difference between gurmukh and manmukh.
2 Suggest three things that Sikhs might do to become gurmukh, and three things that would lead them to becoming manmukh.
3 Explain the meaning of the story of 'The two villages'.

The oneness of humanity and the equality of all

Guru Nanak, the founder of Sikhism, was born into a country influenced by both the Muslim and Hindu religions. After his revelation, he strongly believed that God was One and that there were many ways of approaching God, not just one way. He said, 'God is neither Hindu nor Muslim and the path I follow is God's'. Sikhs believe in the **oneness of humanity** and do not feel the need to convert others to Sikhism – they believe that there are many different paths to God and each individual can find their way, with support from their community and by God's good grace. All these approaches to God are equally valid and deserve respect. Therefore, Sikhism is a tolerant and inclusive faith. Sikhs are expected to honour and protect the rights of others to practise their faith.

> ❝ Call everyone exalted; no one seems lowly. The One Lord has fashioned the vessels, and His One Light pervades the three worlds. ❞
>
> *Guru Granth Sahib 62*

Sikhs believe that all creatures are created by God. God intended them to be created and it is his will. People do not know why they were created; this is something that only God knows. However, humans are unique among the creatures. They can make judgements, they can distinguish between right and wrong, and within them is a divine spark that is from God.

Guru Ram Das taught: 'There is only one breath; all are made of the same clay; the light within all is the same. The One Light pervades all the many and various beings.' (Guru Granth Sahib 96). So humans are 'one' and of equal worth. There can be no distinctions that are made by humans which God recognises.

If God is within all people, then living and working with others in peace and harmony is essential. No one should be rejected or neglected.

> ❝ … the Lord is said to be permeating each and every heart. He looks alike upon the high and the low, the ant and the elephant. Friends, companions, children and relatives are all created by Him. ❞
>
> *Guru Granth Sahib 319*

■ The langar: equality in practice

It was the belief in the **equality of all** that led Guru Nanak to introduce the langar, a free meal. All gurdwaras continue this custom. The practice demonstrates the Sikh belief in the oneness of humanity and the equality of every human being. All eat together, men and women, rich and poor, people of different faiths and of none. The food is always vegetarian,

Objectives

- Understand Sikh beliefs in the oneness of humanity and in the equality of all, and their importance for Sikh life.
- Know and understand the significance of the five Ks as symbols of the Sikh faith.

Key terms

- **oneness of humanity:** the belief that since all humans were created by God, they all have within them the divine spark which unites them
- **equality of all:** the state of all humans being equal, especially in status, rights and opportunities
- **amritdhari:** a Sikh who has been initiated into the Khalsa; sometimes known as a 'Khalsa Sikh'. See page 24–25 to learn more about amritdhari.

> ❝ Recognise the Lord's Light within all, and do not consider social class or status; there are no classes or castes in the world hereafter. ❞
>
> *Guru Granth Sahib 349*

⭐ Study tip

Learn two or three key phrases from the quotations on this page. This will help you when discussing the oneness and equality of human beings.

Links

To find out more about the langar, see pages 22–23 and 42–43.

which means that those who have different rules about how meat is prepared and eaten, and those who do not eat particular kinds of meat, are not offended and everyone can eat together. Any Sikh, male or female, may prepare, cook and serve the food.

■ Equality within the Sikh community

Within the Sikh community, all are regarded as equals. Everyone is treated with respect and honoured, irrespective of gender, disability, race, class or wealth, and the importance of the unity of the community is emphasised. Both Sikh men and Sikh women take part in worship, reading the Guru Granth Sahib, playing music, and cooking or serving in the langar. Any man or woman, regardless of their status, can be initiated and become **amritdhari** Sikhs.

■ The five Ks

Amritdhari Sikhs are required to wear the five Ks to remind them of their faith, wherever they are and whatever they are doing. Many other Sikhs, who are not yet initiated, also wear some or all of the five Ks. These items are a symbol of the unity and equality within their faith community. In whichever part of the world Sikhs live, the five Ks can be seen, and are daily reminders of the Sikh faith. They also remind Sikhs of their responsibilities as members of the community of Sikhs.

1 **Kesh (uncut hair):** Sikhs believe that their hair is a gift God has given to all humans; it was intended to be worn naturally and not cut. It is covered with a turban (seen as a 'crown') to keep it clean. The turban itself is not one of the five Ks.

2 **Kanga (a wooden comb):** This is carried to maintain the tidiness of the kesh and to remind Sikhs of the need to keep their body and mind in a healthy state.

3 **Kara (a steel bracelet):** As a circle the kara represents an unbreakable bond of devotion to God, and a pledge to live in harmony with the divine will. It reminds Sikhs to be hardworking, generous, ethical, and accountable.

4 **Kachhehra (cotton underwear):** This underwear is comfortable and modest. It is reminder of the traditional role of Sikhs as soldiers, being prepared to act quickly and with dignity, and of the need for self-control and chastity (and also a reminder not to commit adultery and to have self-control).

5 **Kirpan (a small sword):** This represents the inner strengths of wisdom and virtue, and the need to uphold goodness in the world and to defend the downtrodden. It reminds Sikhs to maintain a noble, kind and courageous character.

▲ *A special langar meal organised in India, on the occasion of Guru Nanak's birthday anniversary*

▲ *The Sikhs in this photo are wearing karas, to symbolise an unbreakable bond with God*

Activities

1 List the different ways in which Sikhs show that everyone is equal.

2 Draw a grid with two columns, headed 'The five Ks' and 'Importance'. In the left-hand column, draw each of the five Ks. In the right-hand column, write the meaning of each one.

3 'Wearing the five Ks reminds Sikhs of their belief in the equality of all.' What is your opinion? Give reasons to support your point of view.

Summary

You should now understand Sikh beliefs in the oneness of humanity and the equality of all. You should also understand the symbolism and importance of the five Ks.

Discussion activity

Discuss the importance for Sikhs of wearing the five Ks. What are the advantages and/or disadvantages of wearing visible symbols of a faith?

Guru Nanak's life

Guru Nanak was the founder of the Sikh faith. He was born in April 1469 CE in Talwandi, a village in the Punjab. No one is sure what he looked like but Sikhs use paintings of the Guru to represent him and his message. His family were Hindus, but when he was about 13 years old, he rejected the sacred thread ceremony which Hindu boys often take part in when being initiated into the Hindu faith. His father was an accountant and worked for local government run by Muslims. As a child, Guru Nanak was well educated and learnt Arabic and Persian. He had both Muslim and Hindu friends. He married while still a teenager and later had two sons. He worked as a storekeeper for some time but early in the mornings and in the evenings he could be found meditating and singing, accompanied by his Muslim friend, Mardana.

The river experience

One day Guru Nanak went down to wash at the river Bain as usual but did not return. His clothes were still by the bank. Three days later he reappeared at the same spot but at first seemed to be in a trance and was silent. Later he told people that he had had a vision. He had been to God's court. This experience is described in the Guru Granth Sahib:

> ❝ My Lord and Master has summoned me, His minstrel, to the True Mansion of His Presence. He has dressed me in the robes of His True Praise and Glory. The Ambrosial Nectar of the True Name has become my food. ❞
>
> *Guru Granth Sahib 150*

He was changed. He gave up his job and gave all his belongings to people living in poverty. He believed that all religious people were searching for the same God whose Name was Truth. The various ceremonies and rituals that they performed were only ways of trying to connect with a God who was literally wonderful and indescribable. He told people: 'There is no Hindu, no Muslim.' All humanity is created by God and is equal.

Guru Nanak's teaching on equality

Guru Nanak is said to have travelled widely across India and the Middle East, including visits to Sri Lanka, Makkah and Baghdad. He always showed great respect to those who held different religious beliefs and spent time teaching about God.

Guru Nanak believed in the equality of man and woman. He taught that all humanity, created by God, was equal in value. He respected both men and women and believed that they could take an equal share in worship and within the Sikh community. In the time of Guru Nanak, women were often treated less favourably than men and they played a

▲ *Guru Nanak*

Links

To learn more about the river experience and its significance, see page 109.

⭐ Study tip

It is important to know about Guru Nanak's teaching and his influence on Sikhism.

very small part in religious and social life. Guru Nanak believed in the equality of all and wanted to change this.

> **"** From woman, man is born; within woman, man is conceived; to woman he is engaged and married. Woman becomes his friend; through woman, the future generations come. When his woman dies, he seeks another woman; to woman he is bound. So why call her bad? From her, kings are born. From woman, woman is born; without woman, there would be no one at all. **"**
>
> *Guru Granth Sahib 473*

In about 1520, he settled in Kartapur and this new town became a Sikh community, working, praying and learning together. He had been concerned about the inequality and hardship caused by the Hindu caste system, in which people of different castes did not eat together and he wanted to underline the importance of everyone being equal. So he developed the idea of a free kitchen, a **langar**, which provided hospitality for everyone, not just for Sikhs, and served only vegetarian food. Sikhs, male and female, prepared, cooked and served the food and all ate together. This tradition has continued since the time of Guru Nanak. The Rehat Maryada, the Sikh code of conduct, sets out the reasons for this practice:

> **"** Guru's kitchen-cum-eating House [the langar]. The philosophy behind the Guru's kitchen-cum-eating house is two fold: to provide training to the Sikhs in voluntary service and to help banish all distinction of high and low, touchable and untouchable from the Sikhs minds. **"**
>
> *Rehat Maryada, article 21*

The teaching and practice of the langar was continued by the Gurus. In fact, Guru Amar Das decided that no one, however important, would be able to talk with him until they had first shared a meal in the langar.

▲ *In the langar, all are considered equal through the sharing of a meal*

Discussion activity

'Gender equality is to do with how people are treated and valued rather than whether people of different genders are capable of doing the same things.' Discuss this with a partner or a small group.

> **" All human beings, high or low, and of any caste or colour may sit and eat in the Guru's kitchen-cum-eating house.** No discrimination on grounds of the country of origin, colour, caste or religion must be made while making people sit in rows for eating. **"**
>
> *Rehat Maryada, article 21*

Activities

1 Explain how Guru Nanak's upbringing may have influenced his teaching.
2 Why did Guru Nanak believe that eating together was an important activity?
3 Explain why Guru Nanak believed that women were of equal status to men.

Extension activity

Use the internet to research more about Guru Nanak's life and find out about the Janam Sakhis (stories about the life of Guru Nanak). Write down a list of events that you think influenced his teaching.

Summary

You should now know and understand the importance of Guru Nanak for Sikhism and the contribution he made to the belief in the equality of all.

1.9 Equality and Guru Gobind Singh

■ The Ten Gurus

After Guru Nanak died, the Sikhs were led by nine other Gurus in human form, who all contributed to Sikh history and beliefs in different ways. Some of their teaching is also included in the Guru Granth Sahib. The list of the Ten Gurus gives the dates during which they led the Sikh community. In the case of Guru Nanak, the first date marks the date of his experience in the river Bain, which changed his life and began the Sikh faith.

The Ten Gurus	Dates
Guru Nanak	1469–1539
Guru Angad	1539–1552
Guru Amar Das	1552–1574
Guru Ram Das	1574–1581
Guru Arjan	1581–1606
Guru Hargobind	1606–1644
Guru Har Rai	1644–1661
Guru Har Krishnan	1661–1664
Guru Tegh Bahadur	1664–1675
Guru Gobind Singh	1675–1708

■ Guru Gobind Singh

Guru Gobind Singh was nine years old when he became the tenth Guru. He was influenced by his father, Guru Tegh Bahadur, who had supported equality and freedom of belief and been martyred for refusing to become a Muslim. His death was seen to support the rights of Hindus as well as Sikhs to follow the faith they chose, and Guru Gobind Singh continued his work.

During Guru Gobind Singh's rule, the Sikh community developed and was strengthened by his leadership. The Guru was a great poet and wrote much poetry. After his death, a follower, Bhai Mani Singh, collected the poems together in a book, which became known as the Dasam Granth, the book of the Tenth Guru.

In 1708, when Guru Gobind Singh knew he would not recover from a wound he had received, he declared that, after his death, the Guru Granth Sahib would be the final Guru. He believed that 'the living Guru' would teach and lead the Sikh community. Sikhs now use exact copies of the Guru Granth Sahib as he had established it.

■ The Khalsa

One of the most important actions Guru Gobind Singh took was to establish the **Khalsa**, the body of committed Sikhs into which Sikhs would be initiated. He did this at the festival of Vaisakhi in 1699 in a very dramatic way that people would remember.

Key terms

- **Khalsa:** the community of the 'pure ones'; the body of committed Sikhs
- **amrit:** a mixture of water and sugar crystals prepared by the Panj Piare, used in the ceremony of initiation and sometimes in a birth ceremony

▲ *Guru Gobind Singh*

Links

To find out more about the festival of Vaisakhi, see pages 48–49.

Stories from Sikh tradition

The Panj Piare

Guru Gobind Singh explained to the Sikhs, who had come to celebrate Vaisakhi, that they were living in a dangerous time and it was important that the weakness of the community was replaced with unity and strength. He drew his sword and asked the crowd 'Who will die for God and his Guru?' At last, one Sikh came forward and was led into the Guru's tent. There was a swish of the sword followed by a thud, and the Guru emerged from the tent with blood on his sword. He asked the same question again and another Sikh came forward. He also went into the tent. The same noise was heard and the Guru came out again with blood on his sword. This happened three more times and some people began to leave, feeling confused and frightened. Then the Guru came out of the tent with the five men, dressed in special clothes. They had shown absolute loyalty to the Guru and his beliefs. They were then given **amrit**, a mixture of water and sugar crystals prepared by the Guru and his wife, in an iron bowl, stirred by a two-edged sword.

The five men (the Panj Piare) who had shown such commitment were from different backgrounds. However, as they emerged from the tent, dressed identically in the new uniform of the Khalsa, Sikhs understood that this represented their equality. The five men gave up family ties to particular groups, or castes, their previous jobs (which had shown their place in society) and any rituals or customs they had kept. They were now 'saint-soldiers' who would defend the faith, work for justice and equality, and were committed to God.

After the Panj Piare were initiated, Guru Gobind Singh and his wife, Mata Sahib Kaur, were both initiated. The Guru stated that once initiated, a woman would take the name 'Kaur' meaning 'princess' (showing the value of women in Sikhism). A man would take the name 'Singh' meaning 'lion' (representing the strength and courage Sikhs would show in protecting and upholding the faith). The common last names were intended to eliminate caste names and emphasise the equality of all. This ceremony of initiation is known as Amrit Sanskar. Men and women are treated equally and all may be initiated, becoming known as **amritdharis**.

▲ Five Sikhs lead this procession in London to represent the original Panj Piare ('Five Loved Ones')

Links

For details about the rules that amritdhari Sikhs keep, see page 31. To read more about Amrit Sanskar, see pages 58–59.

Activities

1 What is meant by 'the living Guru'?
2 Explain the meaning of the names 'Kaur' and 'Singh' and their importance.
3 Write a newspaper report on the events surrounding the initiation of the Panj Piare, including the reactions of the five men and the crowd.
4 Why was the establishment of the Khalsa important for Sikhism?

Summary

You should now know and understand the importance of Guru Gobind Singh for Sikhism and the contribution he made to the belief in the equality of all.

Discussion activity

Discuss the effect of the experience of the Sikh community at Vaisakhi in 1699. In what ways was Sikhism strengthened by the creation of the Khalsa?

⭐ Study tip

You do not need to know the names of all the Sikh Gurus but it is important to know ways in which Guru Nanak and Guru Gobind Singh influenced Sikh beliefs about equality.

Equality in the Guru Granth Sahib and in Sikhism today

■ The Guru Granth Sahib

Guru Nanak wrote many hymns and his successors, Guru Angad and Guru Amar Das, collected and preserved them. Guru Arjan decided to make a collection that would have authority for all Sikhs and so, with the help of Bhai Gurdas, a compiler, the first collection, known as the Adi Granth, was put together. It contained the hymns of the first four Gurus and also the writings of other saints, including Hindu and Muslim writers whose ideas about God were similar to those of the Sikhs. In this way, Guru Arjan showed the inclusiveness of Sikhism, the equality of all before God and the unity of all religions. The **Guru Granth Sahib** was completed in 1604 and installed in the Golden Temple which Guru Arjan had built in Amritsar. Later, Guru Gobind Singh added writings from his father, Guru Tegh Bahadur, and modestly, only one of his own hymns.

The Sikh Gurus spoke Punjabi and in writing their hymns they developed a new writing script, Gurmukhi, which means 'from the mouth of the Guru'. The Guru Granth Sahib is written on 1430 pages and the words are always written on the same pages and lines on all copies of the scriptures.

■ The Eternal Guru

When the time came for Guru Nanak and Guru Angad to appoint a successor, they placed five coins and a coconut in front of the person they had chosen. Tradition says that when Guru Gobind Singh was dying from a wound he had received, he took five coins and a coconut and placed them before a copy of the Guru Granth Sahib and said:

▲ *A page of the Guru Granth Sahib, written in the Gurmukhi script*

> ❝ Let anyone who wishes to see the Guru come and see the Guru. Whoever wishes to hear the Guru's word should wholeheartedly read the Granth or listen to the Granth being read. ❞

This symbolic act meant that he was choosing the Guru Granth Sahib to be the final and the Eternal Guru, 'the living Guru', which would teach and lead the Sikh community. So the Spirit of the Gurus, God's messengers, would be present wherever Sikhs met before the Guru Granth Sahib.

■ The equality of all in the Guru Granth Sahib

Here are a few quotes from the Guru Granth Sahib which illustrate the Sikh belief in equality:

Objectives

- Know how the Guru Granth Sahib was compiled and what it contains.
- Understand the influence of the Guru Granth Sahib on Sikh beliefs about equality.

Key term

- **Guru Granth Sahib:** the holy scriptures of the Sikh faith, regarded as the ultimate authority

Discussion activity

With a partner discuss whether you think the UK is a community in which all are 'equal'.

> **❝** All beings and creatures are His; He belongs to all. **❞**
>
> *Guru Granth Sahib 425*

> **❝** The God-conscious being looks upon all alike, like the wind, which blows equally upon the king and the poor beggar. **❞**
>
> *Guru Granth Sahib 272*

> **❝** God's Kingdom is steady, stable and eternal. There is no second or third status; all are equal there. **❞**
>
> *Guru Granth Sahib 345*

> **❝** As Gurmukh, look upon all with the single eye of equality; in each and every heart, the Divine Light is contained. **❞**
>
> *Guru Granth Sahib 599*

■ Equality in Sikhism today

Today, there are approximately 30 million Sikhs worldwide and the signs of their belief in equality are clear to see. All gurdwaras have a langar, which accepts people of every race, gender, and class, whether or not they follow a religion. Men and women play an equally important part in both the rituals of worship and in performing sewa (selfless service). In the home, Sikh men and women share in the bringing up of children and are present in the community, doing both paid and voluntary work.

Sikhism and equality

Jaswinder Singh, a Sikh from Canada, explains his reasons for choosing Sikhism: 'Sikhism is truly a religion that has broken down barriers between religions, to show the world that 'anyone' can reach God by immersing themselves in His love. That is why Hindu and Muslim saints' divine hymns from God are also recorded in Guru Granth Sahib.

Sikh Gurus are not only honouring the achievements of these Saints throughout time, but are sending a message to the world. Sikhism is not the property of those who are born in Punjab or to Sikh families. It is a religion for all of humanity, men and women, be they of any caste, creed or colour and be they born to any religion in the world. Sikhism is for all of humanity.'

Activities

1. Look at the quotations from the Guru Granth Sahib. Copy each quotation and under each one, explain what it is saying about the belief in equality.
2. Explain why the Guru Granth Sahib is called the 'Eternal Guru'.
3. How do Jaswinder Singh's words show the Sikh belief in equality?

Research activity

Sikhs believe that there have been many messengers of God who have not been Sikhs. Try to find out who they are.

▲ *A woman reads from the Guru Granth Sahib in a gurdwara in Gravesend*

⭐ Study tip

Try to learn little phrases from some of these quotations, which will help you to remember what the Guru Granth Sahib teaches about equality.

Summary

You should now know how the Guru Granth Sahib was compiled and understand its importance in promoting the equality of all.

1.11 Sewa

■ What is sewa?

Sewa, meaning 'selfless service', is a way of life for Sikhs. It cannot be done to achieve any personal gain. Serving other people is one way of worshipping and serving God and is part of what Sikhs need to do to get close to God. This is one of the reasons why Sikhs do not believe in living a solitary existence, like a monk or nun, or a hermit, because to fulfil sewa, each individual needs to live within a community. Sikhs are encouraged to work as volunteers in hospitals, community centres and care homes, wherever there are people who need help.

▲ *Sikhs performing sewa by cleaning the premises of the Golden Temple*

There are three kinds of sewa:

- Tan: physical sewa. This involves using the body to help others by preparing, cooking or serving in the langar, or cleaning shoes or floors, for example. These are physical tasks which benefit others.
- Man: mental sewa. This relates to using the mind and mental skills to help others, for example reading the Guru Granth Sahib or teaching people. It will also include using skills in organising, communicating or inspiring others.
- Dhan: material sewa. Sikhs expect to use their material wealth to help others. Many give a tenth (dasvandh) of their income to the sangat, the Sikh community, or to charities.

Objective

- Know and understand the meaning of sewa and its importance for Sikhs.

Key term

- **sewa:** selfless service

Discussion activity 💬

Discuss the benefits of doing voluntary work for the volunteers themselves.

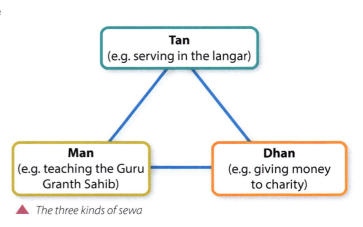

▲ *The three kinds of sewa*

■ The importance of sewa

Sikhs believe that sewa is an important part of a way of life that will lead them to God and help them to become gurmukh. Selfless service helps Sikhs to move away from pride (ahankar), greed (lobh) and self-centredness, and to develop virtues such as humility, compassion and love. Sikhs believe that God is in everyone, and so to love others is to show love for God. Sewa also provides opportunities to use God-given talents, skills and wealth to benefit the community. It demonstrates their belief in the equality of all people. In serving others, there can be no distinctions of race, beliefs, age or class. In living and serving in this way, Sikhs show the oneness of humanity.

> ❝ One who performs selfless service, without thought of reward, shall attain his Lord and Master. ❞
>
> *Guru Granth Sahib 286*

Ramesh Seth

This is a story of what happened to a traveller in India, Ramesh Seth.

He was travelling by train from Delhi to Amritsar with his wife. At dawn the train stopped before it reached the next station. It had rained heavily and the track ahead was submerged. Three Sikhs approached the train and offered the couple cups of tea. It was most welcome. They received two cups of tea and the man asked how much he owed them. They replied, 'Sir, we are from the gurdwara,' pointing to a building near the track. 'We are doing sewa. We saw the train was stranded and thought the people on it would like some tea.' It was cold and pouring with rain. The man and his wife were impressed with their dedication. As the three Sikhs came back down the train, the man offered a contribution for the gurdwara fund. They were reluctant to accept it, but he said to them, 'This is my sewa for your gurdwara.'

> ❝ One who works for what he eats, and gives some of what he has – O Nanak, he knows the Path. ❞
>
> *Guru Granth Sahib 1245*

Activities

1 Explain the different kinds of sewa and give examples of each.
2 How does sewa help Sikhs to avoid evils and develop virtues?
3 Read the story about Ramesh Seth and then answer these questions.
   a Why were the travellers impressed with the offer of tea?
   b Why do you think the Sikhs were unwilling to accept money for the tea?
   c Why did they do so eventually?

> ❝ Through selfless service, eternal peace is obtained. ❞
>
> *Guru Granth Sahib 125*

▲ *Teaching is a type of mental sewa; here schoolchildren are being taught about Sikhism on a visit to a Sikh temple in London*

Activities

1 'For Sikhs, sewa is the most important way of becoming gurmukh.' Evaluate this statement. In your answer, make sure you include more than one point of view.
2 Make a spider diagram suggesting as many ways as possible in which Sikhs could offer mental sewa (Man).

⭐ Study tip

Use the diagram on page 28 to help you learn about the different kinds of sewa.

Summary

You should now understand what is involved in sewa and why Sikhs believe it is a very important part of their faith.

1.12 The role and importance of the sangat

■ The origins of the sangat

Guru Nanak began to establish groups of disciples on his travels. They met to learn, to recite his hymns and to eat together, and he referred to these groups as the **sangat**. The Gurus believed that being involved in a community of believers would help people to be closer to God. This community became known as Sat Sangat, which means 'True Congregation'. Together, Sikhs would meditate on the Name of God, and such worship and meditation would help Sikhs to become God-centred (gurmukh). Guru Nanak urged people to join this group and find God.

> ❝ Join the Sat Sangat, the True Congregation, and find the Lord. The Gurmukh embraces love for the Lord. ❞
>
> *Guru Granth Sahib 22*
>
> ❝ Sitting in the Sangat, the True Congregation, the mind is comforted and consoled by the True Name. ❞
>
> *Guru Granth Sahib 69*

Objectives

- Understand the role and importance of the sangat.
- Consider how the role of the sangat is represented in the Khanda symbol.

Key terms

- **sangat:** the company of Sikhs meeting in the presence of the Guru Granth Sahib; Sat Sangat means the 'True Congregation'
- **sahajdhari:** a Sikh who is not born into a Sikh family; he or she believes in the Ten Gurus and the Guru Granth Sahib but has not been initiated into the Khalsa

■ The role of the sangat

In the time of Guru Nanak, the 'sangat' referred to the community of Sikhs living in a particular place. Today it is used to describe a gathering of Sikhs in a gurdwara, or perhaps in another place, when the Guru Granth Sahib is present. In this way, it means the community as it meets for learning, prayer or for a ceremony. The word 'sangat' reminds Sikhs of their duty to develop spiritual understanding and so get closer to God. The sangat may chant hymns, listen to the musicians praising God, hear a Sikh who is trained in Sikh religion, history or practice give a religious lecture, or discuss local social and community issues.

▲ *Sikhs gather together in a gurdwara for worship*

■ The importance of the sangat

Sikhs believe that being part of the sangat is essential if there is to be progress in the spiritual life of the individual. It enables people to develop their religious understanding and practice and is inspiring. In addition to worship and meditation, the presence of the sangat provides opportunities for sewa (selfless service). Here a Sikh may look after the shoes of the congregation as they go before the Guru Granth Sahib in bare feet, they may swing the large hand-fans to keep everyone cool on a hot day, or they may prepare and serve food. All these things help to keep God in mind and to develop spiritual and moral values.

Discussion activity

Discuss with a partner why Sikhs believe that coming together as a community is so important.

Links

For more information on amritdhari Sikhs, see pages 24–25.

Bhai Gurdas, one of the compilers of the Guru Granth Sahib, wrote:

> **"** … in establishing the dharamsal [a gurdwara] at Kartapur, with its holy fellowship, Guru Nanak brought the heaven on earth. **"**
> *Bhai Gurdas*

▲ *Sikh flags with the Khanda symbol*

■ Amritdhari Sikhs

Once Sikhs are initiated they become amritdharis. Amritdhari Sikhs are expected to offer daily prayers, wear the five Ks, pay tithes, take the names Singh and Kaur, and practise the Sikh virtues. They are also expected to be strictly vegetarian and to obey the code of conduct as set out in the Rehat Maryada. This includes reciting morning and evening prayers each day, attending the gurdwara for worship, and performing sewa. Tobacco, alcohol and illegal drugs are forbidden; so too is adultery.

Most people in the sangat, members of Sikh families, are not 'Khalsa Sikhs' or amritdharis. Many Sikhs choose not to be initiated, perhaps because, while they are committed to Sikhism, they do not wish to keep the very strict rules or because they simply do not yet feel ready for this stage. Other believers may be sahajdharis. These Sikhs do not come from Sikh families but believe in the Ten Gurus and the Guru Granth Sahib; they have no other religion but have not undergone initiation.

■ The Nishan Sahib and the Khanda

The Nishan Sahib is the flag which is always seen outside a gurdwara. It is a sign that the building is a Sikh gurdwara in which the sangat meets. The flagpole will be covered with cloth and will have a small double-edged sword (khanda) at the top. The symbol on the flag represents some of the most important values of the Sikh faith. It is called the Khanda, after the double-edged sword in the centre of the design. It consists of three symbols:

1 **Chakra:** like a spinning wheel of energy, chakra is used here to represent the eternal and infinite nature of God, without beginning or end, a divine oneness that unifies and connects all creation.

2 **Khanda:** a double-edged sword which is finely balanced. It symbolises one God; one edge represents divine justice and the other represents freedom and authority, which is present through moral and spiritual values.

3 **Two kirpans:** two noble swords which Guru Hargobind, the sixth Guru, began to wear to symbolise that worldly or political power (Miri) must be led and guided by the power of spiritual wisdom and virtues (Piri) to avoid tyranny, greed and exploitation, and to empower people to help the world to flourish.

Activities

1 What does the word 'sangat' mean?

2 What makes the sangat special and different from any gathering of Sikhs?

3 Draw out the separate parts of the Khanda symbol and label them. Underneath each part, summarise its meaning.

4 'Getting close to God is much easier when praying or meditating at home.' Evaluate this statement. Include different views and religious teachings in your answer.

5 Make a table to help you remember the rules which amritdhari Sikhs are expected to keep. In the left-hand column write the rules and in the right-hand column draw a symbol to represent the rule.

Extension activity

Guru Hargobind introduced martial art and weapons training for Sikhs. Try to find out why.

▲ *Khanda, the symbol of Sikhism*

Summary
You should now know and understand the role and the importance of the sangat.

⭐ **Study tip**

Learning the meaning of the Khanda symbol will help you to remember and explain important Sikh beliefs.

Key beliefs – summary

You should now be able to:

- ✔ explain about the nature of God as expressed in the Mool Mantra
- ✔ know and understand the significance of the Mool Mantra (Guru Granth Sahib 1)
- ✔ explain the Sikh belief in God as Creator, including different aspects of God's relationship with creation; God shown in and through the universe and God as separate from the universe
- ✔ understand the Sikh belief that the nature of human life is an opportunity to unite with God, including the development of Sikh virtues: wisdom, truthful living, justice, temperance, self-control, patience, courage, humility, contentment
- ✔ explain Sikh beliefs in karma, rebirth, and the aim and meaning of mukti, including the different aspects of mukti (positive and negative)
- ✔ understand the five stages of liberation and the barriers to mukti (illusion, self-centredness, anger, lust, greed, worldy attachment and pride)

- ✔ explain the Sikh understanding of the importance of being God-centred (gurmukh) rather than man-centred (manmukh) and the elimination of pride or ego (haumai).

The nature of human life – summary

You should now be able to:

- ✔ explain Sikh beliefs in the oneness of humanity and in the equality of all, including complete equality of women with men
- ✔ know and understand the expression of the equality of all in the lives of the Gurus, including Guru Nanak and Guru Gobind Singh, in the Guru Granth Sahib and in Sikhism today
- ✔ explain the Sikh practice of sewa: the importance and priority of service to others, including physical (tan), mental (man) and material (dhan)
- ✔ explain the role and importance of the sangat (religious community).

Sample student answer – the 4-mark question

1. Write an answer to the following practice question:

   Explain two ways the Sikh belief in sewa influences Sikhs today. **[4 marks]**

2. Read the following sample student answer:

   "Sikhs show their belief in sewa by taking part in the langar. Guru Nanak set up the langar to show the equality of all people, so Sikhs offer their service voluntarily in the preparation or serving of food and drink to all those who wish to take part. Sikhs give money to provide the food and do not employ caterers because sewa is seen as an important part of the worship of God.

   Sikhs also give money as part of sewa. This is called dasvandh. They give a tenth of their income to the Sikh community so that it can be used to help others, for example by providing free food and drink to the public at festival times."

3. With a partner, discuss the sample answer. Can you identify two different ways in which beliefs influence behaviour? If so, are they simple or detailed? How accurate are they? Can the answer be improved? If so, how?

4. What mark (out of 4) would you give this answer? Look at the mark scheme in the Introduction (AO1). What are the reasons for the mark you have given?

5. Now swap your answer with your partner's and mark each other's responses. What mark (out of 4) would you give the response? Refer to the mark scheme and give reasons for the mark you award.

Sample student answer – the 6-mark question

1. Write an answer to the following practice question:

   Explain two Sikh teachings about God the Creator.

   Refer to sacred writings or another source of Sikh belief and teaching in your answer. **[6 marks]**

2. Read the following sample student answer:

   "Sikhs believe that God is the creator of the world and he created everything in it. In fact he created the universe and any other universes which may exist. The Guru Granth Sahib says this. They also believe that God is present in all things he created and is present in the heart of all human beings who understand the difference between right and wrong, unlike the other creatures. So God is able to show himself to people because they can see him through the creation and in the hearts of people."

3. With a partner, discuss the student answer. Can you identify two different pieces of relevant and accurate teaching? If so, are they simple or detailed? How accurate are they? Is there a clear reference to scripture or sacred writings? Is there anything important missing from the answer? How can it be improved?

4. What mark (out of 6) would you give this answer? Look at the mark scheme in the Introduction (AO1). What are the reasons for the mark you have given?

5. Now swap your answer with your partner's and mark each other's responses. What mark (out of 6) would you give the response? Refer to the mark scheme and give reasons for the mark you award.

Sample student answer – the 12-mark question

1. Write an answer to the following practice question:

'Guru Gobind Singh taught Sikhs more about equality than Guru Nanak.'

Evaluate this statement. In your answer you should:

- refer to Sikh teaching
- give detailed arguments to support this statement
- give detailed arguments to support a different point of view
- reach a justified conclusion.

[12 marks]
[+ 3 SPaG marks]

2. Read the following sample student answer:

"I believe that Guru Gobind Singh taught Sikhs more about equality because he was the Guru who set up the Khalsa and made it clear that all Sikhs were equal. When initiated the five Panj Piare who came from different sections of society drank out of the same bowl and all wore the five Ks. The Khalsa sent a clear message of equality to people about the equal worth of everyone. He believed in the value of every human being whom God had created and the equality between men and women and showed this by expecting all Sikh men to take the name Singh (lion) and all Sikh women to take the name Kaur (princess). He also established the Guru Granth Sahib as the living Guru and because it contains writings from the Hindu and Muslim faith as well as writings of the Gurus, it shows that he expected all Sikhs to believe in equality. It also meant that there could be no dispute about the leadership of the Sikhs which could have divided them and made one group feel they were better than another.

However some people would say that Guru Nanak did more for equality because he showed by the company he kept that people who had different religions could mix with each other. He knew and respected Hindus and Muslims, and Mardana, whom he went on his travels with, was a Muslim. He said 'There is no Hindu and no Muslim' and believed that all religions were making the same effort to get close to the One God. He first established practices which showed his dislike of the caste system and his belief in equality, the most obvious of which was the langar. All were welcome to eat and all food was vegetarian so no one could be offended by not having meat prepared in the right way. Sikhs were expected to share in the tasks of preparing and serving food – this was to demonstrate equality and lack of status. Traditionally castes in India did not mix and would not eat together.

Although both Gurus did a great deal to work for equality I think Guru Gobind Singh did more by establishing the Khalsa."

3. With a partner, discuss the sample answer.

- Does it accurately refer to and develop Sikh teachings, applying them to the quote?
- Is the first argument developed well?
- Is the alternative point of view well developed?
- Is there a valid conclusion and does it reflect the arguments it is based on?
- What is good about the answer? How would you improve the answer?

4. What mark (out of 12) would you give this answer? Look at the mark scheme in the Introduction (AO2). What are the reasons for the mark you have given?

5. Now swap your answer with your partner's and mark each other's responses. What mark (out of 12) would you give the response? Refer to the mark scheme and give reasons for the mark you award.

Practice questions

 1   Which **one** of the following describes liberation from the cycle of birth, death and rebirth?

A) Karma   B) Mukti   C) Sewa   D) Gurmukh   **[1 mark]**

 2   Give **one** word which is used to describe God in the Mool Mantra.   **[1 mark]**

> ⭐ **Study tip**
>
> If a question asks you to 'give' a piece of information, you do not need to give any explanation.

 3   Explain **two** kinds of service which Sikhs may offer.   **[4 marks]**

 4   Explain **two** Sikh beliefs about the nature of human life.

Refer to sacred writings or another source of Sikh belief and teaching in your answer.   **[6 marks]**

> ⭐ **Study tip**
>
> Make sure you read the question carefully and provide everything it asks for in your answer.

5   'Service to others is the most important Sikh belief.'

Evaluate this statement. In your answer you should:
- refer to Sikh teaching
- give reasoned arguments to support this statement
- give reasoned arguments to support a different point of view
- reach a justified conclusion.   **[12 marks]**
     [+ 3 SPaG marks]

> ⭐ **Study tip**
>
> This question is worth as many marks as the previous four questions. You should think carefully about the statement before you start writing. When you have finished writing, make sure you read what you have written to make sure you have included all the question asks you to provide.

> ⭐ **Study tip**
>
> These five questions try to cover as much of the section on key beliefs as possible. You should aim to revise this section thoroughly.

■ The gurdwara

The **gurdwara** is the Sikh place of worship, sometimes called a temple. The word means 'the door of the Guru', and originally it meant the place where Sikhs could meet to hear the human Guru speak and to worship God. Now it can be used to describe any place in which the Guru Granth Sahib, the living Guru, is installed and treated with proper respect. This is often a separate building for public worship but it could be a room in someone's home. The gurdwara is open to all, whatever their nationality, religion or class.

■ Outside the gurdwara

Gurdwaras that have been built specially often have a dome and decorations on the outside. In the UK, some gurdwaras have been built especially for Sikh worship, but some are buildings which Sikhs have adapted for use as their place of worship. From the outside, therefore, some Sikh gurdwaras may not look very different from other buildings, except that there will be a Sikh flag, the Nishan Sahib. The flag is usually yellow with the Khanda symbol in blue, and flies from a flagpole that is often wrapped in yellow cloth.

■ Features of a gurdwara

The two main areas inside a gurdwara are the prayer hall (Darbar Sahib) and the langar (see pages 42–43). The prayer hall is a large space with a raised platform or 'throne' at one end. It is important to remember that the Guru Granth Sahib is regarded as a living Guru, so the features of the gurdwara traditionally reflect the respect and honour in which the Gurus are held. The 'throne' (**takht**) on which the Guru Granth Sahib is placed is similar to an honoured seat that one of the human Gurus would have been offered. The seat will be covered in fine cloth and is usually surrounded by flowers. There may also be an Ik Onkar or Khanda symbol. At the front of the platform, there are places for money and food offerings, and a bowl containing karah parshad, a sweet food to be shared among the congregation.

Objectives

- Know the features of a gurdwara.
- Understand their use and importance.

Key terms

- **gurdwara:** a Sikh place of worship; it literally means 'the door of the Guru'
- **takht:** 'throne'; the raised platform and the structure inside on which the Guru Granth Sahib rests
- **palki:** a canopy which is placed above the raised platform, above the Guru Granth Sahib

▲ *A gurdwara in Leamington Spa, Warwickshire*

⭐ **Study tip**

Learn the names and the importance of some of the features of the gurdwara, especially the takht and the palki.

Near the takht is another raised area from where the musicians will play. The walls may be decorated with pictures of the Gurus or verses from the scriptures. There is no seating in the prayer hall; people sit on the floor below the level of the Guru Granth Sahib.

The takht

The takht is a raised platform designed as a 'throne' within which the Guru Granth Sahib is placed. It is the most noticeable feature of the prayer hall.

The palki

The **palki** is the domed structure used to cover the raised area where the Guru Granth Sahib is placed. The canopy may be engraved at the top with verses from scripture or the word Waheguru, which means 'Wonderful Lord'.

The manji

The manji is, literally, a small bed on which the Guru Granth Sahib is placed during the day in the prayer hall. It has a wooden frame and legs and, like some beds, has a webbing material placed over the frame. A white sheet and three pillows are placed on top of the frame, on which the Guru Granth Sahib rests.

The chanani

The chanani is a large canopy, made of decorated cloth, which is placed over the palki near the ceiling of the prayer hall.

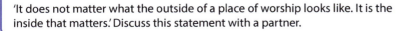
▲ *Sikhs wait to show their respect to the Guru Granth Sahib and to make offerings*

Links

To find out more about the use of music in worship and the musicians (ragis), see pages 40–41.

Extension activity

Find a website for a gurdwara that includes pictures of the prayer hall. See if you can identify the different features in the pictures.

Activities

1 Explain the meaning of the word 'gurdwara'.

2 Suggest two features which show how the Guru Granth Sahib is treated as a living Guru.

3 Explain how someone would know from the outside that a building was a gurdwara.

4 Draw a diagram of the takht and label it carefully. This will help you to remember the key terms.

Discussion activity

'It does not matter what the outside of a place of worship looks like. It is the inside that matters.' Discuss this statement with a partner.

Summary

You should now know the features of a gurdwara and understand their use and importance.

The Guru Granth Sahib

■ Respect for the Guru Granth Sahib

The Guru Granth Sahib contains the verses of many of the Sikh Gurus as well as saintly figures from other faiths, including Muslims and Hindus. It is regarded as the Eternal Living Guru, the eleventh Guru. It is therefore treated with great respect and honour. There are many ways in which Sikhs show their respect towards it:

- It is called Sahib, which is a term of respect, also shown to the ten Sikh Gurus.
- All printed copies of the Guru Granth Sahib have 1430 ang (the respectful word meaning 'limb' of the Guru, that Sikhs use to refer to pages of the Guru Granth Sahib). Each copy that is made is identical worldwide, in that the pages, their length and the numbering are the same. It is written in Gurmukhi script. This is one way in which Sikhs show that the scripture is holy and greatly respected – its words do not change and each copy has the same words on the same page.
- Sikhs sit on the floor for worship so that they are lower than the Guru Granth Sahib.
- They make sure that they do not point their feet towards the Guru Granth Sahib when they are sitting down.
- Worshippers bow before the Guru Granth Sahib as they enter the gurdwara.
- **Rumallas**, which are square or rectangular decorated cloths, sometimes made from silk, are used to cover the Guru Granth Sahib when it is not being read. Rumallas are often given by Sikhs to the gurdwara.
- There are special customs observed in the gurdwara, in which the Guru Granth Sahib is treated as a human Guru would have been treated.

Chauri (Chaur Sahib)

The **chauri** is a fan often made from yak's hair, which is waved from time to time over the Guru Granth Sahib. Honoured teachers would have been offered this service in India to provide cool air and keep flies away. It is a sign of respect for the Guru Granth Sahib and an acknowledgement of its authority.

The resting room

When worship is finished for the day, the Guru Granth Sahib is closed and wrapped in clean cloth. In a procession, it is then carefully carried on the head of a Sikh, who has been initiated into the Khalsa, to its resting room, where it stays overnight. It is, in effect, put to bed. The room is sometimes called Sach Khand, which means 'the realm of Truth' or 'the place where

Objectives

- Understand the importance of the Guru Granth Sahib for Sikhs.
- Consider the respect in which the Guru Granth Sahib is held.
- Understand the role and importance of an akhand path.

Key terms

- **rumalla:** a highly decorated, rich cloth used to cover the Guru Granth Sahib
- **chauri (chaur sahib):** a fan that is waved over the Guru Granth Sahib as a sign of respect
- **Ardas:** the prayer with which Sikhs begin and complete worship

Links

To find out about how the Guru Granth Sahib was compiled and its status as the Eternal Guru, look back to pages 26–27.

▲ The Guru Gobind Singh Gurdwara in Manchester

the True God lives'. The following morning, it will be brought back in the same way to the prayer hall for the Prakash ceremony, during which mantras are recited and a shortened form of the **Ardas** prayer is said.

■ The importance of the Guru Granth Sahib

The Guru Granth Sahib contains the Gurus' teachings about God, who is often described in it as Har (Lord) or Waheguru (Wonderful Lord). Sikhs believe that it provides teaching and guidance about ways in which they may approach God and can become gurmukh. In particular, it encourages meditation on the name of God and keeping God in the centre of people's thoughts. There is no gurdwara unless the Guru Granth Sahib is present. It contains the writings of the Sikh Gurus; since it is the Eternal Living Guru, there will be no need for any more human Gurus. The Mool Mantra and other daily prayers said in Sikh homes come from the Guru Granth Sahib.

▲ *A young Sikh boy reading from the Guru Granth Sahib*

■ The akhand path

The akhand path is a continuous ceremonial reading of the whole of the Guru Granth Sahib, all 1430 pages, which is usually completed within 48 hours. Readers, men and women, will take a turn to read, and reserves are appointed in case someone is ill or there is any emergency. The reading must be clear and accurate and not too fast, so that all can hear it clearly and understand it. An akhand path usually takes place just before a festival begins. It can take place at times of great joy or sorrow, for example before a marriage, to celebrate the birth of a baby or on the death of a family member. Karah parshad is distributed just before an akhand path begins and immediately after it ends.

Sometimes the Guru Granth Sahib will be taken from the gurdwara to a new business or a new home in order to perform an akhand path. If a homeowner or a business owner requests an akhand path, they and their family are expected to take part and listen to the words of the living Guru for some time during the 48 hours. It is believed to be a great blessing, and is not an empty custom to be performed lightly.

> **Discussion activity** 💬
>
> What is the effect on Sikhs of treating scripture in the same way as a holy and honoured human being would be treated? What difference does it make to their faith?

> **Research activity** 🔍
>
> Use the internet to research different occasions on which an akhand path has been performed by Sikhs in the UK, and make a note of these.

> ⭐ **Study tip**
>
> Write a list of the occasions on which an akhand path might be performed and refer to it when studying.

> **Summary**
>
> You should now be able to describe the respect in which the Guru Granth Sahib is held, and understand the role and importance of an akhand path.

> **Activities**
>
> 1 Write a list of different ways in which the Guru Granth Sahib is shown respect or draw a series of pictures to remind you of these practices.
>
> 2 Explain exactly what an akhand path is and how it is organised.
>
> 3 'Asking for an akhand path before a marriage provides a good start for a couple.' What do you think of this statement? Explain your reasons.

2.3 Worship in the gurdwara

The importance of worship

For Sikhs, worship is a way of life. It begins when an individual decides to dedicate him or herself to follow the teaching in the Guru Granth Sahib. True worship is therefore to keep God in one's mind and serve him. Calling to mind the name of God is central to Sikh worship (**diwan**). Worship can include listening and meditating, singing and reciting, working and serving people. It is the approach to all these things that makes it 'worship'. Sikhs believe God is present throughout the universe, and may be found whenever Sikhs or others bring God to mind and remember and recite his name. However, special reverence is also shown to gurdwaras and places of pilgrimage.

> ❝ Worship in adoration that True Lord; everything is under His Power. ❞
>
> *Guru Granth Sahib 521*

> ❝ Worship the True Lord, and believe in the True Guru; this brings the merit of making donations to charity, kindness and compassion. ❞
>
> *Guru Granth Sahib 688*

> ❝ Worship and adore Him, and you shall be at peace forever. ❞
>
> *Guru Granth Sahib 896*

Worship in the gurdwara

Some worship in the gurdwara may last up to five hours but people are not expected to stay for the whole time. Rules about attendance are relaxed and people come and go. Sikhs remove their shoes and cover their heads as a sign of respect before entering the prayer hall. They also wash their hands and may wash their feet as well. They walk towards the Guru Granth Sahib, bow and touch the floor as a sign of respect to the Eternal Living Guru. At this point, it is also common to make an offering of money to help with the running of the gurdwara and the gurdwara's work in the community.

Worshippers sit on the floor of the prayer hall so that the Guru Granth Sahib remains at a higher level, and to show their belief in equality. Men and women usually do not sit together but on different sides of the room. Sikh worship includes the singing of hymns (**kirtan**) and prayer in which the word 'Waheguru' will be said by the congregation a number of times to show their agreement. A sermon or talk may be given, sometimes by a visitor. A reading at random (**hukam**) of the Guru Granth Sahib is performed, which provides a divine order at the start or end of a service. The worship is led by any Sikh, male or female, who is known to be knowledgeable.

Objectives

- Consider how Sikhs worship in the gurdwara.
- Understand how the worship emphasises Sikh beliefs.

Key terms

- **diwan:** originally a royal court; means 'in the court of the Guru'; refers to an act of worship of the Sikh community in a gurdwara
- **kirtan:** devotional singing of the hymns from the Guru Granth Sahib
- **hukam:** the act of opening the Guru Granth Sahib at random and reading a verse

Research activity

Try to find a clip on the internet that shows Sikhs engaged in kirtan. Notice the musicians and the musical instruments used.

▲ *A Sikh praying in the gurdwara*

All services of worship start and end with the recitation of the Ardas prayer, which can be brief or last about 15 minutes. Sikhs stand when it is said, and one person stands in front and leads the prayer. Sikhs are reminded to remember God and the Ten Gurus and, in addition to special prayers for individuals, prayers are said for the welfare of all people everywhere. The prayer begins as below:

> " *There is One Being, all victory belongs to / the Wonderful Guru,*
>
> *May the divine Might help us. / The Tenth Guru's Ode to the divine Might.*
>
> *First remember the divine Might, then think of Guru Nanak, / Next Gurus Angad, Amar Das and Ram Das, / may they stand by us. / Gurus Arjan, Hargobind and Har Rai, / Think of Guru Harkrishan, that sight dispels all suffering. / Remember Guru Tegh Bahadur, / who brings the nine treasures to our home.*
>
> *May they support us everywhere. / May the Tenth Guru, Gobind Singh, support us everywhere.*
>
> **The light of the Ten Gurus shines in the Guru Granth Sahib,** / Consider its sacred word, envisage its sacred sight, / And proclaim: Vaheguru, the Wonderful Guru! "
>
> *Ardas prayer*

Activities

1 How would a Sikh explain what worship is?

2 Explain why a service of worship in a gurdwara might last some hours.

3 Explain the importance of kirtan for worshippers.

4 Explain two ways in which the distribution of karah parshad to everyone reflects Sikh beliefs.

> " At the Gurdwara, the Guru's Gate, the Kirtan of the Lord's Praises are sung. Meeting with the True Guru, one chants the Lord's Praises. "
>
> *Guru Granth Sahib 1075*

■ Kirtan

Kirtan is the singing of God's praises and includes shabads (verses) from the Guru Granth Sahib. These shabads are accompanied by music. Sikhs enjoy singing and listening to kirtan. It is believed that in doing this, they are inspired in their efforts to focus on the meaning of the words and encouraged to concentrate on God and his name. Singing the shabads also helps Sikhs to remember the words and therefore to bring God to mind clearly and frequently. As langar and karah parshad nourish the body, so kirtan nourishes the soul.

▲ *Children singing with ragis in a London gurdwara*

Ragis

Ragis are musicians who sing or play accompaniment for kirtan. The musical instruments most often played are harmoniums and tabla (drums). Some Sikh groups also use traditional stringed instruments or modern guitars to accompany the singing.

■ Karah parshad

The end of a gurdwara service is always marked by the distribution of karah parshad. This is a sweet food, made from semolina, butter, sugar, flour and water, and is distributed to everyone. The sharing of this food is a symbol of the equality of all and is based on the idea that all people belong to God's family. It means that no one leaves the presence of the Guru 'empty-handed'; it symbolises what the Guru may offer spiritually to an individual. It is sweet as are the blessings that come from God.

★ Study tip

Remember that calling to mind the name of God is central to Sikh worship. This will help you remember the different ways in which Sikhs worship God.

Summary

You should now understand how Sikhs worship in the gurdwara, and the importance of worship for Sikhs.

2.4   The langar

The term **langar** is used both to describe the kitchen or canteen in which food is prepared and served, and to describe the meals that are served there. In the langar, only vegetarian food is served. Food is served free to all, regardless of their faith, race, gender, wealth or background. Food is served throughout the day, every day of the year. The food is simple and may include rice, dal (lentils), vegetables and chapatis. The food must be served by Sikh volunteers (paid caterers are not allowed) and its cost is met by voluntary contributions from Sikhs. The process of preparing, serving and sharing the langar should be done while remembering God.

Sometimes, especially at festivals, langars are held in the open air. In India many thousands of people may be given a meal during these celebrations.

■ Origins of the langar

In the fifteenth century, when Sikhism was started by Guru Nanak, India had a caste system which grouped people according to the work they did. The social status of an individual depended on the caste they were in and, generally, castes did not mix. There were rules to prevent people from marrying someone of a different caste and different castes did not eat together. Guru Nanak believed in equality and thought that one of the best ways of showing this in a practical way was to ensure that all were given opportunities to eat together. When Guru Nanak established a Sikh community at Kartapur, he gave the langar a central place and worked on his farm to provide food to contribute to the langar.

When the second Guru, Guru Angad, succeeded Guru Nanak, he was already married to Mata Khivi. Many people came to visit the Guru and Mata Khivi was in charge of the langar. Everyone who came was given the best possible food and treated with great respect.

▲ *Boys receiving food at a langar*

Objectives

- Understand the role of the langar in a gurdwara.
- Appreciate the meaning and significance of the langar as an expression of sewa.

Key term

- **langar:** 1. Guru's kitchen or the free kitchen within each gurdwara; 2. the food that is served in the kitchen

> ❝ The Langar — the Kitchen of the Guru's Shabad has been opened, and its supplies never run short. ❞
>
> *Guru Granth Sahib 967*

Links

Remind yourself about Guru Nanak's part in establishing the langar by looking back to pages 22–23.

> ❝ … Khivi, the Guru's wife … distributes the bounty of the Guru's Langar; the kheer — the rice pudding and ghee, is like sweet ambrosia. ❞
>
> *Guru Granth Sahib 967*

Extension activity

Use the internet to find out what other Gurus taught about the langar, for example Guru Ram Das and Guru Arjan.

Through her work and devotion, the Sikhs gained a reputation for hospitality and kindness. She is the only woman to be mentioned in the Guru Granth Sahib.

It is said that when Guru Gobind Singh, the tenth Guru, was dying, some of his last words were 'Keep the langar ever open', indicating that he believed this practice to be a central part of the Sikh faith. In their prayers, Sikhs make a request to God: 'may the hot plates of the langars remain ever in service.'

▲ Sikhs serving in the langar in Southall, London

Langars in London

The Sikh Welfare and Awareness Team help to provide food and drink for homeless people in London. Every Sunday evening, their van is parked in the same place on the Strand in central London. Each time, Sikh volunteers provide about 250 people with drinks, hot soup, chocolate and other snacks. Those who would like this opportunity for a free meal, very few of whom are Sikhs, line up to receive this service. One of them, John Davidson, said, 'We come here because we get food … A hot meal. It's a luxury for me.'

Many people with different needs benefit from the free meals that Sikh gurdwaras provide in towns and cities across the UK. In Southall, a district in west London, the Guru Singh Sabha Gurdwara, which is believed to be the largest gurdwara outside India, serves approximately 5000 meals each day of the week and 10,000 at weekends. Surinder Singh Purewal, who helps to run the gurdwara, explained that all Sikhs have a duty to perform sewa, which means both helping to provide the necessary food and drink and volunteering to serve it. He said, 'It means we're never short of donations or volunteers to help prepare the langar.'

■ Importance of the langar

The langar is important to Sikhs for a number of reasons:

- Taking part in the langar is one way in which Sikhs perform sewa (selfless service). Through performing sewa, God is worshipped.
- It is one way in which the whole Sikh community, men, women and children, can be involved in service for the good of all.
- The langar is a public expression of the Sikh belief in equality. All are equal because they are created by God, whatever their religion, race, class or background may be.
- The langar is also an expression of the Sikh belief that all humans belong to one communal family, and there is a divine spark in each human being.
- Sikhism teaches that the resources of the world should be shared.
- Sikhs believe in living in a community, not on their own, and including everyone in the life of their community.
- The welcome and hospitality given to all in the langar provides some security and protection for all.
- The langar is to ensure that no one is in such extreme poverty that they cannot eat. This may also prevent a person turning to crime in order to feed their family.

Activities

1. Why did Guru Nanak believe it was important to establish langars?

2. Explain why Mata Khivi is remembered by Sikhs.

3. 'The langar is the most important way in which Sikhs worship God.' Suggest two different views people might hold about this statement and give developed arguments to support them.

⭐ Study tip

It is helpful to understand how important the langar is as an expression of sewa.

Summary

You should now understand the role of the langar as a form of sewa and its importance to Sikhs.

2.5 Prayer in the home and meditating on God's name

■ Prayer at home

Sikhs are expected to remember God at all times, which includes reciting daily prayers at home. Some Sikh families have a copy of the Guru Granth Sahib in their homes, which they are expected to treat in a special way. They do not simply place it on a bookshelf with other books. It should have a room, or at least an area of the house, to itself and it is then treated with respect in the same way as in the gurdwara. In fact, when this happens, the room becomes a gurdwara, because the Guru Granth Sahib is present. However, most Sikhs do not have a copy of the Guru Granth Sahib at home but use a prayer book, a **gutka**. The gutka is also treated with great respect. When not in use, it is wrapped in a special cloth and Sikhs wash their hands before picking it up.

> ❝ One who calls himself a Sikh of the Guru, the True Guru, shall rise in the early morning hours and meditate on the Lord's Name. Upon arising early in the morning, he is to bathe, and cleanse himself in the pool of nectar. Following the Instructions of the Guru, he is to chant the Name of the Lord, Har[1], Har. All sins, misdeeds and negativity shall be erased. Then, at the rising of the sun, he is to sing Gurbani[2]; whether sitting down or standing up, he is to meditate on the Lord's Name. One who meditates on my Lord, Har, Har, with every breath and every morsel of food — that GurSikh becomes pleasing to the Guru's Mind. ❞
>
> *Guru Granth Sahib 305*

[1] the infinite God; [2] hymns from the Guru Granth Sahib

These words, written by Gur Ram Das, set out instructions for Sikhs on how to start each day by remembering God. It is a demanding routine but Sikhs are expected to grow in self-discipline and commitment as they follow this path. As Sikhs are able to concentrate and think less about themselves, they become gurmukh, centred on God.

Sikhs bathe in the morning to remind them that God is all around them, to help them separate meditation from other tasks, and to prepare them for concentration on the meditation. Sikhs are asked to repeat the **Japji**, a prayer given by Guru Nanak, and the Jap and Swayyas prayers written by Guru Gobind Singh, at dawn. These prayers help them to meditate on the name of God. Some Sikhs also use a mala, prayer beads with

▲ *A Sikh family praying at home*

Objectives

- Consider the role of prayer in the home.
- Understand the significance of meditating on the name of God in daily life and in the gurdwara.

Key terms

- **gutka:** a prayer book which contains some of the daily or regular prayers from the Guru Granth Sahib
- **Japji:** a Sikh prayer
- **nam japna:** meditating on the name of God

⭐ **Study tip**

This passage from the Guru Granth Sahib about morning prayer is a set text. Make sure you know what instructions it gives.

108 knots. They pass the beads through their fingers as they repeat 'Waheguru'. Some Sikhs may also attend early morning worship at the gurdwara before they go to work. In the evening, a prayer, Rahiras, is recited at dusk and another, Sohila, when going to bed.

▲ *A mala is used to help Sikhs meditate on God's name*

> ❝ Hearing the Word, we plumb the depths of virtue,
>
> Hearing the Word, we rise to the statue of sages and kings,
>
> Hearing the Word, the path is lit for the blind,
>
> Hearing the Word, the fathomless is fathomed.
>
> Says Nanak, the devout enjoy eternal bliss,
>
> Hearing the Word banishes all suffering and sin. ❞
>
> *Japji prayer, verse 11*

■ Meditation on the name of God

Sikhs have three responsibilities that they are expected to fulfil. The first is to meditate on the name of God (**nam japna**). The others are doing honest work while remembering God (kirat karna), and sharing all they have and giving to charity (vand chhakna). Sikhs believe that the more they are able to think about God, the less selfish they will become. Doing honest work and giving to charity, as well as performing sewa (selfless service), will flow more naturally once God is at the centre of their lives. So keeping God always in mind is assisted by morning and evening prayers at home and by attending worship at the gurdwara. However, ideally God should be remembered throughout the day. Meditating on the name of God can be achieved by quietly reciting God's name (Nam) to oneself, which cannot be heard by others, or by saying God's name out loud, either individually or more commonly in a community recitation, and it is this that is usually called nam japna.

> ❝ Those who have the treasure of the Lord's Name deep within their hearts – the Lord resolves their affairs. ❞
>
> *Guru Granth Sahib 305*

> ❝ If there be a home for praise / and thoughts of the Creator,
>
> Let that home sing in celebration / and remember our Designer.
>
> You sing a hymn of glory / to my Fearless One,
>
> I offer myself to the hymn of glory / which brings everlasting joy. ❞
>
> *Sohila prayer, verse 1 and refrain*

Extension activity

Using a library or the internet, look up the prayers written by Guru Gobind Singh, the Jap and the Swayyas, and write down some quotations which show the importance of meditating on the name of God.

Activities

1 Write a list of the things a Sikh would be expected to do in early morning prayers.

2 'Calling to mind the name of God is all a Sikh needs to do to live a good life.' Consider this statement and explain your reasons for agreeing or disagreeing with it.

3 Consider the opening words of the Sohila prayer said by Sikhs before going to bed. Look carefully at the prayer and identify the different Sikh beliefs it includes.

Summary

You should now know how Sikhs pray at home and understand the importance of meditating on God's name.

2.6 The role of the gurdwara within the Sikh community

■ The management of the gurdwara

The gurdwara is run by Sikhs, most of whom do the work needed voluntarily. There are very few paid posts attached to gurdwaras; the preparations, cleaning, maintenance and organisation are done by Sikhs as part of sewa. In villages or small towns a **granthi** will be appointed to manage and maintain a gurdwara. In larger towns and cities, a management team or committee manage the finances and administration of the gurdwara and oversee the appointment of a granthi. Many gurdwaras are open for 24 hours a day and are open to those of any religion or no religion. A gurdwara acts as a community centre and a base for local voluntary and charitable activities. It is funded by donations and offerings from Sikhs.

■ The role of the gurdwara within the Sikh community

Sikhs believe that true worship affects every part of life. Gurdwaras in the UK have a number of facilities that help to serve the sangat, the congregation of Sikhs, and the local community. These include:

- The prayer hall, where worship takes place and all are welcome. On special occasions, Sikhs may invite members of the local community to share with them in worship and celebrations.
- The langar, which provides free food and drink for Sikhs and the community. All are welcome to eat together and, again, food is prepared and served by volunteer Sikhs performing sewa.
- Toilet and washroom facilities for men and women, and somewhere to place shoes.
- A room or rooms for meetings and education. The gurdwara arranges for children to learn Punjabi (sometimes spelled Panjabi) and Gurmukhi, the script in which the Guru Granth Sahib is written. Studies in the scriptures are also provided. The language lessons help the younger generations to keep in touch with relatives, such as grandparents who live in the Punjab and cannot speak English. There may also be a room for a library of Sikh literature.
- Rooms that may also be used for committee meetings, music classes, a youth club or for women's groups.

In the UK, gurdwaras often act as social centres for the Sikh community, and weddings and funerals often take place in gurdwaras. In India such functions would often be held outside. Other services may be provided, too. For example, a firm of solicitors offers a free legal clinic once a week at a gurdwara in Leicester.

▲ *Young boys learning to read Punjabi at a gurdwara*

46

Some gurdwaras, especially in the Punjab, may also include:

- a guest room or rooms for travellers or pilgrims to stay overnight
- accommodation for the granthi
- a dispensary or clinic.

■ The granthi

The word 'granthi' means someone who reads the Guru Granth Sahib. Granthis are amritdhari Sikhs, members of the Khalsa. They may be men or women. They are expected to be of good character and to live according to the Sikh Code of Conduct, the Rehat Maryada, showing devotion to God and humility. There are several places of training for granthis, the most famous being the Shahid Sikh Missionary College at Amritsar in the Punjab. In the UK, Sikhs often appoint a granthi who has trained in the Punjab. There is no ceremony of ordination because granthis are not priests. They do not have a higher status than other Sikhs, and are equal to other Sikhs in every way, but they are highly respected.

Granthis arrange the daily religious services, including the readings from the Guru Granth Sahib, and teach and advise community members. Many granthis live on the premises of a gurdwara and are responsible for its maintenance and security. Some may be paid a small salary in addition to free accommodation and food. Depending on their duties, some have other jobs as well.

The most important work for a granthi is taking care of the Guru Granth Sahib. They arrange the ceremonies to bring the Guru Granth Sahib from the resting room to the prayer hall in the morning and return it in the evening. Granthi may also lead kirtan, the devotional singing of hymns. A granthi conducts rites-of-passage services, such as marriages and funerals, and is responsible for the performing of an akhand path (the continuous reading of the Guru Granth Sahib), which may take place in the gurdwara, in private homes or at a business premises.

▲ *A granthi removes the rumalla from the Guru Granth Sahib*

Activity

Adam Holloway, the former Member of Parliament for Gravesham, England, said that, 'Every time I visit the gurdwara I am reminded of how lucky we are to have it in the constituency, and how much the members do to help those less fortunate than themselves.'

Give some of the likely reasons why Adam Holloway thinks his community is lucky to have a gurdwara.

Discussion activity

Discuss the importance of the gurdwara as a community centre for Sikhs.

Activities

1 Explain the education that gurdwaras provide and why Sikhs believe this is important.
2 Make a list of the duties of a granthi.
3 Explain how the granthi is paid.
4 What would you expect to be included in the training for a granthi?
5 In pairs, test each other on your knowledge of the facilities and activities the gurdwara provides.
6 'The work of the gurdwara helps to ensure that those Sikhs who are poor or vulnerable feel part of their community.' What do you think? Explain your answer.

⭐ Study tip

It is useful to remember that the granthi has a special role but he or she is not a priest.

Summary

You should now know what the gurdwara provides and how it is managed. You should also understand the importance of the role of the gurdwara within the Sikh community.

■ The origins of Vaisakhi

Vaisakhi was an ancient wheat harvest festival and is still celebrated in many parts of India with a variety of names. Originally it was celebrated at a time when farmers were grateful for a good harvest and prayed that all would go well for them in the coming year. Vaisakhi is a Sanskrit word named after a month in the Indian calendar. It is said that Guru Nanak was born in the month of Baisakh. It is normally celebrated on 13 or 14 April.

■ The importance of Vaisakhi for Sikhs

Vaisakhi is now a very important festival for Sikhs, following the actions of the tenth Guru, Guru Gobind Singh, at the festival of Vaisakhi in 1699. During this time there was much religious persecution. Guru Gobind Singh wanted to combat this and during the festival he established the Khalsa, the body of committed Sikhs. In the future, those who were prepared to commit themselves to the faith, and to the principle of freedom of belief for everyone, were to agree to keep certain rules and wear special symbols of their faith (the five Ks).

Some Sikhs will also take time at Vaisakhi to remember sad occasions from the past when Sikhs were persecuted and killed. One such event took place in April 1919 at Jallianwala Bagh where Sikhs had gathered to celebrate Vaisakhi. A British general, acting on the orders of the Lieutenant Governor of the Punjab, tried to prevent Sikhs from coming together and many were shot and killed. Freedom to practise religion is an important Sikh principle, and is now one of the human rights listed in the Universal Declaration of Human Rights (1948).

▲ A Vaisakhi procession in Birmingham, UK

■ Celebrations at Vaisakhi

Many of the celebrations at Vaisakhi are common to all Sikh communities across the world. Every gurdwara will hold an akhand

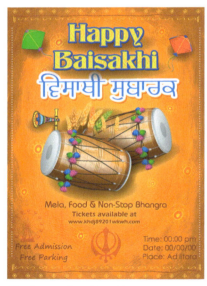

▲ A poster for a Vaisakhi event

path, a continuous reading of the Guru Granth Sahib, followed by an act of worship. Sikhs recite the Ardas prayer. Community meals form an important part of the celebrations and Sikhs may cater for large numbers of people. Other customs which Sikhs may take part in are:

- making a commitment to follow the Sikh way of life by becoming an amritdhari Sikh
- performing kirtan
- holding cultural celebrations
- sending Vaisakhi cards to family and friends
- wearing new clothes, especially the children
- voting for elected committees for the gurdwara.

In many towns in Britain, as well as in the Punjab, Sikhs organise processions. They carry the Guru Granth Sahib on a decorated float, accompanied by Sikhs singing and dancing. The route will often be lined with stalls offering free food and soft drinks to passers-by and the local community. Special jalebi sweets, made from flour and sugar syrup, are made and given away to people at the festival. This is also a popular time for Sikhs to be initiated into the Khalsa in memory of Guru Gobind Singh's actions in 1699.

During this festival the Sikh flag (the Nishan Sahib), which stands in the grounds of a gurdwara, is taken down and a new flag, donated by members of the sangat (the Sikh congregation), will replace it. The flagpole itself is taken down and washed carefully in yoghurt and milk, and then with water as a symbol of purity and cleanliness. The saffron-coloured cloth in which the flagpole is wrapped is also replaced.

In India, large fairs are organised with sporting competitions and Sikhs demonstrate traditional martial arts skills. Bhangra dancing and folk music are popular too. At Anandpur Sahib, there are special celebrations at the Keshgarh Sahib gurdwara, since it was here that Guru Gobind Singh began to initiate Sikhs into the Khalsa. Some Sikhs travel a long way to go to the celebrations at the Golden Temple. In other towns, Vaisakhi celebrations may include a market for buying and selling animals, political rallies and sports events.

Extension activity

Indarjit Singh is a journalist, broadcaster and member of the House of Lords. He has said that when Guru Gobind Singh urged Sikhs to help others, there was an urgent need to challenge oppression. But now, after three centuries, although people's needs have changed, the same kind of commitment to others (rather than oneself) has never been more important.

Explain ways in which this commitment to others rather than oneself is important for Sikhs.

▲ *Sikh musicians celebrating at Vaisakhi*

Research activity

Find out more about how Sikhs celebrate Vaisakhi in the largest towns and cities in Britain.

⭐ Study tip

Using the internet, try to find and watch a video clip of Vaisakhi celebrations in Britain. This will help you to remember what happens during the celebrations.

Activities

1 Explain how religious persecution of the Sikhs and the establishment of the Khalsa are connected.
2 Describe what is done to the flagpole and flag during Vaisakhi and consider why Sikhs think these actions are important.
3 Give two ways in which Sikhs celebrate Vaisakhi in Britain.
4 Explain why many Sikhs are initiated into the Khalsa at Vaisakhi.
5 'For Sikhs, Vaisakhi celebrates the beginning of the Sikh religion.' Develop some arguments to support this statement and some arguments to support a different point of view.

Summary

You should now be able to explain the origins of Vaisakhi, how Sikhs celebrate the festival and its importance for Sikhs.

2.8 The festival of Divali

■ The origins of Divali

Divali, the festival of light, is celebrated widely in India by Hindus and Sikhs in October or early November. For Sikhs it has a special significance linked to Sikh history. Sikhs call it Bandi Chhor Divas, which means 'day of liberation from captivity', and they celebrate the values of hope, faith, solidarity and freedom demonstrated by the sixth Sikh Guru.

Guru Hargobind

During a time of persecution in 1619, the sixth Guru, Guru Hargobind, and 52 Hindu princes were imprisoned in the fort of Gwalior by the Mughal authorities. All were arrested for political reasons. When Jehingir, the emperor, announced his release, the Guru refused to leave prison unless the princes were released as well. Jehingir replied that as many as could hold onto the Guru's clothes as he walked out of a narrow gate could be released. The Guru had a special cloak sewn with 52 long tassels attached to it and each prince was able to hold onto the cloak. So all were freed. On his return to the Golden Temple at Amritsar, the Guru was welcomed by Sikhs who had decorated the temple and the surrounding pool. The Guru became known as 'Bandi Chhor', the deliverer from prison, and the day became known as 'Bandi Chhor Divas'.

The martyrdom of Bhai Mani Singh

During Divali, Sikhs also remember the martyrdom of Bhai Mani Singh, who was the granthi at the Golden Temple and who transcribed the final version of the Guru Granth Sahib at Guru Gobind Singh's request. He had gained permission for a gathering of Sikhs to celebrate Bandi Chhor Divas at the Golden Temple in 1737, in return for a large tax that the Mughal emperor demanded. However, he later discovered that the emperor was intending to kill many Sikhs at this gathering and cancelled the meeting. The emperor then ordered his death.

■ Sikh celebrations for Divali

An akhand path (continuous reading of the Guru Granth Sahib) is held at the gurdwara, and lights and lamps are lit. Sikhs remember Sikh history, the values of the Gurus and God's light.

In India, in addition to spectacular firework displays, bonfires will be lit. The Golden Temple at Amritsar and the surrounding pool and buildings are decorated with

▲ *Guru Hargobind: his cloak enabled the freedom of 52 Hindu princes*

▲ *Sikhs light Divali candles outside a gurdwara in Britain*

Activities

1 Describe some of the ways in which Divali is celebrated by Sikhs in Britain today.

2 Explain why Bhai Mani Singh is especially remembered at Divali.

3 'The festival of Divali is celebrated by Sikhs mainly to remember the courage shown by Guru Hargobind.' Do you agree with this statement? Give some reasons for your answer.

thousands of lights. Many Sikhs travel to the Golden Temple to join in the celebrations. Langars are often held, some in the open air, and hundreds or thousands of people attend.

■ The importance of Divali for Sikhs

For Sikhs, Divali is a celebration of freedom. Not only was Guru Hargobind seen to be innocent of the charges and freed from prison but he managed to obtain the release of 52 innocent Hindu princes who had been imprisoned only for their political beliefs. Sikhism has always supported freedom to follow and express religious beliefs – not just for Sikhs, but for all people. Therefore, this was an important victory, particularly so in a time of persecution.

Sikhs celebrate the way in which leaders have supported religious freedom and the equality of all people. They also show respect for those, such as Bhai Mani Singh, who have opposed injustice and oppression. The festival also remembers the courage of Sikhs prepared to stand up for the faith in the face of persecution or adversity. The compassion and consideration Sikhs have shown, and their willingness to pursue their beliefs in equality of treatment for all, are celebrated. Sikhs encourage each other to follow the examples of Guru Hargobind and Bhai Mani Singh, both in promoting and protecting religious faith.

Research activity

Use a library or the internet to find out why candles and lights are important in religious celebrations.

⭐ **Study tip**

Check that you can write down a list of reasons why Divali is an important festival for Sikhs.

Summary

You should now know the origins and significance of the Sikh celebration of Divali and its importance for Sikhs in Britain today.

Extension activity

Investigate the reasons why Guru Hargobind was arrested and why the Hindu princes were also imprisoned.

Gurpurbs

Gurpurbs are celebrations which take place at anniversaries, usually of the birth or death of one of the Gurus. 'Gur' comes from the word Guru and 'purb' means a festival or holiday in Punjabi. Throughout the world, four gurpurbs are widely celebrated by Sikhs; others are celebrated only at the sites of the original event. The four that are widely celebrated are:

- the birthday of Guru Nanak (October/November)
- the birthday of Guru Gobind Singh (December/January)
- the martyrdom of Guru Arjan (May/June)
- the martyrdom of Guru Tegh Bahadur (November/December).

A fifth gurpurb that is also popular is the installation of the Guru Granth Sahib in the Harimandir Sahib at Amritsar (held in August).

Before each gurpurb, Sikhs will prepare themselves by reading the Guru Granth Sahib.

Celebrations in the community

Gurpurbs may be celebrated by the Sikh community in the following ways:

- The Guru Granth Sahib is carried in procession. Sometimes, it is carried on a float with members of the Khalsa on either side to protect it and show it respect. During the time of the Gurus, important people might have been similarly carried through the streets with guards to protect them and make sure the way was safe. In front of the Guru Granth Sahib are five Sikhs who represent the first five members of the Khalsa, the Panj Piare.
- Local bands or groups of musicians perform kirtan.
- Passers-by are offered food or refreshments.
- Local competitions may be organised and prizes given.
- Cards may be exchanged.
- Special langars are held for all those taking part in the celebrations.

Celebrations in the gurdwara

Before each gurpurb, gurdwaras will hold an akhand path, the continuous reading of the whole of the Guru Granth Sahib. This helps Sikhs to prepare for the gurpurb. It begins about 48 hours before the gurpurb, so that it will be completed by dawn on the day of the anniversary. During this time, people will come and go to and from the gurdwara, and langar and karah parshad are available throughout. Worship includes singing hymns composed by the Guru whose anniversary is being celebrated, and listening to stories or talks about the life of the Guru. The langar provides hospitality throughout the day.

Objectives

- Know how gurpurbs are celebrated in Great Britain and in India.
- Understand the importance of gurpurbs for Sikhs.

Key term

- **gurpurb:** 'festival of a Guru'; festivals which celebrate the anniversary of the birth or death of a Guru

▲ Guru Arjan was the first martyr of the Sikh faith

Links

To read more about an akhand path, see page 39.

❝ The stories of one's ancestors make the children good children. ❞

Guru Granth Sahib 951

■ Guru Nanak's birthday

Guru Nanak's birthday is the most important of the gurpurbs. Celebrations will begin early in the gurdwara and in some parts of the UK there will be a procession in the streets. Candles are lit in the gurdwara as well as in homes, shops and offices. Firework displays also are organised to celebrate the occasion. In the Punjab, children are given new clothes and they have a holiday from school.

■ The martyrdom of Guru Tegh Bahadur

▲ *Sikh children celebrating Guru Nanak's birthday*

Guru Tegh Bahadur lived at a time of persecution for Sikhs. In 1675, he appointed his son, Guru Gobind Singh, as his successor and then left with three other Sikhs to try to persuade the emperor to stop the persecution. They were all arrested and imprisoned. The three Sikhs were executed in front of Guru Tegh Bahadur, and he, like them, refused to become a Muslim. He was invited to perform a miracle to show that he was a man of God but he refused and so was executed.

■ Differences between celebrations in Great Britain and India

- The dates of these celebrations vary within 28 days because they are based on a lunar system. In India, celebrations take place on the actual anniversary date of the original event whereas in Britain, Sikhs sometimes celebrate the gurpurbs on the Sunday nearest the actual date.
- In India, schools are often closed for some of the gurpurbs but in Britain, the festival will be held at the weekend.
- In India, the gurpurb will be marked by colourful processions through towns, and firework displays and fairs. In Britain, celebrations are generally quieter and more local, often centred on the gurdwara. There may, however, be a local procession or a firework display.
- In Britain, possibly influenced by the tradition of sending cards at Christian festival times, Sikhs sometimes send cards to each other.

■ The importance of gurpurbs

Gurpurbs provide an opportunity for Sikhs to celebrate the religion's history and to remind themselves of the important principles of their faith. They help to strengthen the faith of individual Sikhs as they come together to celebrate and worship. The akhand path is a reminder of Sikh priorities, calling on God's name and putting him in the centre of life. The gurpurbs enable children to learn about the Gurus and their beliefs, their teaching and their example. Gurpurbs are also an opportunity for Sikhs to share their faith with the wider community and to practise sewa.

Activities

1 What is meant by the word 'gurpurb'?
2 Explain two different ways in which gurpurbs are celebrated in India and Britain.
3 Explain what Sikhs could learn from the martyrdom of Guru Tegh Bahadur.

Research activity

Research the martyrdom of Guru Arjan. What would Sikhs learn from this story?

Extension activity

Find out more about how Sikhs celebrate gurpurbs in the Punjab. You may be able to watch clips on the internet or study photos of celebrations.

★ Study tip

It is important to know about the celebrations for Guru Nanak's birthday.

Summary

You should now know how gurpurbs are celebrated and the differences between celebrations in Britain and India. You should also understand their importance.

■ The Harimandir Sahib: the Golden Temple

Many Sikhs visit the Punjab where the Sikh faith began. Most who visit will make a pilgrimage to **Harimandir Sahib**, the Golden Temple. This is located in Amritsar, a city in the northern part of the Punjab, close to the border with Pakistan. The Golden Temple is the most famous place of worship for Sikhs. The word Harimandir means 'the temple of God' and Sahib is a term of respect.

The Harimandir Sahib is surrounded by a pool of fresh, clear water (the Amrit Sarover), brought there by the River Ravi. Amritsar is named after the pool. The gurdwara is a two-storey building with four entrances, one on each side to symbolise that people from all corners of the world are welcome, whatever their caste, class, race or religious beliefs. It is known as the Golden Temple because, in the upper storey, the white marble from which it is built is overlaid with gold leaf. It has a Golden Dome that is believed to represent an inverted lotus flower, its petals pointing down to the earth, reminding Sikhs that they should be concerned about the world's problems. The temple is approached by a causeway called the Guru's Bridge. At the northern entrance steps go up and then down again into the temple, symbolising the need to be humble and respectful in the presence of the Guru Granth Sahib.

Inside the temple, the walls are covered in wooden panels inlaid with gold and silver. The original Adi Granth, the first version of the scripture compiled by Guru Arjan, is installed on a takht (throne) under a canopy set with jewels. A continuous reading of the Guru Granth Sahib is performed each day in three-hour shifts.

▲ The Golden Temple: a spiritual place for Sikhs

Objectives

- Understand Sikh attitudes to pilgrimage.
- Understand why Sikhs may wish to visit historical gurdwaras.
- Consider the importance for Sikhs of the Golden Temple.

Key term

- **Harimandir Sahib:** the Golden Temple, the temple of God

■ Akal Takht: the throne of religious authority

The Akal Takht (which means the 'Throne of the Timeless One') is the most important political building for Sikhs and faces onto the causeway which leads to the Golden Temple. It is where the spiritual leader of the Sikhs works and is the centre of religious government, dealing with both spiritual and more practical or earthly (temporal) matters relating to the Sikh community. It is the place where judgements about religious matters are made.

It houses the resting room for the Guru Granth Sahib. Every morning, at 4 am in the summer and 5 am in the winter, Sikhs carry the Guru

Discussion activity

Discuss what pilgrimage may contribute to the faith of an individual. Consider the effects of planning the visit, travel arrangements and taking part as an individual or a group.

Extension activity

Use the internet to find out more about the history and importance of the Akal Takht for Sikhs.

Granth Sahib across the causeway lit by lamps to the Golden Temple where the prakash ceremony is performed. In the evening, at 10 pm, the sukhasan ceremony is performed and the Guru Granth Sahib is returned to the Akal Takht.

▲ *Sikh pilgrims on the Guru's bridge*

■ Visiting the Golden Temple

Pilgrims visiting the Golden Temple can bathe in the sacred water, which is believed to have healing properties. They visit the gurdwara, listen to kirtan and hear readings from the Guru Granth Sahib. They spend time in reflection and meditation, reciting the name of God. Every day, volunteers maintain the Golden Temple buildings and prepare and serve the langar. Tens of thousands of pilgrims are able to receive a free meal and the costs are met from donations.

> **"** The spiritual wisdom given by the Guru is the True sacred shrine of pilgrimage … **"**
>
> *Guru Granth Sahib 687*

■ The role of pilgrimage in Sikh life

Guru Nanak and the other Gurus believed that ritual and ceremony could sometimes get in the way of true faith and wisdom. Such ritual could not be seen to earn merit or take the place of the effort to understand God and meditate on his name. For example, many of the gurdwaras in the Punjab have pools but the Gurus were clear that bathing in them would do nothing if people were not clean inside. It was the spiritual state of mind of the individual that was important.

Sikhs do not have to complete any pilgrimage but many do. Many believe that the effort to make such a pilgrimage, and the spiritual reflection that places like the Golden Temple encourage, will provide time and inspiration to deepen their faith and understanding. A visit to the Golden Temple may also help them learn about the stories of the courage and faith of Sikh Gurus and leaders, and help them to meditate on the name of God and the important principles of the Sikh faith. Pilgrims may also visit other historical gurdwaras in India and Pakistan to understand more about the beginning of their faith and about the history of the Sikhs. There are many gurdwaras associated with one or more of the Ten Gurus, in places where they lived and worked, or where a particular visit of a Guru is remembered.

One of these places is Goindval, where Guru Amas Das built a deep well that has 84 steps into it. Sikhs sometimes recite the Japji on each of these steps as they go down to bathe. However, the emphasis is always on focusing on God and his name, not on the ritual itself.

> **"** One who bathes in the Ambrosial Water of spiritual wisdom takes with him the virtues of the sixty-eight sacred shrines of pilgrimage. The Guru's Teachings are the gems and jewels; the Sikh who serves Him searches and finds them. **There is no sacred shrine equal to the Guru. "**
>
> *Guru Granth Sahib 1328*

Activity

'They go and bathe at sacred shrines of pilgrimage, but their minds are still evil, and their bodies are thieves. Some of their filth is washed off by these baths, but they only accumulate twice as much. Like a gourd, they may be washed off on the outside, but on the inside, they are still filled with poison. The holy man is blessed, even without such bathing, while a thief is a thief, no matter how much he bathes.' (Guru Granth Sahib 789)

Read this quotation carefully and write down the important ideas it contains. How does it explain Sikh beliefs about faith and pilgrimage?

⭐ Study tip

Learning short quotations can be very useful, for example 'a thief is a thief, no matter how much he bathes'.

Summary

You should now have considered Sikh attitudes to pilgrimage, and the importance of visiting historical gurdwaras. You should also understand the importance of the Golden Temple for Sikhs.

2.11 Birth and naming ceremonies

■ The naming ceremony in a gurdwara

About two weeks after a baby is born, as soon as the mother has recovered from the birth, the family takes the baby to the gurdwara, inviting their friends and family to be present. This can be during a normal service of worship at the gurdwara. As in any worship service, everyone bows before the Guru Granth Sahib and makes offerings of food or money. At the end of the ceremony, karah parshad is distributed to all. The family may also offer something special to the gurdwara such as a rumalla.

The Mool Mantra is said in thanksgiving for the new life. Hymns of joy or thanksgiving will be recited or sung. The baby will be given a spoonful of **amrit**, a mixture of sugar and water. The granthi recites the first five verses of the Japji as he or she stirs the amrit with a khanda, a two-edged sword. The granthi then dips the sword in the amrit and lightly touches the baby's tongue and head with the tip of the sword. The rest of the amrit is given to the baby's mother to drink.

> 66 The True Guru has truly given a child. The long-lived one has been born to this destiny. He came to acquire a home in the womb, and his mother's heart is so very glad. A son is born – a devotee of the Lord of the Universe. This preordained destiny has been revealed to all. In the tenth month, by the Lord's Order, the baby has been born. Sorrow is dispelled, and great joy has ensued. The companions blissfully sing the songs of the Guru's Bani. This is pleasing to the Lord Master. The vine has grown, and shall last for many generations. The Power of the Dharma has been firmly established by the Lord. That which my mind wishes for, the True Guru has granted. I have become carefree, and I fix my attention on the One Lord. As the child places so much faith in his father, I speak as it pleases the Guru to have me speak. This is not a hidden secret; Guru Nanak, greatly pleased, has bestowed this gift. 99
>
> *A hymn of joy on the birth of a child, Guru Granth Sahib 396*

■ The naming of the child

After the ceremony with amrit, the granthi opens the Guru Granth Sahib at random. As the pages fall open, he or she will read out the top section of the left-hand page. The first letter of the first word of the first hymn on the left-hand page will decide the first letter of the child's name. The parents decide on a name and the granthi then announces it to the congregation and says a blessing. The congregation sings Anand Sahib and offers a prayer of thanksgiving. They then say prayers for the child, including a hope that the child will become a true Sikh, showing devotion to God. They say the Ardas prayer and then share out karah parshad to everyone present.

▲ *The first letter of a Sikh's name is taken from the Guru Granth Sahib during the naming ceremony*

Some of the names that Sikhs may choose can be given to girls or boys, for example Jaswant or Harminder.

If the mother is not well enough to attend the gurdwara or the family does not have a gurdwara nearby, the ceremony can be performed at home and the gutka, the prayer book which Sikhs often keep at home, is used instead of the Guru Granth Sahib.

> **Links**
>
> For information about the gutka look back at pages 44–45.

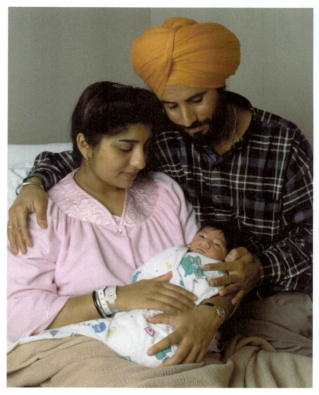

▲ *The naming ceremony happens about two weeks after a baby is born*

■ The surnames of Kaur and Singh

Some Sikhs use their family name but others follow Guru Gobind Singh's practice of giving all women the surname 'Kaur' (princess) and men the surname 'Singh' (lion). Soon after the appointment of the Panj Piare at the time of Vaisakhi in 1699, Guru Gobind was known as Guru Gobind Singh and his wife as Mata Sahib Kaur. This showed the Sikh belief in the equality of all and prevented discrimination based on what caste in India any individual had come from.

> ❝ The Transcendent Lord has given me His support. The house of pain and disease has been demolished. The men and women celebrate. The Lord God, Har, Har, has extended His Mercy. O Saints, there is peace everywhere. The Supreme Lord God, the Perfect Transcendent Lord, is pervading everywhere. The Bani of His Word emanated from the Primal Lord. It eradicates all anxiety. The Lord is merciful, kind and compassionate. Nanak chants the Naam, the Name of the True Lord. ❞
>
> *A hymn of thanksgiving, Guru Granth Sahib 628*

> **Activity**
>
> Write a letter that a Sikh might write to a friend describing the naming ceremony of a baby in their family.

■ The importance of birth and the naming ceremony

Sikhs believe that each individual has many reincarnations and the birth of an individual as a human is a great gift of God, providing the opportunity for that individual to come to know God and be united with him. So it is a time to celebrate and give thanks to God.

> **Summary**
>
> You should now be able to describe a Sikh naming ceremony and understand its significance and importance for Sikhs.

 Study tip

Try to remember that it is the first letter of the first word of the first line of the left-hand page that settles the first letter of the child's name.

2.12 The initiation ceremony (Amrit Sanskar)

■ Initiation into the Khalsa

Sikhs who are prepared to be fully committed to the Sikh faith take part in the **Amrit Sanskar** ceremony. Sometimes this ceremony of initiation is called a baptism. This is an important event in the life of the individual Sikh and for the Sikh community. In agreeing to undergo this ceremony, a Sikh is making a commitment to become a member of the Khalsa, and this will involve not only wearing the five Ks but also keeping to the rules set out for the Khalsa. Both men and women can become members and are then known as amritdhari. Sikhs need to be old enough to recognise the importance and seriousness of the responsibilities of the Khalsa, so this ceremony is not usually performed until individuals are in their later teens or sometimes well into adulthood. For example, some Sikhs may not feel that they can commit fully to the rules until they are much older. As this ceremony ends, Sikhs are expected to take the surname Singh or Kaur, a practice Guru Gobind Singh began.

■ The ceremony: Amrit Sanskar

The person to be initiated is required to bathe and wash their hair, cover their head, and wear clean clothes for the ceremony. They also wear the five Ks and then take part in a ceremony with at least six amritdhari Sikhs. Five of these, who represent the first Panj Piare initiated by Guru Gobind Singh, conduct the ceremony. The other Sikh, the granthi, reads the Guru Granth Sahib. Those who have presented themselves are asked whether they wish to be initiated and are reminded about what it means to be a member of the Khalsa. In turn, each one of the Panj Piare recites one of the five prayers. They use a khanda to stir the amrit in a steel bowl. The granthi opens the Guru Granth Sahib at random (hukam) and reads a hymn. Everyone recites the Ardas prayer.

The person being initiated then drinks amrit from the bowl five times, saying, 'Waheguru Ji Ka Khalsa, Waheguru Ji Ki Fateh', which means 'The Khalsa belongs to God, victory belongs to God.' The Panj Piare sprinkle amrit on their eyes and hair five times. Those being initiated share the rest of the amrit, all drinking from the one bowl. They recite the Mool Mantra, and any person who does not already have a Sikh name is given one. Everyone eats a share of karah parshad.

■ The requirements for members of the Khalsa

There are strict rules, set out in the Rehat Maryada, concerning the Amrit Sanskar ceremony to ensure that all those who are

▲ *Five Sikhs represent the Panj Piare, the five loved ones, at the Amrit Sanskar ceremony*

amritdhari understand their commitment. At the end of the ceremony, one of the five Sikhs representing the Panj Piare has to explain to the Sikhs who have just taken part in the ceremony the importance of their membership of the Khalsa. This includes the following words:

> ❝ Today you are reborn in the true Guru's household, ending the cycle of migration, and joined the Khalsa Panth (order). Your spiritual father is now Guru Gobind Singh and, spiritual mother, Mata Sahib Kaur. Your place of birth is Kesgarh Sahib and your native place is Anandpur Sahib. You, being the sons of one father, are, inter-se [among] yourselves and other baptised Sikhs, spiritual brothers. You have become the pure Khalsa, having renounced your previous lineage, professional background, calling (occupation), beliefs, that is, having given up all connections with your caste, descent, birth, country, religion, etc. You are to worship none except the One Timeless Being – no god, goddess, incarnation or prophet. You are not to think of anyone except the ten Gurus and anything except their gospel as your saviour. ❞
>
> *Rehat Maryada, article 24*

Members of the Khalsa are expected to recite or hear recited at least the following prayers each day: the Japji Sahib, the Jap Sahib, the Ten Swayyas, the Sodar Rahiras and the Sohila. They are reminded that they should always wear the five Ks and that they should keep the following rules:

- They must worship only one God, and accept the teachings of the Ten Gurus and the Guru Granth Sahib.
- They must not cut their hair; they should keep it clean and wear a turban.
- They should not eat meat which has been ritually slaughtered, and most amritdhari Sikhs understand this to mean they should be vegetarian.
- They must not cohabit with anyone who is not their husband or wife.
- They should not use tobacco.

Other prohibitions include:

- not to drink alcohol
- not to steal or gamble
- not to arrange a son or daughter's marriage for financial gain
- not to believe in any superstition or magic
- women are not to wear a veil.

▲ A Sikh woman has amrit sprinkled on her eyes and hair

Links

To remind yourself about the origins of the Amrit Sanskar ceremony, see pages 24–25.

Discussion activity

Discuss with a partner why initiation ceremonies are important for religious believers.

Extension activity

Research Sikh history and see whether you can find, in the life or teaching of the Gurus, reasons for some of the prohibitions.

⭐ **Study tip**

Try to learn the first five rules which amritdhari Sikhs are expected to keep.

Summary

You should now understand the meaning and importance of the Amrit Sanskar and what membership of the Khalsa means for amritdhari Sikhs.

Activities

1 Draw a diagram of amrit in a steel bowl being stirred with a kirpan. Around the edge of the diagram, starting on the left of the page, write the series of actions and words in the ceremony in order. This will help you to remember it.

2 Consider all the prohibitions listed on this page. Explain how each of these fits in with Sikh beliefs.

Worship and service – summary

You should now be able to:

✔ explain the religious features of the gurdwara: design, furniture and artefacts, including the palki and the takht; explain religious practices in the gurdwara, including worship that is associated with these features and their importance

✔ explain the role of the gurdwara within the Sikh community

✔ explain the role of prayer in the home, including an understanding of Guru Granth Sahib 305:4

✔ explain the role and importance of the akhand path

✔ explain the meaning and significance of langar as an expression of sewa

✔ explain the significance of meditating on the name of God (nam japna) in daily life and in the gurdwara.

Festivals and lifestyle – summary

You should now be able to:

✔ know and understand the Sikh festivals of Vaisakhi (Baisakhi) and Divali, including their origins and significance and their importance for Sikhs in Britain today

✔ know and understand the origins and significance of gurpurbs, including Guru Nanak's birthday, and their importance for Sikhs in Britain, including differences in the way gurpurbs are celebrated in India and Britain

✔ explain the importance of visiting Sikh historical gurdwaras, including the Golden Temple (Harimandir Sahib) in Amritsar

✔ explain birth and naming ceremonies, including their meaning and significance

✔ explain the initiation ceremony (Amrit Sanskar), including the meaning and importance of the Khalsa and the five Ks

✔ explain the different perspectives of sahajdhari and amritdhari Sikhs

✔ explain the significance and use of the names Singh and Kaur.

Sample student answer – the 4-mark question

1. Write an answer to the following practice question:

   Explain two different ways in which Sikhs can follow their faith by being amritdhari or sahajdhari. [4 marks]

2. Read the following sample student answer:

   "Many Sikhs believe that they should follow the example set by Guru Gobind Singh and join the Khalsa. In so doing they agree to keep quite a lot of rules as well as being true to the one God. They must wear the five Ks and follow a set series of prayers each day. They must not drink alcohol or smoke. They must not cut their hair and must wear a turban to keep it tidy and clean. They must not have sex except with their husband or wife and must not eat meat that has been ritually slaughtered. They believe that living a strict life like this will bring them closer to God because they will bring God's name to mind all the time and not worry so much about material things.

Sahajdhari Sikhs are Sikhs who hold all the beliefs of Sikhism and try to follow the teachings of the Gurus, but they may not wear any or all of the 5Ks, although many wear a kara. They may intend to become amritdharis later in their lives and usually bring up their children in the Sikh faith. Sikhs take very seriously the decision to become amritdhari and breaking the Khalsa code of conduct is seen to be a great sin, so Sikhs understand that it is better not to become amritdhari than to fail afterwards. Sahajdhari Sikhs do not use tobacco or eat halal meat."

3. With a partner, discuss the sample answer. Is the focus of the answer correct? Is anything missing from the answer? How do you think it could be improved?

4. What mark (out of 4) would you give this answer? Look at the mark scheme in the Introduction (AO1). What are the reasons for the mark you have given?

5. Now swap your answer with your partner's and mark each other's responses. What mark (out of 4) would you give the response? Refer to the mark scheme and give reasons for the mark you award.

Sample student answer – the 6-mark question

1. Write an answer to the following practice question:

   Explain **two** ways in which the akhand path is important for Sikhs.

   Refer to sacred writings or another source of Sikh belief and teaching in your answer.

   [6 marks]

2. Read the following sample student answer:

   "The akhand path is the continuous reading of the Guru Granth Sahib. It takes about 48 hours to read it and there are a team of readers who take it in turns. It has to be read clearly and steadily. It is usually done in a gurdwara but it can be done in someone's home or in a business. Sikhs come to listen to it but can come and go as they like. Sikhs believe it is important because it is the living Guru from whom they can learn about the faith and it helps them to make God the centre of their attention. The Guru Granth Sahib is scripture and arranging a special reading before a wedding, for example, can bring great blessing on the couple who are preparing for an important stage in their lives."

3. With a partner, discuss the sample answer. It makes some good points but it fails to do something which is important. How do you think the answer could be improved?

4. What mark (out of 6) would you give this answer? Look at the mark scheme in the Introduction (AO1). What are the reasons for the mark you have given?

5. Now swap your answer with your partner's and mark each other's responses. What mark (out of 6) would you give the response? Refer to the mark scheme and give reasons for the mark you award.

Sample student answer – the 12-mark question

1. Write an answer to the following practice question:

   'The lives and teachings of the Ten Gurus are more important for the Sikh faith than the Guru Granth Sahib.'

   Evaluate this statement. In your answer you should:

   • refer to Sikh teaching
   • give reasoned arguments to support this statement
   • give reasoned arguments to support a different point of view
   • reach a justified conclusion.

   [12 marks]

2. Read the following student sample answer:

   "I think the lives and teachings of the Ten Gurus are much more important for the Sikh faith than the Guru Granth Sahib. Without the Ten Gurus there would be no Sikh faith. The Guru Granth Sahib was written by the Gurus anyway so it just contains their teaching. Guru Nanak was very important indeed because he started the faith and showed Sikhs how to live in harmony with others, to be tolerant and to welcome everyone. He started the langar which showed his belief in the value of all human beings and which challenged the practices of the caste system and the bad treatment of women. Some Gurus lost their lives because they stood up for their faith and for the rights of others for freedom of worship. The Gurus wrote the hymns which Sikhs sing now, many of which are in the Guru Granth Sahib, and Guru Arjan built the Golden Temple which, with its four doors, demonstrates the welcome to all people whatever their race or religion or background. Guru Gobind Singh began the Khalsa which has helped to make for a strong Sikh community and helped to complete the Guru Granth Sahib which he said would be the living Guru.

   However I can see that some people would say the Guru Granth Sahib was more important because it is here now for Sikhs to study and contains all the wisdom needed for faith in God. It does not change and the Gurus are just part of history really – they were important but they are not now.

   Overall, I think it is clear that the Ten Gurus are important for the Sikh faith. They developed the beliefs and practices of the religion. Guru Nanak gave Sikhs the Mool Mantra which is the basis of faith and all the Sikh festivals remember the Gurus.

   Of course the Guru Granth Sahib is important for wisdom and for worship but it is based on what the Gurus gave to the Sikh faith."

3. With a partner, discuss the sample answer. Consider the following questions:

   • Does the answer refer to Sikh teachings and if so what are they?
   • Is there an argument to support the statement and how well developed is it?
   • Is a different point of view offered and how developed is that argument?
   • Has the student written a clear conclusion after weighing up both sides of the argument?
   • What is good about this answer?
   • How do you think it could be improved?

4. What mark (out of 12) would you give this answer? Look at the mark scheme in the Introduction (AO2). What are the reasons for the mark you have given?

5. Now swap your answer with your partner's and mark each other's responses. What mark (out of 12) would you give the response? Refer to the mark scheme and give reasons for the mark you award.

Practice questions

1 In which city is the Golden Temple?
  A) Delhi   **B)** Amritsar   **C)** Kartarpur   **D)** Varanasi   **[1 mark]**

2 Give **one** of the Sikh five Ks.   **[1 mark]**

> **Study tip**
>
> This question only requires the naming of one of the five Ks and one mark will be given for a correct answer. Do not waste time by answering in sentences.

3 Explain **two** different ways in which Sikhs show respect for the Guru Granth Sahib.   **[4 marks]**

> **Study tip**
>
> This question asks you to *explain*, which means that more than just naming a way of showing respect is needed. Do not forget to develop the points you are making. You should choose *only two* ways in which Sikhs show respect and develop your answer by explaining the meaning of each action, rather than just writing a list of *all* the things that are done to show respect. Make sure the two ways are sufficiently different.

4 Explain **two** ways in which the Sikh birth and naming ceremonies are important.

Refer to sacred writings or another source of Sikh belief and teaching in your answer.

      [6 marks]

5 'The most important duty of a Sikh is to become a member of the Khalsa.'

Evaluate this statement. In your answer you should:
- refer to Sikh teaching
- give reasoned arguments to support this statement
- give reasoned arguments to support a different point of view
- reach a justified conclusion.   **[12 marks]**

> **Study tip**
>
> Read the statement carefully and make sure that your answer is focused fully on what it is saying.
>
> You should aim to develop different viewpoints to show differences between those who agree with the statement and those who think the other duties of a Sikh, such as meditating on the name of God, are more important. You should aim to refer to Sikh teaching in your arguments. You should develop your answer by giving examples or further explaining your arguments. You should also reach a justified conclusion.

Part 2: Thematic studies

3 Relationships and families

3.1 Religious teachings about human sexuality

■ Sikh attitudes to human sexuality

Human sexuality refers to the way people express themselves as sexual beings. It is natural for young people to begin to have an interest in sex when they reach puberty. They are going through physical and psychological changes, which can lead to forming an opposite-sex (**heterosexual**) relationship (between a man and a woman) and to reproduction (having children).

Sikhs believe God is present within creation; therefore sex is seen as a wonderful creative act that has the potential to bring a new soul into the world. It is also a means of spiritual growth as couples express love, companionship and intimacy within a marriage. The Guru Granth Sahib compares the soul's relationship with God to the union between husband and wife, describing it as joyous and infinitely pleasurable.

For Sikhs it is important to remain pure (chaste) before marriage since the body contains the divine spark of God, so should be kept clean and perfect. Lust (a strong sexual desire) is one of the barriers to mukti (liberation) and can harm others, so Sikhs believe that sexual relationships should only take place within marriage.

■ Sikh attitudes to same-sex sexual relationships

A same-sex sexual relationship is a sexual relationship between a man and another man or a woman and another woman. The Guru Granth Sahib does not mention same-sex sexual relationships, but it does encourage opposite-sex marriage and the life of a householder (family life). Many Sikhs, therefore, believe that since the only marriage mentioned in the Guru Granth Sahib is that of a man and woman, same-sex marriage is wrong. Lust is condemned as one of the five vices in the Guru Granth Sahib and in the Sikh Code of Conduct (Rehat Maryada). Some

▲ *Sikhs are expected to remain chaste before marriage*

Objectives

- Understand Sikh teachings about human sexuality.
- Consider contemporary British attitudes towards these relationships.

Key terms

- **human sexuality:** how people express themselves as sexual beings
- **heterosexual:** sexually attracted to members of the opposite sex

Discussion activity

Sikhism discourages dating. Discuss the advantages and disadvantages of this for a young Sikh.

Sikhs interpret this teaching as a condemnation of same-sex sexual relationships. However, others say that the teaching against lust applies equally to opposite-sex sexual relationships, and that Guru Nanak's teaching on equality and brotherhood requires respect for the rights of people who are attracted to people of the same sex. What is clear is that Sikh teaching does not condemn a person's sexual orientation. Sikhs do not approve of discrimination against anyone, regardless of race, religion, gender or sexuality. The gurdwara is open to all and people who are attracted to people of the same sex are free to participate in services.

■ Contemporary British attitudes

Today in Britain, sex before marriage, multiple sexual partners, children outside of marriage, affairs (adultery) or same-sex sexual relationships are more common. Same-sex relationships are legal and same-sex couples can marry or convert civil partnerships into marriage if they wish.

Like many Sikhs, many British Christians believe that the only place for sex is within marriage and that opposite-sex sexual relationships fulfil God's purposes for humanity. But within Christianity, as within Sikhism, there are those who accept same-sex sexual relationships as part of life and see them as just as valid as opposite-sex sexual relationships.

The age of consent

In the UK, the age of consent for anyone to have sex is 16 years old, which means you are legally old enough to freely agree to have sex. The law tries to protect anyone under 16 from exploitation and abuse. Sikh teachings do not specify an age of consent, but it is not considered desirable or proper to marry very young. Sikh parents would only arrange for their children to be married when they are mature enough to enter into such a commitment. Sikhs generally accept the laws of the country in which they live.

▲ *Sikh girls dress modestly*

> 66 O sexual desire, you lead the mortals to hell; you make them wander in reincarnation through countless species. You cheat the consciousness, and pervade the three worlds. You destroy meditation, penance and virtue. But you give only shallow pleasure, while you make the mortals weak and unsteady; you pervade the high and the low. 99
>
> *Guru Granth Sahib 1358*

> 66 Lust, anger, greed, attachment, and pride,
>
> may they all leave me.
>
> Says Nanak, I have come to Your refuge,
>
> grant me Your blessing, my supreme Guru. 99
>
> *Sukhmani prayer, section 6 introduction*

Contrasting beliefs

Find out more about Christian teachings on same-sex sexual relationships. Do Christian beliefs agree with or differ from Sikh beliefs on this issue?

⭐ Study tip

It is important to remember that for Sikhs sex has a moral dimension. It should only be engaged in responsibly within an opposite-sex marriage.

Activities

1 Explain Sikh attitudes towards human sexuality.
2 Explain why many Sikhs consider same-sex marriage to be wrong.
3 'There is too much sexual freedom in contemporary British society.' Evaluate this statement.

Summary

You should now be able to explain Sikh attitudes to human sexuality, including opposite-sex and same-sex sexual relationships.

3.2 Sexual relationships before and outside marriage

■ Sexual relationships before marriage

As we have seen, Sikhs consider marriage the only appropriate place for a sexual relationship. **Sex before marriage** is expressly forbidden. The Sikh Code of Conduct (Rehat Maryada) says that anyone who has sexual relationships without marriage is not a true Sikh.

> ❝ For a moment of sexual pleasure, you shall suffer in pain for millions of days. ❞
>
> *Guru Granth Sahib 403*

Family honour is important, and girls especially must be modest. Anything that might lead to lust, one of the five evil vices, must be avoided. For example, Sikhs avoid dancing or mixing intimately with the opposite sex so that they are not tempted to be impure. Sikhs share the views of many other religious people that premarital sex can lower a person's self-respect and respect for others who hold God's divine spark within them. It can also lead to unwanted consequences, such as pregnancy or sexually transmitted infections.

▲ *Sikhism teaches that sex should be reserved for marriage*

■ Sexual relationships outside marriage

Like all religions, Sikhism teaches faithfulness in marriage. **Adultery** or **sex outside marriage** is considered a serious sin. Sikh marriage is a sacred bond and adultery breaks that bond, betrays trust and brings shame on the family. It is one of four misdeeds (kurahat) that members

Objectives

- Understand Sikh beliefs and teachings about sexual relationships before marriage and outside marriage.
- Consider contemporary British attitudes towards sexual relationships before marriage and outside marriage.

Key terms

- **sex before marriage:** sex between two unmarried people
- **adultery:** voluntary sexual intercourse between a married person and a person who is not their husband or wife
- **sex outside marriage:** sex between two people where at least one of them is married to someone else; adultery; having an affair

Activities

1. Explain the difference between 'sex before marriage' and 'sex outside marriage'.
2. Explain two ways in which sex before marriage could harm the people involved.
3. Explain why Sikhs believe that adultery is a serious sin.

of the Khalsa must not commit. The kachhehra (underwear worn by men and women, and one of the five Ks) reminds Sikhs that they must be faithful and sexually pure in marriage. A Sikh should respect another man's wife as he would his own sister or mother, and avoid looking lustfully at someone else's wife (Guru Granth Sahib 274).

> ❝ He who regards another man's daughter as his own daughter, regards another man's wife as his mother, has coition [sex] with his own wife alone, he alone is a truly disciplined Sikh of the Guru. ❞
>
> *Rehat Maryada, article 16*
>
> ❝ The blind fool abandons the wife of his own home, and has an affair with another woman. ❞
>
> *Guru Granth Sahib 1165*

Contrasting beliefs

Find out more about Christian teachings on sexual relationships before marriage, and compare them with Sikh attitudes to this issue.

⭐ **Study tip**

Try to learn some quotations from the Guru Granth Sahib and Rehat Maryada so that you can support your explanation of Sikh beliefs about sexual relationships.

■ Contemporary British attitudes

In contemporary Britain, sex before marriage is now widely accepted. Many magazines, films and television programmes reflect the common belief that it is usual for couples who are dating to have sex. There is often peer pressure on young people to have sexual experiences before marriage and it is commonly argued that couples should see whether they are sexually compatible before they marry. Young British Sikhs can sometimes feel caught between the values of their religion and the values of the culture in which they live.

▲ *Young people sometimes feel pressured into having sex before marriage*

Sikh views on sex before marriage are similar to those held by many Christians and other religions in Britain today. However, some liberal Christians are more tolerant of loving, committed sexual relationships that are conducted ethically and responsibly, even if the partners are not married.

Adultery is often reflected in the media and popular culture too. But many people, both religious and non-religious, would regard unfaithfulness in marriage as wrong. The lies and deception that adultery brings to a relationship often lead to divorce. The great majority of British Sikhs would consider all forms of sex outside marriage to be wrong.

Summary

You should now be able to explain Sikh beliefs about sex before and outside marriage, and the reasons for these beliefs.

3.3 Contraception and family planning

What is contraception?

Contraception is a way of preventing pregnancy when a couple have sex. There are three main forms: artificial, natural and permanent.

- Artificial forms include the pill, diaphragm, condom, spermicidal jellies, coil and morning after pill.
- Natural contraception, for example the rhythm method, usually involves only having sex at certain times of the month in order to reduce the chance of pregnancy. The withdrawal method (withdrawing the penis before ejaculation) is also a natural form.
- Sterilisation (a surgical operation) of the man or the woman is more permanent.

▲ *Contraception may be necessary for health reasons*

Objectives

- Examine different types of contraception.
- Understand Sikh beliefs about family planning and the use of contraception.
- Consider contemporary British attitudes towards family planning and the use of contraception.

Key terms

- **contraception:** the methods used to prevent a pregnancy from taking place
- **family planning:** the practice of controlling how many children couples have and when they have them

Sikh beliefs about contraception and family planning

Like Catholic and Orthodox Christianity, Sikhism teaches that sex before marriage is wrong, so contraception is only considered in the case of married people. Sikhs are expected to marry and have children. Sensible **family planning** is accepted by the community as morally responsible behaviour.

Sikh scriptures give no specific guidance about contraception, so couples can decide for themselves whether to use contraception for the sake of the woman's health or the welfare of their other children. Sikh couples choose their own methods. Most have no objection to artificial methods but sterilisation would only be used if medically necessary. For Sikhs, contraception should not be used to prevent having children altogether or to cover up an adulterous affair. Some Sikhs prefer natural methods because they are less disruptive to the natural cycle of procreation. Since the scriptures teach that God does not intend humans to suffer, contraception can be seen as a positive way of helping a couple to plan to have children at a time when they are ready to welcome them into their lives.

▲ *Having children is an important part of marriage for Sikhs*

As in Christianity, there are some Sikhs who disagree with the use of contraceptives because they believe sex is a God-given gift that should be used to have children. These Sikhs consider some forms of contraception, such as the morning after pill, as killing life. Some Sikhs take the view that excessive sex without allowing children to be conceived is lust, and if a couple is using contraception, there is no reason for them to engage in the act of intercourse other than fulfilling sexual desire and giving in to lust.

> **"** Those who are deluded by sensual pleasures, who are tempted by sexual delights and enjoy wine are corrupt. **"**
>
> *Guru Granth Sahib 335*

One Sikh's opinion about family planning

One Sikh has posted the following online giving their view on using contraception:

'Using any kind of contraceptive or birth control is not in accordance to gurmat (the Guru's way). Sexual relations [are only acceptable] within marriage … which is a part of 'gristi' (life of a householder). Sexual relations are necessary for a householder life as this is the only way a child is born. A Gursikh doesn't engage in 'kaam' (lust). If a couple is using birth control, there is no other purpose other than fulfilling lust and sexual desires. Accepting Guru Sahib's hukam (will) includes accepting how many children he gives us. Birth control is wrong from that angle as well. Traditionally Sikh families are large, providing spiritual [strength] to the couple and helping the Panth to gain strength and remain strong. Whenever we're confused about an issue we can ask ourselves, 'Would puraatan (ancient) Gursikhs have done this or approve of this?' The answer to birth control is clearly, 'No."

■ Contemporary British attitudes

Most people in Britain, religious and non-religious, accept the use of contraception for family planning. Some believers, such as Catholic and Orthodox Christians, oppose artificial methods but accept natural ones. Many people think that the medical advances in preventing unwanted pregnancies should be welcomed and used responsibly, not just for personal reasons but also to control population growth and prevent the spread of sexually transmitted diseases. Most British Sikhs would agree that the use of some forms of artificial contraception within marriage is acceptable if used for the right reasons. They would also agree that in cases where contraception involved the killing of a fertilised egg (that is, after conception) it would be a sin because it would involve destroying life.

Research activity 🔍

Find out more about different methods of artificial contraception and how they work. What moral considerations would a religious believer have when deciding which to use?

Activities

1 Explain two reasons why some Sikh couples might wish to use contraception.
2 Why do Sikhs usually oppose sterilisation?
3 Explain two different Sikh attitudes about the use of contraception within marriage.
4 'Using artificial contraception encourages selfishness.' Evaluate this statement.

Contrasting beliefs

Find out more about Christian beliefs on the use of different forms of contraception, both natural and artificial, and note any beliefs that differ from Sikh views on this issue.

⭐ Study tip

Remember that Sikhs do not all agree about contraception. Try to use phrases such as 'some Sikhs believe…' and 'other Sikhs believe…' when describing Sikh beliefs about this issue.

Summary

You should now be able to explain Sikh attitudes to family planning and the use of different methods of contraception.

Marriage in contemporary Britain

Marriage is a serious, lifelong, public commitment. It is a legal contract that brings security to a relationship and protects the rights of each partner. Until recently, marriage in the UK was defined as the legal union of a man and a woman. In 2004, same-sex couples were allowed to register their union in a **civil partnership**, which gave them the same legal rights as married couples. **Same-sex marriages** became legal in England, Wales and Scotland in 2014, and in Ireland in 2015. In Britain, fewer couples are getting married. Some couples choose to live together without getting married. This is called **cohabitation**.

Sikh beliefs about the nature and purpose of marriage

For Sikhs, marriage is a religious act, a spiritual opportunity to become one spirit within two bodies. The wedding ceremony is called Anand Karaj, meaning 'blissful union'.

▲ *A Sikh wedding, in front of the Guru Granth Sahib*

Marriage helps the two people experience God's love within their relationship. For this reason, the Gurus taught that the life of the householder was the highest spiritual path. Sikhs are expected to marry, and they believe it is the way God intended men and women to live. Marriage is more than a social contract; it is a union witnessed by God, shown by the presence of the Guru Granth Sahib at the wedding ceremony. The ideal marriage is one of faithfulness, happiness, love and loyalty. Sikhs regard men and women as equal. The husband should gently guide and support his wife, while recognising her individuality and equality. A wife should loyally show her love and respect for her husband, and share life's joys and

Objectives

- Consider Sikh beliefs about the nature and purpose of marriage.
- Explore Sikh and non-religious responses to same-sex marriage and cohabitation.

Key terms

- **marriage:** a legal union between a man and a woman (or in some countries, including the UK, two people of the same sex) as partners in a relationship
- **civil partnership:** legal union of same-sex couples
- **same-sex marriage:** marriage between partners of the same sex
- **cohabitation:** a couple living together and having a sexual relationship without being married to one another

> ❝ They alone are called husband and wife, who have one light in two bodies. ❞
>
> *Guru Granth Sahib 788*

Discussion activities

1 With a partner or in a small group, discuss the qualities you think are important for a marriage to succeed.

2 Discuss the advantages and disadvantages of parents helping their children to find a marriage partner.

sorrows with him. At their wedding the couple are advised to try to achieve a harmonious union, intellectually, emotionally, physically, materially and spiritually.

For Sikhs, the purpose of marriage is companionship and the spiritual development of the partners, more than sexual enjoyment. Some Sikhs believe it is a great virtue to deny themselves sexual intercourse in order to concentrate on divine love. However, for all Sikhs the purpose of marriage is also to contribute to God's creation by having children.

In Britain, young Sikhs have the final word in their choice of marriage partner, but parents and other relatives still like to be involved. Sikh scripture says that caste or birth should not matter and everyone is equal. As long as both man and woman profess the Sikh faith, they may be married in the Anand Karaj ceremony.

▲ *Companionship is a purpose of marriage*

■ Cohabitation and same-sex marriage

Many young couples in Britain choose to cohabit, although they may decide to marry when they want to start a family. Some live together for financial reasons or because they want to see if the relationship will work. Others never marry but live in committed relationships throughout their lives. Same-sex couples may cohabit until they decide to seek a civil partnership or marry.

Sikhs do not approve of cohabitation because they believe a sexual relationship should only occur within marriage. Sikh teachings make it clear that opposite-sex marriage is intended by God and is the natural state in which people should live. Therefore many Sikhs, like some other religious people, were opposed to the changes in the law that made same-sex marriages legal. The supreme Sikh religious body, the Akal Takht, issued an edict condemning same-sex marriage. A Sikh leader echoed its words by saying:

> ❝ The advice given by the highest Sikh temporal authority to every Sikh is saying that it [same-sex marriage] is unnatural and ungodly, and the Sikh religion cannot support it. ❞
>
> *Manjit Singh Kalkatta*

However, some Sikhs, like some liberal Christians, value the love and commitment of couples who wish to marry whatever their gender, and respect their desire for equal rights. These Sikhs believe the family lifestyle that the Gurus encourage can be developed by two members of the same gender.

Activities

1 Explain three Sikh beliefs about the purpose of marriage.
2 Explain why many Sikhs disagree with cohabitation and same-sex marriage.
3 'Sikhs should accept same-sex marriage as morally right.' Evaluate this statement.

Research activities

1 Use the internet to find the text of the four Lavan (marriage hymns that are recited at a Sikh wedding). What do the Lavan teach about the nature and purpose of marriage?
2 Find out some teachings about Sikh marriage in the Rehat Maryada, chapter 11, article XVIII.

> ❝ By the affair of this marriage, truth, contentment, mercy and faith are produced … ❞
>
> *Guru Granth Sahib 351*

⭐ Study tip

Some Christians, like Sikhs, regard marriage as a union witnessed by God. Try to keep in mind beliefs and teachings that other religions share as well as those with which they disagree.

Summary

You should now be able to explain Sikh beliefs about the nature and purpose of marriage, and religious and non-religious responses to same-sex marriage and cohabitation.

■ Divorce in Britain

In 2021, in England and Wales, an estimated 42 per cent of all marriages ended in **divorce**. Divorce is allowed after one year of marriage if the marriage cannot be saved. A legally recognised civil divorce must be obtained through a court. **Remarriage** is allowed as many times as people wish, to a different partner or to a person's original spouse.

Reasons for divorce

There are many different reasons why a marriage can fail. One of the most common causes of divorce is adultery. People can change, grow apart and fall out of love. Illness, addiction, work or money pressures and domestic violence or abuse can cause the complete breakdown of a relationship.

■ Religious and non-religious attitudes towards divorce

All religions believe marriage is for life, but they recognise that some marriages break down. Sikhs, like many other religious believers, have to balance ethical arguments between the sanctity of their marriage vows and compassion for people whose marriage has broken down. While many would say that promises made before God are sacred and should never be broken, others may believe that there may be circumstances when it is more compassionate to allow divorce.

Most non-religious people accept divorce and remarriage from a practical point of view. They might take a utilitarian position: if divorce causes the least harm in the situation, then it is morally right. Atheists and humanists do not believe that marriage promises are made before God, so it is up to the couple to decide on the future of their relationship. The main priority for religious and non-religious people is the wellbeing of any children involved.

■ Sikh teachings about divorce and remarriage

Marriage should be for life; the couple should be 'one spirit in two bodies' (Guru Amar Das). They have sealed their marriage before God to love and honour each other for life. The Rehat Maryada teaches that in general no Sikh should marry a second time if their first spouse is alive. However, Sikhs reluctantly accept civil divorce. The couple's families will do everything they can to prevent the separation. The Sikh community may also be involved in helping the couple to resolve their differences, and if that is not possible they may give permission for the couple to part. The grounds for divorce include adultery, cruelty, desertion, insanity and change of religion. Widowed Sikhs who wish to marry again are encouraged to do so in the gurdwara. The Rehat Maryada says

Objectives

- Explore different reasons for divorce in Britain today.
- Understand Sikh teachings about divorce and remarriage.
- Consider ethical arguments related to divorce, including those based on the sanctity of marriage vows and compassion.

Key terms

- **divorce:** legal ending of a marriage
- **remarriage:** when someone marries again, after a previous marriage or marriages have come to an end

Discussion activity 💬

Read the case study about divorce on page 73 and discuss with a partner or in a small group. Why should a divorce affect the local community? Do you agree that divorce might be harder on Sikh women than on men? What do you think are the changes that are referred to in the last paragraph that mean young couples feel less supported when they go through difficult times?

▲ Sikh scriptures forbid the drinking of alcohol, which, if abused, can lead to conflict

that a widow or widower may remarry if they find someone suitable. The remarriage may be conducted in the same manner as a normal Sikh wedding ceremony (called Anand Karaj):

> **❝❞** If a woman's husband has died, she may, if she so wishes, finding a match suitable for her, remarry. For a Sikh man whose wife has died, similar ordinance obtains. The remarriage may be solemnised in the same manner as the Anand marriage. **❞**
>
> *Rehat Maryada, article 18*

> **❝❞** Having one woman as wife he (the Sikh) is a celibate and considers any other's wife as his daughter or a sister. **❞**
>
> *Bhai Gurdas*

▲ *The support of the Sikh community may help couples to overcome problems in their marriage*

⭐ Study tip

It is worth remembering that although some Sikhs may feel that divorce is increasing among Sikhs, a recent survey showed that only 4–10 per cent of British Sikhs were divorced or separated – a very low rate compared to the rest of the UK.

Divorce in the Sikh community

Written by a 32 year old married Sikh woman, who is also an Amritdhari, about her childhood friend:

'I was shocked to hear that one of my Sikh friends was having problems in her marriage and they eventually divorced. Both she and her husband, and their respective families were well known in the local Sikh community as devout Sikhs; we saw them as good Sikh role models. I feel very distraught for her and also worry at a community level. While the divorce rates in the Sikh community may be relatively low, the effects on young women like my friend are enormous.

While she was worried sick about the long-term consequences for her and "loss of family honour", her husband and in-laws appeared full of bravado and carefree. She seems to be suffering more which is unfair, and at odds with the prominence that our faith gives to women.

She seemed to have it all: an enthusiastic and practising Sikh, full of respect for her husband and in-laws, highly educated and in a well-paid job. I don't know how to explain things or figure out how the Sikh faith will survive the impact of increasing divorce.

Marriage is at the heart of a Sikh life at many different levels and until recently the immediate families and community would have found ways to support and help any couple going through difficult times. Things are changing rapidly for the worse: family and community structures are changing rapidly; young couples not able to cope with difficulties have little support; community and faith organisations haven't yet developed new support networks to help; families seem unable to respond with any meaningful interventions.'

Activities

1. **a** Explain three reasons why some marriages fail.
   b Are these reasons grounds for divorce, or do you think couples could overcome some of these difficulties?
2. Explain different religious and non-religious attitudes towards divorce in contemporary Britain.
3. Write a short summary of Sikh teaching about divorce and remarriage.
4. Explain how a belief in a) the sanctity of marriage vows and b) compassion could affect someone's attitude towards divorce.
5. 'Sikh couples who are having problems should stay together for the sake of their children.' Evaluate this statement. Be sure to include different views and religious teachings in your answer.

Summary

You should now understand some reasons for divorce and religious and non-religious attitudes to divorce and remarriage in contemporary British society, including ethical arguments based on the sanctity of marriage vows and compassion. You should be able to explain Sikh beliefs about divorce and remarriage.

The nature of families in Britain today

In contemporary Britain, the types of families may have changed but the **family** is still considered to be the best environment for bringing up children and keeping society stable. The basic unit of mother, father and children (a **nuclear family**) is still the most common in the UK, although now approximately 25 per cent of children live in single-parent families. There are more 'step families', where divorced people with children marry new partners with children of their own. **Same-sex parents** may have children from previous relationships, legally adopt children, and conceive through in vitro fertilisation or donor insemination, or use surrogates. In the past, families were larger, and often included grandparents and other relatives (an **extended family**) all living together. For many non-Western cultures, the extended family unit is still very common.

Sikh beliefs about the family

> " The householders assert their faith in family life. "
>
> *Guru Granth Sahib 71*

The family is the essential social unit in Sikh society. Guru Nanak preached that the life of the householder was the highest path to spirituality, rather than the ascetic life (a life of severe self-discipline, free from material possessions) that other religions promoted at the time.

> " Immersed in family life, the Lord's humble servant ever remains detached; he reflects upon the essence of spiritual wisdom. "
>
> *Guru Granth Sahib 599*

All the adult Gurus were married and they believed that the family was the basis for a strong, safe, secure society. The family is where children are trained in Sikh virtues such as practising sewa (selfless service), and where the traditions of the religion are passed down. Sikhs believe that the values learned in the family are needed to achieve prosperity and world peace.

> " Gazing upon his family, he blossoms forth like the lotus flower... "
>
> *Guru Granth Sahib 92*

Objectives

- Explore the nature of families in the twenty-first century.
- Understand Sikh beliefs and teachings about the nature of families and the role of parents and children, including the topics of polygamy and same-sex parents.

Key terms

- **family:** a group of people who are related by blood, marriage or adoption
- **nuclear family:** a couple and their dependent children regarded as a basic social unit
- **same-sex parents:** people of the same sex who are raising children together
- **extended family:** a family which extends beyond the nuclear family to include grandparents and other relatives as well
- **polygamy:** the practice or custom of having more than one wife at the same time
- **bigamy:** the offence in the UK of marrying someone while already married to another person

▲ *Sikhism teaches respect for older members of the family*

Unlike Islam, which allows a man to have more than one wife (**polygamy**) under certain circumstances, Sikhs believe in monogamy (having one husband or wife). Polygamous marriages cannot be performed in Britain because **bigamy** is illegal.

▲ *An extended Sikh family*

■ The role of parents and children

Sikhism teaches that men and women are equal and each family member is expected to play their part in family life. When a Sikh mother gives birth, she usually takes on the main role of bringing up the child for the first few years. The father will take on other household duties so that the family's work is shared evenly. Traditionally, fathers were expected to work to support the family, but in contemporary Britain it is not unusual for both parents to work and share domestic responsibilities. As children grow older, they too are expected to help with chores.

> **Links**
>
> For more about gender equality see pages 78–79.

Sikh parents are expected to love and care for their children, set a good example for them, teach them right from wrong and bring them up in the Sikh faith. Baptised (amritdhari) Sikhs and many non-amritdhari Sikhs do not cut their children's hair.

> **❝** A Sikh … should not [tamper] with the hair with which the child is born … A Sikh should keep the hair of his sons and daughters intact. **❞**
>
> *Rehat Maryada, article 16*

When the children are older, parents often support their children in finding a suitable marriage partner. Grown-up children see it as their duty to support their elderly parents because they supported them when they were young.

Sikhs do not approve of same-sex parenting, because the ideal is for children to grow up with a male and female role model as parents, as the Gurus showed. Since many Sikhs consider same-sex sexual relationships and same-sex marriage morally wrong, they do not believe that same-sex parents would be able to set a good example to their children. Some liberal Sikhs who do not object to same-sex sexual relationships think that it is more important for children to be raised in a secure and loving family, regardless of the gender of their parents.

> **Activities**
>
> 1 Explain briefly the difference between a nuclear family and an extended family.
>
> 2 Explain the role of parents in Sikhism. Refer to scripture or sacred writings in your answer.
>
> 3 'Sikhs who disapprove of same-sex parenting are right.' Evaluate this statement.

> **Discussion activity**
>
> Discuss the reasons why some Sikhs do not approve of same-sex parenting.

> ⭐ **Study tip**
>
> Try to keep in mind beliefs about the nature of marriage and the role of parents that all people share, as well as the things over which they disagree.

> **Summary**
>
> You should now understand Sikh beliefs about the nature of families and the role of parents, including the issues of polygamy and same-sex parents.

3.7 Religious teachings about the purpose of families

The purpose of families

The basic social unit in all societies is the family. It serves a number of purposes:

- It controls sexual behaviour because it is where **procreation** mainly takes place.
- It creates **stability** for family members and also for society itself.
- It provides for the **protection of children**, supplying their basic needs and safeguarding them from harm.
- It is where children learn how to relate to others so they can grow up and contribute positively to society.
- It helps provide safety and security for the sick, elderly and disabled.
- For religious parents, it involves **educating children in a faith**.

The purpose of families in Sikhism

The Sikh family is considered a noble institution whose purpose is to procreate and continue the existence of society. A strong family life ensures stability and safety for the members of the family and for the Sikh community as a whole. It is the place where the emotional, spiritual, physical and economic needs of its members are provided for, and where Sikh values, culture and religious beliefs are passed on to the next generation.

As we have seen, the Gurus taught that family life was the highest path to spirituality. It is through the family that husband and wife, who are one spirit in two bodies, reach liberation from the cycle of birth, death and rebirth.

The Sikh community is itself a family. Sikhism teaches that human beings are sons and daughters of the same universal father (God), and that Sikhs should base their lives on universal brotherhood, love for one another, equality and the welfare of all.

Guru Arjan described an ideal family where the mother is central to its happiness:

> **“** She is blessed with all sublime attributes, and her generations are unblemished. Her Husband, her Lord and Master, fulfils her heart's desires […] She is the most noble of all the family. She counsels and advises her hope and desire. How blessed is that household, in which she has appeared. **”**
>
> *Guru Granth Sahib 371*

> **“** It is a Sikh's duty to get his children educated in Sikhism. **”**
>
> *Rehat Maryada, article 16*

Objectives

- Explore the purpose of families in contemporary British society.
- Understand Sikh beliefs and teachings about the purpose of families, including procreation, stability, the protection of children and educating children in a faith.

Key terms

- **procreation:** bringing babies into the world; producing offspring
- **stability:** safety and security; a stable society is one in which people's rights are protected and they are able to live peaceful, productive lives without continuous and rapid change
- **protection of children:** keeping children safe from harm
- **educating children in a faith:** bringing up children according to the religious beliefs of the parents

> **“** The faithful uplift and redeem their family and relations. **”**
>
> *Guru Granth Sahib 3*

Links

See pages 74–75 for more about the roles of parents and children in Sikhism.

■ Educating children in the Sikh faith

The mother has a particularly strong role in educating her children in their faith. Her own example as a devout and loving mother is the biggest influence, but she will also teach her children to pray and meditate, and to learn the stories of the Gurus and history of the religion. She will also introduce them to the Sikh community in weekly worship at the gurdwara.

Traditionally, a Sikh son brings his wife home to live with his parents after marriage, so both the father and grandparents are very involved in the upbringing of the children. Baptised (amritdhari) Sikhs initiate their children into the wearing of the five Ks and explain why they do not cut their hair. Sikh parents rise early, bathe and begin the day meditating on God. It is hoped that if children grow up seeing this example, they will follow in their parents' footsteps.

Many Sikh children have close relationships with their grandparents. This has mutual benefits, including providing security for elderly family members in their later years. Most Sikhs would not consider putting their elderly parents in a care home. They do not regard their parents as a burden, but rather see it as an honour to be able to repay them for the love and support they gave them as children.

▲ *Sikh parents have an important role in passing down the faith to their children*

> **❝** The stories of one's ancestors make the children good children. **❞**
>
> *Guru Granth Sahib* 951

South London Sikh Youth

South London Sikh Youth was set up to educate the younger generation in the Sikh faith and to enable them to experience with other young people what it means to be a Sikh in contemporary Britain. Their aims include:

- Education: inspiring young people to grow mentally, physically and spiritually.
- Wellbeing: supporting and encouraging young people to understand the benefits of a healthy diet and exercise.
- Mentoring: providing support and guidance to help individuals to develop.

They use events and trips, talks and question-and-answer sessions, and classes and music lessons to teach young people the message of the Guru Granth Sahib.

Activities

1   Make some notes on how South London Sikh Youth helps parents educate their children in their faith.
2   Explain three purposes of the family in contemporary Britain.
3   Explain two ways in which Sikh families might differ from non-religious families in contemporary Britain.
4   Explain different beliefs in contemporary Britain about caring for the elderly.

⭐ Study tip

Remember that the 'nature' of families can refer both to the different types of families in Britain and what they should ideally be like. The 'purpose' of families refers to what families are for.

Summary

You should now understand Sikh beliefs and teachings about the purpose of families.

Religious attitudes to gender equality

Gender equality in contemporary Britain

Many people in Britain today agree with the idea of **gender equality** (that people should be give the same rights and opportunities regardless of their gender identity), but there are also many examples where it does not happen. Something that prevents it is **gender prejudice**, which is often based on **sexual stereotyping**. An example of this is the idea that women are more naturally caring or are the weaker sex, so they should look after the home while men go out to work. Sexual stereotyping can lead to **gender discrimination**, perhaps by not giving a man a job that involves looking after young children or not employing a woman on a building site.

The Sex Discrimination Act (1975) made gender discrimination illegal in the UK. Despite this, women generally earn lower pay than men. Some are paid less than men who are doing the same jobs. Women make up roughly half of the workforce, but men hold a higher proportion of senior positions.

> ### Links
> For information on other types of prejudice and discrimination, and the role of women in religion, see pages 160–163.
>
> For Sikh teachings on gender equality, see pages 22–23.

Sikh beliefs about gender equality

Unlike other religious leaders of his time, Guru Nanak (1469–1539) spoke up on behalf of women as vessels who carry not only the next generation, but also the culture and values of a community.

The third Guru, Guru Amar Das, spoke out against the practice of sati (where a widow was burned to death on her husband's funeral pyre). He also condemned the wearing of the veil to cover a woman's face (see Rehat Maryada, article XVI). Fifty-two of the missionaries Guru Amar Das sent out were women. The early codes of conduct for the Khalsa required Sikhs to break ties with those who committed the sin of female infanticide (killing baby girls). The teaching of the Gurus changed Indian society as more women began to take part in social, religious and political matters. Their contribution as equal partners of men was recognised by others outside Sikhism.

In Sikh teachings, women and men are equal before God, who is beyond gender. All human beings are judged only by their deeds, not by their caste, gender or race. Baptised (amritdhari) Sikh women use the name 'Kaur' meaning 'princess', which frees them from having to take their husband's name when marrying.

Objectives

- Understand Sikh beliefs and teachings about the roles of men and women, gender equality, and gender prejudice and discrimination.
- Consider examples of gender prejudice and discrimination in contemporary British society.

Key terms

- **gender equality:** the idea that people should be given the same rights and opportunities regardless of their gender identity
- **gender prejudice:** unfairly judging someone before the facts are known; holding biased opinions about an individual or group based on their gender
- **sexual stereotyping:** having a fixed general idea or image of how men and women will behave
- **gender discrimination:** to act against someone on the basis of their gender; discrimination is usually seen as wrong and may be against the law

Activities

1 Explain, using an example, what is meant by sexual stereotyping.

2 Explain Sikh beliefs about the roles of men and women.

3 'Sikh women have equal rights to Sikh men.' Evaluate this statement.

> ❝ He Himself created all women and men; the Lord Himself plays every play. You created the entire creation; O Nanak, it is the best of the best. ❞
>
> *Guru Granth Sahib 304*

A male Sikh is taught to consider all females older than him as his mother, equal in age to him as a sister, and younger than him as a daughter. In other words he is taught to treat all women as though they were family members to whom he owed respect and consideration (see the quotation from Bhai Gurdas on page 73).

The roles of men and women in Sikhism

As we have seen, a Sikh marriage is described as one spirit in two bodies. The strong emphasis on equality that is seen in the scriptures and in Sikh worship applies to family life as well. British Sikh families share responsibilities in the home, particularly as often both parents are working. Many Sikh women are well educated and are encouraged to pursue professional careers. They have always had full rights to own and inherit property equally with their brothers.

Gender prejudice and discrimination

Although Sikhism teaches equality, some Sikh women feel that traditional Indian culture, rather than Sikhism itself, has limited their chances for education, freedom to socialise and express opinions, and has put pressure on them to dress modestly, not to date, and in a few rare cases to accept a marriage proposal even if they have doubts. In some families, girls are expected to do most of the household chores in preparation for married life. A 2013 survey showed:

- 43 per cent of British Sikh females have experienced gender discrimination, as opposed to 14 per cent of British Sikh males
- 71 per cent of British Sikh females who experienced gender discrimination did so within their extended family and 55 per cent did so at their gurdwara
- 15 per cent of British Sikh females said they had been discriminated against at work.

▲ *'Bend it Like Beckham' is a film about a Sikh girl playing football despite her parents' disapproval at first*

Extension activity

Choose one example of gender prejudice and one example of gender discrimination in contemporary Britain. Write a paragraph about each one.

Research activity

Using the internet, try to find out more about restrictions placed on girls and women in traditional Sikh families in Britain. Do you think these restrictions result from cultural or religious ideas?

⭐ Study tip

It is important to remember that 'equal' does not mean 'the same'. Just because women have different roles does not always mean that they are seen to have less value than men.

Summary

You should now be able to explain Sikh and non-religious attitudes to the roles of men and women, gender equality, and gender prejudice and discrimination, including examples.

Discussion activities

1 From your school's staff list, count the number of male and female teachers. Are they about equal? Put a mark next to the teachers who hold positions of responsibility and a different mark next to those who do not. What conclusions might you draw from your findings?

2 Do either men or women experience prejudice or discrimination in their roles as parents?

Sex, marriage and divorce – summary

You should now be able to:

✔ explain Sikh teachings about human sexuality, including opposite-sex and same-sex relationships

✔ explain Sikh beliefs and teachings about sexual relationships before and outside marriage

✔ explain Sikh attitudes to family planning and the use of different forms of contraception

✔ explain Sikh understandings of the nature and purpose of marriage

✔ explain Sikh and non-religious responses to same-sex marriage and cohabitation

✔ explain Sikh teachings about divorce and remarriage

✔ explain contrasting beliefs in contemporary British society about the three issues of same-sex sexual relationships, sex before marriage and contraception, with reference to the main religious tradition in Britain (Christianity) and one or more other religious traditions.

Families and gender equality – summary

You should now be able to:

✔ explain Sikh beliefs and teachings about the nature of families and the role of parents and children, including the issues of polygamy and same-sex parents

✔ explain Sikh beliefs and teachings about the purpose of families, including procreation, stability, the protection of children and educating children in a faith

✔ explain religious beliefs, teachings and moral arguments about the roles of men and women, gender equality, and gender prejudice and discrimination

✔ describe examples of gender prejudice and discrimination in contemporary British society

✔ explain contemporary British attitudes (both religious and non-religious) towards all of the above issues.

Sample student answer – the 4-mark question

1. Write an answer to the following practice question:

   Explain **two** different beliefs in contemporary British society about same-sex sexual relationships.

   In your answer you should refer to the main religious tradition of Great Britain and one or more other religious traditions. **[4 marks]**

2. Read the following sample student answer:

   "Within Sikhism there is a strong emphasis on opposite-sex marriage. Some Sikhs think the teaching against lust in the scriptures means that same-sex sexual relationships are sinful. This means that many Sikhs disapprove of same-sex sexual relationships but they would never discriminate against people who are attracted to people of the same sex and they welcome anyone to the gurdwara. The main religious tradition of Great Britain, Christianity, also emphasises opposite-sex marriage, but Christians themselves have differing opinions about same-sex sexual relationships. Some, like some Sikhs, are opposed to such relationships. But some liberal Christians hold a different view, that people who are attracted to people of the same sex who are in committed relationships should be welcomed."

3. With a partner, discuss the sample answer. Is the focus of the answer correct? Is anything missing from the answer? How do you think it could be improved?

4. What mark (out of 4) would you give this answer? Look at the mark scheme in the Introduction (AO1). What are the reasons for the mark you have given?

5. Now swap your answer with your partner's and mark each other's responses. What mark (out of 4) would you give the response? Refer to the mark scheme and give reasons for the mark you award.

Sample student answer – the 6-mark question

1. Write an answer to the following practice question:

   Explain two religious beliefs about divorce.

   Refer to sacred writings or another source of religious belief and teaching in your answer. **[6 marks]**

2. Read the following sample student answer:

   "Sikhs are not in favour of divorce. Marriage should be for life and the couple are 'one spirit in two bodies'. The Sikh Code of Conduct teaches that in general a man should not marry a second wife if his first wife is alive. But Sikhs accept that marriages do break down. Grounds for divorce in Sikhism include adultery, cruelty, desertion, insanity, and change of religion.

   The Sikh community always tries to help reconcile a couple who are having problems. There is nothing about divorce proceedings in the scriptures. But the community or the Panj Piare may give permission for couples to seek a civil divorce. Sikhs believe it is a very serious matter because the couple have promised to be faithful to each other for life."

3. With a partner, discuss the sample answer. What does the answer contain that is particularly important? How do you think the answer could be improved?

4. What mark (out of 6) would you give this answer? Look at the mark scheme in the Introduction (AO1). What are the reasons for the mark you have given?

5. Now swap your answer with your partner's and mark each other's responses. What mark (out of 6) would you give the response? Refer to the mark scheme and give reasons for the mark you award.

Practice questions

 1 Which **one** of the following is the name given to the practice in some religions of having more than one wife?

A) Procreation   **B)** Contraception   **C)** Stability   **D)** Polygamy   **[1 mark]**

2 Give **one** religious belief about the purpose of families. **[1 mark]**

3 Explain **two** different beliefs in contemporary British society about sex before marriage.

In your answer you must refer to one or more religious traditions. **[4 marks]**

4 Explain **two** religious beliefs about the nature of marriage.

Refer to sacred writings or another source of religious belief and teaching in your answer. **[6 marks]**

> ⭐ **Study tip**
>
> In this question the 'nature' of marriage refers to what marriage is, and what it should be like.

5 'Same-sex parents are just as good at bringing up children as other parents.'

Evaluate this statement. In your answer you:
- should give reasoned arguments to support this statement
- should give reasoned arguments to support a different point of view
- should refer to religious arguments
- may refer to non-religious arguments **[12 marks]**
- should reach a justified conclusion. **[+ 3 SPaG marks]**

> ⭐ **Study tip**
>
> You should aim to develop two different points of view and refer to religious beliefs. You could discuss differences between those who think that same-sex couples can fulfil the same purposes of family life for their children as other couples and those who think that same-sex couples will not be able to fulfil some of those purposes.

■ The universe

The current observable **universe** is about 93 billion light years in diameter. Light travels at a speed of 186,000 miles per second, 671 million miles an hour or about 6 trillion miles a year. If our sun was the size of a one-pence piece, the nearest star, Alpha Centauri, would be about 350 miles away. On this scale, our Milky Way galaxy would be 7.5 million miles across. Astronomers tell us that there are millions of galaxies so the universe is enormous and, according to scientists, still expanding. How did the universe come into existence? Are there more universes than the one we know? For generations scientists have been trying to find answers to these and many more questions about the universe and its origins.

■ Sikh beliefs

Most of the world's religions have produced theories as to how the universe and the world came into existence. Sikhs believe that the universe and everything in it was not the result of an accident, but was made by Waheguru (God). Before Waheguru's creation, he was all that existed. There was no earth, sky, sun or life. Guru Nanak said there was chaos and darkness for a very long time.

Then Waheguru spoke and his word created everything. He willed the whole of creation into existence in an infinitesimal moment. This means that the whole of creation belongs to God, who is in charge of all life. Without God's will (hukam) nothing can exist, change or develop. The Guru Granth Sahib explains the enormity of this creation:

> **❝** The limits of the created universe cannot be perceived. Its limits here and beyond cannot be perceived. Many struggle to know His limits, but His limits cannot be found. No one can know these limits. The more you say about them, the more there still remains to be said. **❞**
>
> *Guru Granth Sahib 5*

God not only created everything, but also rejoices in it and cares for it.

The time when this occurred remains a mystery that only God knows the answer to.

Objectives

- Understand Sikh beliefs and teachings about the origins of the universe.
- Understand the scientific theory of the Big Bang and Sikh views about this.

Key terms

- **universe:** all there is in space, including planets, galaxies and stars; it encompasses all matter
- **Big Bang:** a massive expansion of space which set in motion the creation of the universe

> **❝** For endless eons, there was only utter darkness. There was no earth or sky; there was only the infinite Command of His Hukam. There was no day or night, no moon or sun; God sat in primal, profound Samaadhi [meditation]. **❞**
>
> *Guru Granth Sahib 1035*

▲ *The Hubble space telescope is able to look further into deep space than even the largest telescope on earth*

> ❝ There are planets, solar systems and galaxies. If one speaks of them, there is no limit, no end. There are worlds upon worlds of His Creation. **As He commands, so they exist. He watches over all, and contemplating the creation, He rejoices.** ❞
>
> *Guru Granth Sahib 8*

▲ *Amazing star clusters in deep space*

■ The Big Bang theory

The **Big Bang** theory suggests that around 13.8 billion years ago there was a massive expansion of space. All the material that forms the universe suddenly expanded, flinging everything into space. The universe kept expanding and as the matter cooled, the stars and galaxies were formed. Background microwave radiation consistent with a large expansion has been detected by scientists, but there are still many unanswered questions, for example why the universe appears to be gathering speed in its expansion rather than slowing down. This is opposite to what many scientists expected, but some think that the universe will eventually collapse in what is known as the Big Crunch.

Many scientists believe that most of the universe is made up of dark matter that cannot be seen and its effects are not yet fully understood.

Sikhism does not find itself in conflict with the Big Bang theory, because the theory attempts to explain how things happened rather than why. Sikhs believe that all that has happened is due to God's will. The Guru Granth Sahib supports the idea of an expanding universe.

> ❝ In so many ways, He has unfolded Himself. So many times, He has expanded His expansion. Forever and ever, He is the One, the One Universal Creator. ❞
>
> *Guru Granth Sahib 276*

However, Sikhs believe that the current universe is not permanent and there is a continuous cycle of creation and destruction of the universe.

> ❝ Creation and destruction happen through the Word of the Shabad [God]. Through the Shabad, creation happens again. ❞
>
> *Guru Granth Sahib 117*

Discussion activity

In small groups or pairs, discuss whether you think the universe started by accident or was designed by a creator.

Extension activity

Use the internet or books to find out how the red shift is used by scientists to prove that the universe is expanding. Find out about more theories concerning how the universe started.

⭐ Study tip

Remember that Sikhs believe God has no gender. The terms 'he' and 'him' are only used to be able to talk and write easily about God.

Summary

You should now know what Sikhs believe about the origins of the universe and their views concerning the theory of the Big Bang.

Activities

1 Describe, using examples, the enormous size of the universe.
2 Explain what Sikhs believe about how the universe came into being.
3 Write a paragraph to explain the Big Bang theory.
4 What Sikh teaching supports the idea of an expanding universe?
5 'Sikhs have no problem in agreeing with the Big Bang theory.' Do you agree?

■ How valuable is the world?

As far as we know, the Earth is unique in the universe, so it is priceless. It is impossible to say how valuable it is because the Earth supports all life as we know it. Conditions in the world have allowed the rich variety of flora and fauna to develop and flourish. The world contains gold, diamonds and many other valuable minerals but the real value is seen in the abundant life forms, including the human life that it supports. Therefore, humans have a **responsibility** to care for the world because if it is ruined and destroyed, there are no known alternatives where we could all live.

■ Sikh beliefs

The Guru Granth Sahib explains that the world is priceless because it was created by Waheguru (God), and that God has a divine presence in all of creation.

> ❝ The Lord infused His Light into the dust, and created the world, the universe. The sky, the earth, the trees, and the water – all are the Creation of the Lord. ❞
>
> *Guru Granth Sahib 723*

Everything in the world is God's creation. Its origin was in God and the world operates within God's hukam (will and order) because God's spirit is in everything. The world is sacred and God can be seen through his creation, which he watches over with care and kindness.

Sikhs believe that God created the world as a place where every type of plant and animal could live, so that all life could have the chance to reach mukti (liberation from the cycle of birth and death, reincarnation). There is a divine spark in each living thing that is part of God and this spark or soul is taken back to join God when finally released from the cycle of rebirth. So nature and human life should be treated with respect, because both are equally important. Sikhism differs from Christianity, in which it is perceived that humans have **dominion** over nature and are seen as superior. However, like Christianity, Sikhs believe that humans have been given the task of **stewardship** and the responsibility for living in harmony with the environment and all of God's creation. This means taking care of all nature and avoiding actions that have the potential to ruin or destroy our natural environment.

Objective

- Understand Sikh beliefs about the value of the world and the duty of human beings to protect it.

Key terms

- **responsibility:** a duty to care for, or having control over, something or someone
- **dominion:** dominance or power over something; having charge of something or ruling over it
- **stewardship:** the idea that believers have a duty to look after the environment on behalf of God
- **awe:** a feeling of respect, mixed feelings of fear and wonder
- **wonder:** marvelling at the complexity and beauty of something

▲ *A view from space showing the beauty of the world*

▲ *An example of the Northern Lights (Aurora Borealis)*

Activities

1 Explain why it is vital that the Earth is looked after and valued by humans.

2 Who do Sikhs believe created nature and the world?

3 Explain why Sikhs believe that all life is special.

4 What does it mean to live in harmony with the environment?

5 Explain how nature may cause feelings of awe and wonder.

■ Awe and wonder

For Sikhs, Waheguru's creation is amazing and often **awe**-inspiring. The beauty of living creatures or a glimpse of an incredible landscape may trigger emotions that make people gasp in awe and **wonder** that such remarkable things exist. The roar of the sea, the sight of a colourful butterfly emerging from a chrysalis, the spectacle of millions of migrating birds, beautiful flowers covering a garden or the Northern Lights can take a person's breath away. Such scenes can cause people to reflect on spiritual things and wonder how they have come into existence. Sikhs believe that all the incredible variety of nature reflects God, because nature is part of God. Humans have a responsibility to preserve and care for it. For example, Guru Har Rai developed Kiratpur Sahib as a town of parks and gardens. Situated by the banks of a river, he planted flowers and fruit trees to attract beautiful birds to the town and create an environment where it was an idyllic place to live.

Guru Nanak describes the feeling of awe and wonder that humans may experience in the following passage from the Guru Granth Sahib:

> **❝** … Wonderful are the beings, wonderful are the species. Wonderful are the forms, wonderful are the colours … Wonderful is the wind, wonderful is the water. Wonderful is fire, which works wonders. Wonderful is the earth, wonderful the sources of creation … How wonderful to behold the Lord, ever-present here. Beholding His wonders, I am wonder-struck. O Nanak, those who understand this are blessed with perfect destiny. **❞**
>
> *Guru Granth Sahib 463–464*

Discussion activity

In small groups or pairs, discuss the following statement: 'Looking after the world is the most important duty for a Sikh.'

 Study tip

You should be able to explain what is meant by 'awe' and 'wonder', and know Sikh beliefs about stewardship and people's responsibilities towards nature.

Summary

You should now know Sikh beliefs about the value of the world, the duty of human beings to protect it and that God (Waheguru) can be seen through his creation and nature, because he is an integral part of it.

■ The use of natural resources

Sikhs are very concerned that human exploitation of nature is leading towards an environmental crisis. **Natural resources** are being used up at an ever increasing rate. Oil, gas, copper, zinc and many rarer minerals are in great demand by a growing world population. These are **non-renewable resources** and future generations will be left with less and less of them. The destruction of forests and overuse of land for agriculture and housing is a threat to the planet. The World Wide Fund for Nature (WWF) has estimated that around 50,000 square miles of forest are lost every year. That is the equivalent area covered by 48 football pitches, destroyed every minute. Forests are vital for the world's ecosystem because they soak up carbon dioxide and produce oxygen. They contain many species of flora and fauna not found elsewhere, and some of these plants may potentially provide new medicines in the fight against disease. **Deforestation** is occurring as people respond to the worldwide demand for wood by cutting down trees for furniture and other uses. Huge areas are also cleared for farming, building houses and roads. This human activity is one of the major contributors to climate change and it is estimated that as much as 15 per cent of all greenhouse gases are the result of deforestation.

▲ *Forests are disappearing at an alarming rate*

■ Pollution

Not only is the environment suffering from human **abuse** of natural resources, but modern lifestyles are causing contamination of the atmosphere, land and water. Gas emissions from industry, fires, homes and vehicles pollute the air and cause acid rain. Industrial waste, rubbish, oil and the use of pesticides contaminate the land, streams, rivers and the sea. Wildlife is affected by non-biodegradable and non-reusable materials which are dumped by humans.

▲ Many fish do not survive in polluted water

■ Sikh beliefs

Sikhs believe that people, who are conscious of God and his creation, are motivated to look after the environment and the world's natural resources.

Sikhs seek to live in harmony with nature, attempt to avoid waste and promote **sustainable development**. For example, in Northern India, traditional methods of farming have been dependent on relatively scarce natural resources. Consequently, the traditional lifestyle adopted by Sikhs has ensured that there has been considerable reuse, **recycling** and sharing of the resources that are available. For example, in the Punjab, the Gurus established places by the gurdwaras and community land where water is available. The community land is not farmed but is planted with plants and trees, which provide shade and a source of firewood for those who live in the vicinity to share. For example, Amritsar grew up around the Harimandir (the Golden Temple) and the Amrit Sarovar (the pool of nectar, that is, the water).

Sikhism stresses the importance of mastering the five evils: Lust, Anger, Worldly or Materialistic Attachment, Pride and Greed. Living simply in harmony with nature avoids abusing the world's resources. The Guru Granth Sahib refers to the Earth as the mother that should be treated with respect and, therefore, not exploited. Care should be taken to ensure that no damage occurs to the environment while going about a person's daily life. Trees are regarded as special and some species are named as sacred. The Guru Granth Sahib says that air, water, earth and sky are God's home and temple; so are sacred places that need to be looked after.

> 66 Sikhism teaches that the natural environment and the survival of all life forms are closely linked in the rhythm of nature. The history of the Gurus is full of stories of their love and special relationship with the natural environment, with animals, birds, vegetation, earth, rivers, mountains and the sky. 99
>
> *O. P. Dwivedi*

Activities

1 Why are Sikhs concerned about the use of mineral resources?
2 Explain why deforestation is a problem for the environment.
3 Give examples of pollution caused by human activity.
4 Explain Sikh attitudes to the use of natural resources.

Extension activity

Use the internet to find out about EcoSikh (www.ecosikh.org) and make notes on one project that EcoSikh has been involved in.

> 66 The God-conscious being delights in doing good to others. 99
>
> *Guru Granth Sahib 273*

> 66 Air, water, earth and sky – the Lord has made these His home and temple. 99
>
> *Guru Granth Sahib 723*

⭐ Study tip

Make sure that you not only know the problems resulting from exploiting the environment, but are also able to explain what Sikhs say and do about the situation.

Summary

You should know and understand Sikh beliefs about the use and abuse of the environment, including the use of natural resources.

The use and abuse of animals

■ Treatment of animals

Sikhs believe that it is important to treat animals well, because all creation has a divine presence. Cruelty to animals results in disrespecting God's creation. Sikhs believe that all living creatures are sentient, feeling beings and should be treated with respect and compassion.

All animals, like humans, have souls that go through different life forms until being purified to become one with God. The soul goes through countless cycles of birth and death before being born as a human.

> ❝ In so many incarnations, you were a worm and an insect; in so many incarnations, you were an elephant, a fish and a deer. In so many incarnations, you were a bird and a snake. In so many incarnations, you were yoked as an ox and a horse. Meet the Lord of the Universe – now is the time to meet Him. After so very long, this human body was fashioned for you. In so many incarnations, you were rocks and mountains; in so many incarnations, you were aborted in the womb; in so many incarnations, you developed branches and leaves; you wandered through 8.4 million incarnations. ❞
>
> *Guru Granth Sahib 176*

Objectives

- Understand Sikh beliefs about the use and abuse of animals.
- Explain Sikh attitudes towards animal experimentation and the use of animals for food.

Key terms

- **vegetarian:** a person who does not eat meat or fish
- **vegan:** a person who does not eat animals or food produced by animals (such as eggs); a vegan tries not to use any products that have caused harm to animals (such as leather)

■ The use of animals for food

Many practising Sikhs are lacto-vegetarians (they do not eat meat, fish or eggs). They are guided by Sikh teachings on living compassionately and responsibly, avoiding undue harm or death to people and all other living beings. You may also encounter Sikhs who are not vegetarian, who eat meat and fish so long as the animals are slaughtered quickly and with minimal suffering. However, for religious events and gatherings the food served is strictly vegetarian, most notably in the langar of a Sikh gurdwara.

> ❝ Show kindness and mercy to all beings. ❞
>
> *Guru Granth Sahib 508*

▲ *The food served in langars is always vegetarian*

> ❝ Kabeer, the dinner of beans and rice is excellent, if it is flavoured with salt. Who would cut his throat, to have meat with his bread? ❞
>
> *Guru Granth Sahib 1374*

The food that is served in the langar (gurdwara kitchen) and at Sikh religious events is always vegetarian.

■ Animal testing

▲ *Rats are specially bred to be used for animal testing*

Most Sikhs do not like animal experimentation of any kind because they oppose cruelty. However, many would not take action to stop it if the research is done as humanely as possible in order to find a cure for a disease. If the animal experimentation is done to test cosmetics like lipstick, then Sikhs would see this as humans abusing their power to serve their vanity. The intention is really important; if it is done to relieve suffering by creating medicines, then it can be understood, but to use animals for other purposes such as making money is very much against Sikhism. Christianity has similar views about when it might be acceptable to experiment on animals, but doesn't have the idea that such actions will have an effect on a person's karma.

Discussion activity

In small groups or pairs, discuss the following statements: 'Animal cruelty does not include killing an animal for food' and 'Sikhs should never buy a product which has been tested on animals.'

Contrasting beliefs

Find out more about Christian attitudes towards animal experimentation. Do Christian beliefs agree with or differ from Sikh beliefs on this issue?

⭐ **Study tip**

When you are answering an evaluation question on controversial issues such as animal experimentation or meat eating, you should give arguments for more than one point of view.

Activities

1 Give two reasons why Sikhs believe that it is right to treat animals well.

2 What are amritdhari Sikhs not allowed to eat?

3 Explain why only vegetarian food is served in the langar.

4 Explain Sikh attitudes to animal testing.

Summary

You should now know and understand Sikh beliefs and attitudes to the use and abuse of animals, the use of animals for food and animal experimentation.

4.5 The origins of human life

■ The creation of life

The detail of exactly how and when the first human beings came into existence is not an important question for Sikhs. Much more significant than any speculation about creation stories is the belief that Waheguru (God) created every living thing.

> 66 Without God, there is nothing at all. As one thread holds hundreds and thousands of beads, He is woven into His creation. 99
>
> *Guru Granth Sahib 485*

Sikhs are more interested in the wonder of God's creation rather than its possible origins. Life came about by God's order and will, and creation speaks of his greatness. The real issue is not how it happened, but what is the purpose of this life, and how can that purpose be achieved. The Guru Granth Sahib refers to all living things (including plants, birds and animals) as being made of three elements. These are the material body, soul and prana (breath, or universal energy which flows in currents in and around the body).

The Guru Granth Sahib classifies all life into four categories – 'born of sweat' refers to microbes or bacteria:

> 66 The beings born of eggs, born of the womb, born of the earth and born of sweat, all are created by You. 99
>
> *Guru Granth Sahib 596*

Objectives

- Understand Sikh beliefs about the origins of human life.
- Explore the relationship between evolution and creation.

Key terms

- **evolution:** the process by which living organisms are thought to have developed and diversified from earlier forms of life during the history of the Earth
- **mutation:** the changing of the structure of a gene or chromosome which gives the life form a different feature from that of the parents; this difference may be transmitted to following generations
- **adaptation:** a process of change, in which an organism or species becomes better suited to its environment

▲ *This iguana found on the Galapagos Islands is very different to any wildlife found in Europe*

> 66 From the True Lord came the air, and from the air came water. From water, He created the three worlds; in each and every heart He has infused His Light. 99
>
> *Guru Granth Sahib 19*

■ The theory of evolution

Charles Darwin, a British naturalist, published a book in 1859 called *On the Origin of Species by Means of Natural Selection*. In it he explained the theory of **evolution**. This theory was based on his study of plants and animals during his five-year expedition to places like the Galapagos Islands and Australasia.

He found many species which were quite different from those in Britain, and he put forward the idea that all life had evolved and changed into the species that are around today. He suggested that over millions of years, life evolved from single-cell organisms as a result of random **mutations**, natural selection and the survival of the fittest. If a random mutation were advantageous to the creature concerned, it would survive and breed more of the same kind. Life began first of all in water and over time many sorts of fish evolved. Fish eventually gave rise to amphibians, amphibians to reptiles, reptiles to birds and mammals and finally human beings. Species which were unable to compete or, by a process of **adaptation**, to adjust to changes in the environment, such as the dodo and the dinosaurs, died out. According to this theory, people are the highest and most complex form of life with apes, gorillas and chimpanzees being the closest relatives to humans.

▲ *British naturalist Charles Darwin*

■ Sikhism and evolution

Sikhism does not oppose the idea of life evolving, but the emphasis is on the creation of various forms of life by divine will (hukam) rather than changes taking place by accident because of natural selection. Under Charles Darwin's theory, only the fittest and most successful species survive, but Sikhs believe that Waheguru (God) oversees this natural process of evolution. God created nature and planned everything that happens – it isn't left to random chance.

The process is shown in the idea of rebirth. Sikhs believe that a person's soul is a very minute part of the Eternal Soul and has existed since the time of creation. Eventually it will be re-absorbed into God, but until then it remains separate and is subject to the samsara cycle of birth, life, death and rebirth. During the stages of existence, it evolves from primitive forms of life until it receives the gift of human form. Humans have the ability to communicate, reason, appreciate God's wonderful creation and, most importantly, seek a reunion with God.

 Discussion activity

With a partner or in a small group, discuss the following: 'It is possible to believe in both evolution and Sikh beliefs about the origins of human life.'

⭐ **Study tip**

Learn some relevant quotations from the Guru Granth Sahib and be able to explain how they apply to the creation of life.

Summary

You should now be able to explain Sikh and scientific beliefs about the origins of life on earth, and consider how they relate to each other.

Activities

1 Explain why Sikhs are less concerned about the details of how human life began.
2 Give the three elements that Sikhs believe all life includes.
3 Explain Charles Darwin's theory of evolution.
4 Explain Sikh beliefs about evolution.
5 'Everything has come about by accident, not by the design of Waheguru.' Do you agree? Give reasons for your answer.

4.6 Abortion

The sanctity of life

Sikh teachings state that life begins at conception and is precious because it is God given. Sikhs believe that all human beings are created by Waheguru (God) and that God lives in them. Life is therefore sacred.

Pro-life groups, such as the Society for the Protection of the Unborn Child (SPUC), use the concept of the **sanctity of life** as one of their main arguments against **abortion**.

▲ *People who are pro-life believe that abortion is a form of murder*

The quality of life

Some circumstances make the future prospects for an unborn child very bleak. Some families are already struggling financially and cannot afford another mouth to feed. In some instances, tests show that the child is going to be born with a severe disability. In situations where a child's life will be full of suffering, their **quality of life** will be poor. In contrast to this, a good quality of life enables the person to enjoy happiness, health, freedom, dignity and a good standard of living.

Pro-choice groups, such as Abortion Rights, argue in favour of the woman having the right to choose an abortion, because of issues concerning the potential quality of life for the unborn child or the family.

Abortion and the law

Abortion became legal in the UK in 1967 (except for Northern Ireland), providing certain conditions were met. Under the 1990 Human Fertilisation and Embryology Act, a woman cannot have an abortion past 24 weeks into the pregnancy, except where her physical health is at

> **"** O my body, the Lord infused His Light into you, and then you came into the world. **"**
>
> *Guru Granth Sahib 921*

> **"** In the first watch of the night, O my merchant friend, you were cast into the womb, by the Lord's Command. **"**
>
> *Guru Granth Sahib 74*

risk, or if there is a reasonable chance of a seriously disabled child being born.

An abortion is allowed if two doctors agree that one of the following conditions applies:

- the life or physical health of the woman is at risk
- the mental health of the woman is at risk
- the woman's existing family will suffer
- it is likely that the child will be born with a serious disability.

■ Sikhism and abortion

Sikhs believe that life is a gift from God and so abortions, or action deliberately causing a miscarriage, should not take place because it interferes with God's creative work. The belief that life begins at conception means that deliberately ending it is a sin. They argue that even if there is a definite chance of the unborn child being severely disabled, an abortion should not take place. An abortion might be regarded as acceptable if the pregnancy was a result of rape, or if the woman's life is at risk during pregnancy. Despite this teaching, the aborting of female embryos has been practised by many communities in India, including the Punjabi Sikh community. This has been the result of a cultural preference for boys, because they are seen as breadwinners who will eventually look after their parents. Also the social custom of providing a dowry for their daughters places families under intense financial pressures. However, the Sikh Gurus strongly condemned this practice and Sikhs continue to campaign against female embryos being aborted.

 An abortion is legal after 24 weeks if the woman's life is at risk

An unexpected pregnancy

Saachi is a sixteen-year-old Sikh student who is about to start studying for her A levels. She is hoping to get good results in order to go to university. Her boyfriend is also a Sikh and he is training to be an accountant. They have had a relationship for some time and Saachi began feeling sick every morning. On taking a pregnancy test, the result was positive and now she doesn't know what to do. She is worried about her parents' reaction if she tells them. She thinks that her boyfriend will support her, but doesn't know for sure. She wonders whether she should try to get an abortion, or give up her plans for going to university and have the baby. She knows what her Sikh faith says about abortion.

Activities

1 When do Sikhs believe that life begins?
2 Explain the difference between what is meant by the sanctity of life and the quality of life.
3 Under what circumstances does UK law allow an abortion to take place?
4 Explain what Sikhism teaches about abortion.
5 Read the story about Saachi and her situation. What do you think she should do? Give reasons for your opinion.

Discussion activity

In pairs or in a small group, discuss different circumstances where an abortion might be thought of as an option. Consider whether it would be right for religious believers to join either pro-life or pro-choice pressure groups.

Contrasting beliefs

Research Christian beliefs that are similar to, or different from, Sikh beliefs about abortion. For example, find out Roman Catholic and Methodist views about when life begins and when an abortion might be allowed.

★ Study tip

Be aware that sometimes cultural pressures are so strong that people follow them rather than the teachings of their religious faith.

Summary

You should now understand what is meant by the sanctity of life and quality of life, as well as understanding UK law and Sikh beliefs about having an abortion.

■ What is euthanasia?

Euthanasia is the term usually given to ending a life prematurely on compassionate grounds. If a person is suffering great pain from a terminal illness with no hope of recovery, it is argued that they should be allowed to die. The word 'euthanasia' comes from two Greek words: 'eu' which means 'good' and 'thanatos' which means 'death', so 'euthanasia' literally means 'a good or gentle death'. Euthanasia is illegal in the UK. If euthanasia were legal it would mean that those suffering from a poor quality of life would be permitted to end their life in a painless way. In some European countries, for example Holland and Switzerland, the law is less restrictive than in Britain, allowing euthanasia under certain circumstances.

Doctors in the UK can decide to withhold or withdraw medical treatment or life support that is keeping the person alive because they are not going to get better, or because the person asks them to. Medical professionals call this a non-treatment decision. Controversially, it is also sometimes called passive euthanasia.

Those who are against the legalisation of euthanasia in Britain argue that it is dangerous to allow someone to make a decision about whether a person should live or die. Such a law, some might argue, would be open to abuse. For example, someone wanting to inherit property might persuade their elderly relative to request euthanasia even though there is no need. Those opposing euthanasia might argue that it requires a judgement that life is no longer worth living, but all people are valuable at all times. Even if a sick person were to want to die, they might argue that no one has the authority to take a life away. Medical care that focuses on removing or controlling pain is available through the hospice movement.

On the other hand, some argue that people should be given the right to say when they want their lives to end. They believe that death is a private matter, and people should have the right to self-determination. They should be able to choose to die with dignity, rather than suffer from a prolonged painful end. Keeping a patient alive who has no hope of recovery is expensive. Animals in pain may be put down to avoid further suffering, so humans should have the same choice.

Objectives

- Investigate what is meant by euthanasia.
- Understand Sikh beliefs about euthanasia.

Key terms

- **euthanasia:** killing someone painlessly and with compassion, to end their suffering

Contrasting beliefs

Find out what Christianity teaches about euthanasia. Learn any similarities or differences between Christian and Sikh beliefs.

▲ *Sikhs believe in the importance of sewa (selfless service) and caring for the sick*

■ Types of euthanasia

The three types of euthanasia are as follows:

- Voluntary euthanasia – this is when the person asks a doctor to end their life.
- Non-voluntary euthanasia – when the person is too ill to request it themselves but it is seen as in their best interest.
- Involuntary euthanasia – when the person is able to provide consent but does not, either because they do not want to or because they are not asked, but their life is ended anyway.

■ Sikhs and euthanasia

Sikhs believe that life is sacred and God given. No person has the ability to decide to end a life prematurely, because the timing of birth and death is decided by God.

> ❝ Praise the Great Giver, who gives sustenance to all … Those who are sent, come, O Nanak; when they are called back, they depart and go. ❞
>
> *Guru Granth Sahib 1239*

Sikhs believe that a person may be suffering for unknown reasons related to events and actions in a past life. Escaping this suffering through euthanasia would result in suffering in the next life, so this is one reason why Sikhs oppose euthanasia. Instead Sikhs believe that they should pray for the courage and strength to endure the suffering, rather than ending a life early and causing future karmic consequences. Sikhism teaches that service (sewa) and caring for others is a duty. This suggests that the best response is to provide such good care that euthanasia becomes an unattractive option.

The Gurus began hospitals for the sick and dying, and many Sikhs work in the National Health Service and hospices. Sikhs oppose deliberately ending life, but many do not support artificially prolonging life when a person is in a vegetative state and their life has effectively ended. Keeping a person alive in circumstances where there is no chance of recovery is extending life longer than God intends. In those situations, many Sikhs would support a non-treatment decision, and agree with withdrawing medical provision and turning off life support machines.

Tony Nicklinson

Tony Nicklinson suffered a stroke in 2005 that left him paralysed from the neck down. He described his life as a 'living nightmare'. As a result, he tried to get the courts to allow doctors to end his life. In 2012, the High Court refused his request, so he refused to eat and died a few days later. He had made it clear that he did not want any life-sustaining treatment.

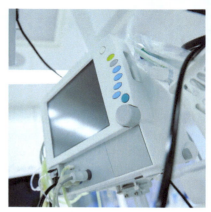

▲ *Life support machines may keep patients alive*

Activities

1 What is meant by the term 'euthanasia'?

2 What does the law say about euthanasia?

3 Give two arguments for and two arguments against euthanasia.

4 Explain briefly the three types of euthanasia.

5 Explain Sikh attitudes towards euthanasia.

Discussion activity

In small groups or pairs, discuss whether you think Tony Nicklinson was right to ask for euthanasia. Would a Sikh agree with your opinion? Give reasons for your conclusion.

★ Study tip

If you are evaluating whether people should support euthanasia, remember to include the fact that there are different types of euthanasia and that it is illegal in Britain.

Summary

You should now be able to explain what is meant by euthanasia and Sikh attitudes to it.

4.8 Death and afterlife

■ Is death the end?

Atheists believe that death is the end and that there is no afterlife. Once a person has died, that is it – oblivion. There is no scientific proof that can establish whether atheists or religious believers are correct in their beliefs. Some people claim that they have had near-death experiences (NDEs) in which they have gone along a tunnel towards a light. In some cases they say that they have met deceased members of their families or a divine figure. Others claim to have seen ghosts or been able to talk to the dead or remember previous lives. Sikhs, like Hindus and Buddhists, believe in **samsara**, the cycle of birth, death and rebirth.

Sikhs sometimes refer to death as like an experience of sleep. Having gone to sleep tired, the person wakes up refreshed the next day, ready for a new life. Excessive crying over death is therefore discouraged. The body is seen as a vessel for the soul, so the body holds no great significance in Sikh funerals. Usually the body is cremated, but burial is acceptable.

■ Is there a judgement?

Karma is the idea that what you sow, you will reap within your life and across lifetimes. Sikhs believe people are affected by karma, but understand that the divine will of God and God's grace also play an important part in their lives. According to one tradition, messengers take the deceased to the one who will judge their actions, Dharam Raj. Two angels, Chitra and Gupta, are called to record and present a balance sheet of the person's actions during their life. The judge then looks at the record of good and evil deeds and makes a judgement. If the balance shows mainly evil deeds, they will go into lower forms of life, whereas if they have done mostly good deeds then they will get a human life again or be liberated from the samsara cycle. Sikhs do not believe that at death a person goes to a physical place called heaven or hell. The Guru Granth Sahib does describe a desolate place of horror, but to most Sikhs it is a symbolic picture to show what it is like to be out of the presence of God.

> **"** In the hereafter, you shall have to cross over the fiery river of poisonous flames. No one else will be there; your soul shall be all alone. The ocean of fire spits out waves of searing flames; the self-willed manmukhs fall into it, and are roasted there. **"**
>
> *Guru Granth Sahib 1026*

To Sikhs, heaven can be experienced by being in tune with God while still alive. On the other hand, the pain and suffering caused by ego can be seen as hell on earth.

Objectives

- Review Sikh beliefs and attitudes about death and an afterlife.
- Understand the impact of these beliefs on the way Sikhs live their lives.

Key terms

- **samsara:** the cycle of birth, death and rebirth
- **reincarnation:** being born again into a new body

▲ *A cremation urn for the ashes of the deceased person*

Discussion activity

In pairs or small groups, discuss what you think happens after death. Do you think Sikhs would agree with you? Give reasons.

■ Reincarnation

Sikhs believe that the soul is immortal and goes through different life forms until purified to become one again with God. Like Hindus, Sikhs believe in **reincarnation**, although no one has seen what exactly happens after death, so it is difficult to understand precisely what happens. Sikhs believe that the soul goes from one body to the next, through countless reincarnations. Good merit or karma brings about a higher spiritual understanding and a closer relationship with God. Further rebirths allow this relationship to develop. When a righteous person dies, he or she may enter into union with God and escape the samsara cycle and all the suffering of this world. To achieve this involves meditating on God and purifying the soul from things like anger, attachment, greed, lust and ego (pride). Failure to worship God and meditate upon him results in more reincarnations. If no effort is made to love God and purify the soul, the result is wandering through the 8.4 million species (Guru Granth Sahib 88).

▲ Sikhs believe that humans can be reborn as 8.4 million different life forms

> **❝** The blind and ignorant fools do not serve the True Guru; how will they find the gate of salvation? They die and die, over and over again, only to be reborn, over and over again. **❞**
>
> *Guru Granth Sahib 115*

Sikhs believe that it is vital to overcome ego and build up good merit by meditating on God, doing good deeds and serving the community. The aim is to achieve liberation while still alive (jivan mukti). A warning is given in the Guru Granth Sahib 526 that what the mind last remembers will affect what happens after death.

> **❝** At the very last moment, one who thinks of wealth, and dies in such thoughts, shall be reincarnated over and over again, in the form of serpents … At the very last moment, he who thinks of women, and dies in such thoughts, shall be reincarnated over and over again as a prostitute … At the very last moment, one who thinks of the Lord, and dies in such thoughts, says Trilochan, that man shall be liberated; the Lord shall abide in his heart. **❞**
>
> *Guru Granth Sahib 526*

Activities

1 What are Near Death Experiences (NDEs)?
2 Explain the difference between karma and samsara.
3 What do Sikhs believe about judgement?
4 Explain Sikh beliefs about reincarnation.
5 How might the belief in reincarnation affect the way a Sikh lives?

Extension activity

Find out what Christianity says about life after death. Learn any similarities or differences between Christian and Sikh beliefs.

Links

To discover more about Sikh beliefs about karma and rebirth, see pages 14–15.

⭐ Study tip

Make sure you can explain the influence Sikh beliefs about karma and life after death may have on their actions in life.

Summary You should now know Sikh beliefs and teachings about death and the afterlife.

The origins and value of the universe – summary

You should now be able to:

✔ explain Sikh teachings, beliefs and attitudes about the origins of the universe, including different interpretations of these

✔ explain scientific views, such as the Big Bang theory, and their relationship with religious views

✔ explain Sikh teachings about the value of the world and the duty of humans to protect it, including the ideas of stewardship, dominion, responsibility, awe and wonder

✔ explain teachings and beliefs about the use and abuse of the environment

✔ explain beliefs about the use of natural resources

✔ explain the problems caused by pollution and Sikh responses to the issue

✔ explain teachings, beliefs and attitudes about the use and abuse of animals

✔ explain religious beliefs about animal experimentation

✔ explain Sikh responses to the use of animals for food.

The origins and value of human life – summary

You should now be able to:

✔ explain Sikh teachings about the origins of human life, including different interpretations of these

✔ explain the relationship between scientific views, such as evolution, and religious views

✔ explain the concepts of sanctity of life and quality of life

✔ explain religious views concerning the issue of abortion, including situations when the woman's life is at risk

✔ explain religious beliefs about euthanasia

✔ explain Sikh beliefs about death and an afterlife, and their impact on beliefs about the value of human life

✔ explain contrasting beliefs in contemporary British society about the three issues of abortion, euthanasia and animal experimentation, with reference to the main religious tradition in Britain (Christianity) and one or more other religious traditions

✔ explain contemporary British attitudes (both religious and non-religious) about all of the above issues.

Sample student answer – the 12-mark question

1.   Write an answer to the following practice question:

'There must be life after death.'
Evaluate this statement. In your answer you:
- should give reasoned arguments to support this statement
- should give reasoned arguments to support a different point of view
- should refer to religious arguments
- may refer to non-religious arguments
- should reach a justified conclusion.

[12 marks]
[+ 3 SPaG marks]

2.   Read the following sample student answer:

"Not everyone believes that there is life after death. Atheists, for example, think that when you die that is it. They don't believe in a soul that lives on. Once the heart stops beating and the brain stops functioning many believe that life is over. There doesn't seem to be any sign of life. No one can prove that life continues in another form. We can't do a scientific experiment to show that it does. Some people have claimed that they have come back from the dead or have had near death experiences but they may not be telling the truth or they may have been misled. So the statement may not be true.

Others would argue that the scriptures say that there is life after death so it must be true. Sikhs believe in reincarnation and the samsara cycle of birth, death and rebirth, which is stated in the Guru Granth Sahib. They believe that the soul is immortal and so there is life after death as the soul is reborn in another being.

Personally I am not sure as no one can prove that there is such thing as a soul and even if there is it cannot be proven what happens to it after a person dies. There might be life after death, but we won't know for certain until we ourselves die and experience what really does happen, if anything."

3. With a partner, discuss the sample answer. Is the focus of the answer correct? Is anything missing from the answer? How do you think it could be improved?

4. What mark (out of 12) would you give this answer? Look at the mark scheme in the Introduction (AO2). What are the reasons for the mark you have given?

5. Now swap your answer with your partner's and mark each other's responses. What mark (out of 12) would you give the response? Refer to the mark scheme and give reasons for the mark you award.

Practice questions

 1 Which **one** of the following means the cycle of birth, death and rebirth?

A) Karma **B)** Samsara **C)** Ardas **D)** Gurmukh **[1 mark]**

2 Give **one** reason why religious believers might oppose animal experimentation. **[1 mark]**

3 Explain **two** different beliefs in contemporary British society about euthanasia.

In your answer you should refer to the main religious tradition of Great Britain and one or more other religious traditions. **[4 marks]**

> ⭐ **Study tip**
>
> Remember to develop the points you are making. This may be done by giving detailed information, such as referring to examples. Be sure to include different beliefs in your answer. This may be done by referring to Christianity and Sikhism.

4 Explain **two** religious beliefs about what happens when a person dies.

Refer to sacred writings or another source of religious belief and teaching in your answer. **[6 marks]**

 5 'Religious believers should not eat meat.'

Evaluate this statement. In your answer you:
- should give reasoned arguments to support this statement
- should give reasoned arguments to support a different point of view
- should refer to religious arguments
- may refer to non-religious arguments
- should reach a justified conclusion.

[12 marks]
[+ 3 SPaG marks]

> ⭐ **Study tip**
>
> A detailed response is required. Focus your answer on the statement. It is about whether it is *right* for religious believers to eat meat, not just a statement suggesting that everyone should avoid eating meat.

5 The existence of God and revelation

5.1 The Design argument

■ Belief in God

A **theist** believes that God created the universe and life on earth for a purpose. Some theists argue that nature is so intricate and complex that God must have designed it. It could not have happened by random chance. An **atheist** believes that there is no God and that there is no evidence that the universe or life on earth were created by God. Atheists argue that the universe just happened and life evolved. An **agnostic** believes that it is impossible to know for certain whether or not God exists. After all, no one can see God or produce God as proof.

■ Sikh beliefs

The Mool Mantra expresses the belief that God is timeless and self-existent (eternal and not created by anyone or anything other than God's self). Guru Nanak taught that the creation and its creator are inseparable, just as an ocean is made up of individual drops of water. In one of his hymns, Guru Nanak says that God made the laws to run the universe, and then made the universe itself.

> ❝ He Himself created Himself; He Himself assumed His Name. Secondly, He fashioned the creation; seated within the creation He beholds it with delight. ❞
>
> *Guru Granth Sahib 463*

Objective

- Consider the Design argument, including its strengths and weaknesses.

Key terms

- **theist:** a person who believes in God
- **atheist:** a person who believes that there is no God
- **agnostic:** someone who thinks there is not enough evidence for belief in God
- **Design argument:** the argument that God designed the universe because everything is so intricately made in its detail that it could not have happened by chance

Many Sikhs believe that the world is so well-ordered to sustain life, and so complex, right down to the internal structure of even the most basic cells, that it could not have evolved from a random collection of smaller, simpler units. DNA gives precise instructions to cells to act in a certain way. Such precision could not come about unintentionally. An intelligent guide or director controlled the process, God.

■ Design arguments

Over the years, philosophers have put forward several versions of the **Design argument** (sometimes called the teleological argument).

▲ *Does the complex, precise structure of DNA prove God designed everything that exists?*

Thomas Aquinas (1225–1274)	Only an intelligent being could keep things in the universe in regular order. The planets, sun, moon and stars rotate in the solar system in a set pattern because God holds them in place.
Isaac Newton (1642–1727)	The human thumb's design is so clever, and unique to every individual, that it alone convinced Newton that there was a designer of the world, God.
William Paley (1743–1805)	The intricate workings of a watch show it was designed deliberately for a purpose. Its pieces could not have come together by themselves. Nature shows evidence of design, for example the eye for sight, birds' wings for flight, etc. The universe is more complicated than a watch and must have had a designer, God.
F. R. Tennant (1866–1957)	If the strength of gravity, the power and speed of the explosion caused by the Big Bang, or the difference in size between a proton and a neutron had been just a tiny bit different, then life would not exist. Therefore the world must have had a designer, God.

■ Strengths and weaknesses of the Design argument

Everyone can appreciate that nature is beautiful, complex and follows orderly laws. Most Sikhs welcome scientific discoveries and see no contradiction between their faith in God as designer of the universe and scientific theories like the Big Bang and Evolution.

> ❝ The One Universal Creator Lord created the creation. He made all the days and the nights. The forests, meadows … the countries, the continents and all the worlds, have all come from the One Word of the Lord. ❞
>
> *Guru Granth Sahib 1003*

Atheists argue that because the process of natural selection (the fittest survive, the rest die out) happens by chance, species designed themselves over time. The thumb, the eye and birds' wings are all the result of evolution, not a designer God. The order in the universe is needed to support life, so it merely gives the appearance of design. Humans impose the order on nature to explain it. Atheists also ask why there is so much suffering in the world if God designed it. Cruelty within nature, wars, disease and earthquakes all suggest the design is faulty. Would a designer God create evil and suffering?

Activities

1 Explain Sikh beliefs about the design of the universe.
2 Explain the Design argument of William Paley.
3 'Evolution proves that the world is not designed.' Evaluate this statement.

Links

See pages 10–11 for more about God the Creator.

⭐ Study tip

Try to learn one of the more detailed Design arguments, such as William Paley's argument.

▲ *The intricate workings of a watch show that it has been designed*

Research activity 🔍

Find out more about the Design arguments of the philosophers mentioned above. Which argument, if any, do you think is the most convincing for the existence of a designer God?

Links

See pages 106–107 for more detail on the problem of suffering and evil.

Summary

You should now be able to explain and discuss the Design argument, including its strengths and weaknesses.

The First Cause argument

Discussion activity 💬

With a partner, trace the events of your life back to the moment of your birth, back to when your parents met, back to when they were born, etc. How far can you go? Was there an original cause for the universe to begin?

People naturally try to find causes for events that take place, including what caused the universe. When you trace your life back in time (see the discussion activity above), you will probably find that there are only two possibilities; either there is a starting point when the universe began, or there is no starting point or beginning: the universe goes back into infinity.

The **First Cause argument**, also called the cosmological argument, relies on the belief that the universe had a beginning and a cause like all other things that exist. The argument goes:

- Everything that exists or begins to exist must have a cause.
- The universe exists and began to exist, so it too must have a cause.
- There had to be something eternal that was not caused by anything.
- The **eternal** first cause is God.
- Therefore God exists.

The Big Bang

Theists claim that God started the chain of events that has led to the present. It would be difficult to explain the existence of the universe if it did not have a beginning.

Most scientists accept that the universe began as a result of the Big Bang. But where did the material that was created at the Big Bang come from? What existed before the Big Bang? There must have been a cause for the Big Bang and the start of the universe. Modern theists, including all Sikhs, would argue that God was the eternal, uncaused cause of the Big Bang. Guru Nanak described God as uncaused when he wrote: 'He Himself created Himself' (Guru Granth Sahib 463).

Thomas Aquinas' First Cause argument

Thomas Aquinas, a thirteenth-century philosopher, said he could prove the existence of God. He argued that everything we observe is caused to exist. Nothing can become something by itself. Nothing equals

Objective

- Examine the First Cause argument for the existence of God, including its strengths and weaknesses.

Key terms

- **First Cause argument:** also known as the cosmological argument; an argument that all things in nature depend on something else for their existence and so must have been started by an independent being, such as God
- **eternal:** without beginning or end
- **creation:** the act by which God brought the universe into being

> ❝ The entire creation came from God. As it pleases Him, He creates the expanse. As it pleases Him, He becomes the One and Only again. ❞
>
> *Guru Granth Sahib 294*

▲ *What caused the Big Bang to happen?*

nothing, and remains nothing unless something is added. For example, a vacuum remains a vacuum for ever, unless some air is let into it, and then it ceases to be a vacuum. Since nothing we observe can cause itself to exist, there are only two possibilities. Either there is an infinite chain of effects preceded by causes, or there must be a first cause, which by definition must be uncaused. But an infinite sequence of causes and effects is impossible, since it would have taken an infinite amount of time to reach us. Therefore, there must have been a first cause that was not itself caused by anything else. Aquinas believed the first cause of the universe was God. We can plainly see that the universe exists, so, Aquinas argued, it must have had a creator to begin with: God.

▲ *Scientists, such as those working at CERN, are still trying to discover more about the origins of the universe*

■ Objections to the First Cause argument

- Atheists say the argument contradicts itself: if everything that exists has a cause, what caused God?
- If you say that God is eternal and has always existed, why can't the universe always have existed too?
- Just because events have causes, it does not mean the universe itself has a cause.
- The Big Bang was a random, spontaneous event, not an action by God.
- Religious **creation** stories are just myths (stories that tell a spiritual, rather than actual, truth).

Theists, including many Sikhs, would counter by saying that only God is eternal, beyond time and space. The cause of the Big Bang is not yet known. Why couldn't it be God?

> ❝ He [God] is not obtained by intellectual recitation or great cleverness; only by love does the mind obtain Him. ❞
>
> *Guru Granth Sahib 436*

Research activity 🔍

Find out about Thomas Aquinas' 'first way' of proving the existence of God. God has been described as the Prime Mover because of this argument.

⭐ Study tip

Try to remember that Sikhs believe God created the world, but they do not all agree with the First Cause argument or the Design argument. Some think that God can only be experienced through devotion.

Activities

1 Explain two strengths and two weaknesses of the First Cause argument.
2 Why do dominoes fall in a domino rally? How could this idea link to the First Cause argument?
3 'The First Cause argument is a stronger argument for the existence of God than the Design argument.' Evaluate this statement.

Summary

You should now be able to explain the First Cause argument and discuss its strengths and weaknesses.

■ What is a miracle?

For theists, a **miracle** is an event performed by God that seems to break the laws of nature. The event should be impossible to contradict, in other words, have no other explanation. It may be a cure from a fatal illness that doctors cannot explain or survival from certain death by a freak occurrence.

According to Sikh tradition (but not mentioned in the Guru Granth Sahib itself), the Gurus experienced miracles. Guru Nanak disappeared in the River Bain for three days and, when he emerged, began his life's work of preaching. He was said to have saved his companion, Mardana, from starving by making some bitter nuts sweet, and on another occasion he stopped a boulder by stretching out his hand. But when asked about his supernatural powers, he replied that he could do nothing against the law of God, and that only God could perform miracles.

Sikhs accept the possibility of supernatural powers, but believe these should not be used selfishly, to prove the greatness of one's religion or to convince people that a religion is true. Guru Arjan and Guru Tegh Bahadur were put to death for refusing to perform miracles.

Some people may call a wonderful event like the birth of a baby a 'miracle', but this is not really a miracle in the same way. Babies are born every day and science can explain the process. If a woman was unable to conceive and then did so after praying to God, she might be justified in describing her pregnancy as a miracle. Whether something is a miracle often depends on interpretation and the faith of the witnesses.

■ Argument from miracles

Theists argue that if there is no scientific explanation for an event, then it must be supernatural, in other words, caused by something outside nature. Since only God is outside nature, then it must be the result of God's intervention in the world. Therefore God exists.

Theists believe that miracles show God's love and care for people. They argue that there are too many accounts of miracles for them not to happen, and some happen to non-believers who become believers because of them. Many miracles are

▲ Miracles are reported to have occurred at the Golden Temple in Amritsar

investigated thoroughly before they are accepted, showing that there is sound medical or scientific proof that they are genuine.

■ Objections to the argument from miracles

Atheists might argue that miracles cannot prove God's existence because:

- miracles are no more than lucky coincidences
- they may have scientific explanations not yet discovered
- miracle healings may be the result of mind over matter on the part of the sufferer, or a misdiagnosis by doctors
- some 'miracles' are fakes, made up by people who want fame or money.

David Hume, an eighteenth-century philosopher, argued against miracles by saying that there can never be enough evidence to deny the laws of nature, and that witnesses to miracles are unreliable as most of them are primitive, uneducated people. Religions depend on miracles to prove they are true, but not all the religions can be right.

Some theists object to miracles because they seem to show God as unfair by picking and choosing who is helped. For example, why save someone from cancer and allow thousands to die in a natural disaster? Since God is all-just and all-loving, they argue, miracles do not happen.

▲ *Does God choose to save only some people?*

Stories from Sikh tradition

Guru Nanak and the boulder

The Guru and his companions were thirsty. They came upon a famous holy person who owned a well at the top of a hill and they asked him for water. He refused them three times, demanding payment which they did not have. Guru Nanak dug into the ground at the bottom of the hill and a spring appeared, so they drank their fill. The holy person was struck by anger and pushed a huge boulder down the hill intending to crush the Guru, but Nanak stretched out his hand and it miraculously stopped.

Extension activity

Interview two people, one from a religious background and one from a non-religious background, to find out their views about miracles. Have they known anyone who experienced a miracle? Do they think miracles are possible?

Activities

1 Explain in detail the reasons why atheists disagree with miracles as evidence for God.
2 'Miracles make God appear unfair.' Evaluate this statement.

Summary

You should now be able to discuss and evaluate the argument from miracles and describe one example of a miracle. You should also be able to explain different beliefs about miracles.

⭐ **Study tip**

Make sure you know how Sikhs and non-believers would explain a 'miracle'.

Further arguments against the existence of God

■ Faith and proof

We have considered three arguments for God's existence: Design, First Cause and the argument from miracles. None of these offer conclusive **proof** that God exists. Theists already have **faith** in God. These arguments may serve to strengthen their faith. If a belief was proved to be a fact, then it would no longer be a matter of faith. The Gurus never spoke about proofs of the existence of God. For them God is too real and obvious to need any logical proof.

■ How science is used to challenge belief in God

Some atheists argue that we do not need to invent a God to make sense of what we do not know at the moment (sometimes called a 'God of the gaps'). Science will eventually discover all the facts about how the universe began. God is not needed.

For atheists, evolution has shown that there is no specific design in the universe and that species have naturally adapted to survive. Again there is no need for God to explain the development of human life. It is just nature.

Science is also close to creating human life. For atheists, this is further evidence that God does not exist.

■ How the existence of evil and suffering is used to challenge belief in God

We live in a world full of **evil** and **suffering**. The news is full of examples of crimes committed against innocent people and natural disasters that destroy lives. Some atheists use the fact that there is evil and suffering in the world to argue that God does not exist. They argue that:

- God is believed to be all-knowing, all-powerful and all-loving.
- God therefore should be aware of evil, should be able to prevent it, and would want to do so.
- God does not do this, so God does not exist.

There is cruelty within nature (cats by nature want to kill mice, for example). Natural disasters are also evidence of poor design. Why would a good God create a world that contains suffering or create humans that choose evil over good?

■ Sikh responses to these arguments

Sikh scriptures and science are seen as complementary, all showing the same divine truth. Scientific discoveries about the origins of the universe and life support teaching in the Guru Granth Sahib.

▲ *Will science replace belief in God?*

> 66 There are planets, solar systems and galaxies. If one speaks of them, there is no limit, no end. There are worlds upon worlds of His Creation. As He commands, so they exist. He watches over all, and contemplating the creation, He rejoices. 99
>
> *Guru Granth Sahib 8*

Links

For more on creation, see pages 82–83.

Sikhs believe that religion and science answer different questions. Science pursues physically measurable information about matter. God who is ultimate truth is beyond human science and cannot be tested in a laboratory. Questions about the purpose of life, why humans exist, and how they should live are appropriate questions for religion and philosophy, not science.

> 66 The concerns of science and religion are not mutually exclusive, but are complementary. Religion can lend meaning to life, whatever the facts that science discovers about the mechanics of life itself. 99
>
> *I. J. Singh*

Sikhs believe that suffering is often the result of a person's own actions and moral choices. God does not inflict suffering or want people to suffer, but God permits it to test people's faith and courage. Whatever happens is God's will, so God has reasons for allowing evil that humans cannot know. If God constantly intervened to prevent evil, humans would not be free.

▲ *Sikhs believe that suffering can be a result of human action*

Discussion activities

1 Look at the photo of the train crash below. Discuss with a partner how human action might have contributed to the crash.

2 With a partner, consider what the consequences would be for human freedom if God intervened to prevent suffering and evil from taking place.

Activities

1 Explain two ways in which atheists use science to argue that God does not exist.

2 Explain two Sikh responses to these arguments.

3 Explain Sikh beliefs about evil and suffering in the world.

4 'When science discovers all the answers, there will be no need for God.' Evaluate this statement.

⭐ **Study tip**

Try to learn arguments both for and against the existence of God and form your own opinion to reach a justified conclusion.

Summary

You should now be able to discuss the arguments against the existence of God based on science and on the problem of suffering and evil.

5.5 Special revelation and enlightenment

■ What is meant by the divine?

Every religion accepts that there is an **ultimate reality** that is eternal and unchanging. Ideas about **the divine** include God, gods or ultimate reality. For example, Buddhists and many Sikhs think of ultimate reality as an eternal truth or principle that governs the universe. Hindus worship one God (Brahman) through different gods and goddesses that reveal different aspects of God.

Sikhs emphasise the oneness of God, the eternal truth and source of all life, in the prayer they recite every morning, the Mool Mantra. In Gurmukhi, it consists of a series of adjectives to describe God.

■ How may God be known?

Some theists say that God cannot be known because God is pure mystery, beyond human understanding. Guru Nanak said that God is not accessible through intellect or clever arguments, but is only revealed through devotion (see Guru Granth Sahib 436). Sikhs accept that God is beyond humans' limited understanding, but believe that it is possible to know something of God's nature and purposes through **revelations**. Humans can only know God if God chooses to reveal himself to people, not through any efforts of their own. There are two main kinds of revelation: special revelation and general revelation.

■ Special revelation

Special revelation is when people experience God directly in a particular event. It might be a dream, a **vision**, a prophecy, a miracle, or hearing 'God's call', either alone or with a group of people. These experiences usually have a huge impact on people and can change their lives.

▲ Sikhs consider the Guru Granth Sahib to be a special revelation from God; it can also be a general revelation to a person reading it today

---

Objectives

- Examine special revelation as a source of knowledge about the divine.
- Understand enlightenment as a source of knowledge about the divine.
- Consider one example of a vision.

Key terms

- **ultimate reality:** an eternal, unchanging truth that governs the universe; theists believe the ultimate reality to be God or gods
- **the divine:** God, gods or ultimate reality
- **revelation:** God showing himself to believers; this is the only way anybody can really know anything about God
- **special revelation:** God making himself known through direct personal experience or an unusual specific event
- **vision:** seeing something especially in a dream or trance, that shows something about the nature of God or the afterlife
- **enlightenment:** the gaining of true knowledge about God, self or the nature of reality, usually through meditation and self-discipline; in Buddhist, Hindu and Sikh traditions, gaining freedom from the cycle of rebirth

Links

You can read about the Mool Mantra on pages 8–9.

Sikhism began with the special revelation of God to Guru Nanak (see the story below). Sikh scriptures describe God's self-revelation through the words of the Gurus that have come directly from God: 'The Creator Lord Himself causes the Guru to chant it' (Guru Granth Sahib 308) and 'By myself, I do not even know how to speak; I speak all that the Lord commands' (Guru Granth Sahib 763).

Stories from Sikh tradition

Three days in the river

Early each morning, Guru Nanak would bathe in the River Bain and sing God's praises. One day he disappeared, leaving his clothes lying next to the riverbank. His friends walked up and down calling his name, but there was no sign of him. They were afraid he had drowned.

But Nanak was far from the reach of any of them. He was in a divine trance in which he was sitting in God's own presence. God gave him a cup of nectar and said, 'I am with you. Go and repeat My Name, and teach others to do the same.' Nanak was so filled with love for God that he sang the words of the Mool Mantra.

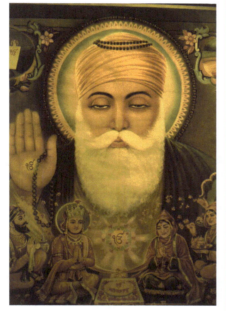

▲ *Guru Nanak received a special revelation while bathing in the River Bain*

God looked upon him with infinite kindness and said, 'My Name is God, and you are the divine Guru.'

Visions

A vision is a form of special revelation that comes as a picture or image. People see holy people, angels or hear messages from God. A vision holds a deep meaning for the person receiving it and enables them to become aware of reality in a new way or with a new intensity. Guru Nanak's experience of drinking a cup of nectar in the court of God is an example of a vision.

Enlightenment

Buddhists do not believe in God or gods. They seek understanding of what is true and what is not, that is ultimate reality. Through meditation and practising the Buddhist way of life, they hope to end suffering and achieve happiness by escaping the cycle of birth, death and rebirth. **Enlightenment** is also a goal of Sikhs and Hindus who believe in God. They seek enlightenment through prayer, meditation and following a religious way of life.

5.6 General revelation

■ General revelation

Unlike special revelation, which is direct and sometimes dramatic, **general revelation** comes through ordinary, everyday experiences that are open to everyone. Some people feel God's presence in **nature** or when they read the **scriptures** of their religion or take part in worship. Some feel sure of God's existence through their reason, conscience or sense of right and wrong. For others, the lives and work of religious leaders who seem particularly close to God reveal something of God's purposes for humans. General revelation is available to anyone, but these experiences do not convince everyone that God is real, because they depend on people's interpretation of them.

Some examples of revelation can be both general and special, depending on the circumstances. For example, reading scripture is open to anyone (general), but it may be the means of a direct personal experience of God for an individual (special). The Guru Granth Sahib is a special revelation of God to the Gurus, but it can reveal truths about God to anyone who reads it with an open mind.

■ Nature as a way of understanding the divine

The beauty of nature, the power of storms and the sea, the wonder of a newborn baby, the complexity of the human body, the order and design in nature reveal God as present within the creation to many people. For Sikhs, the natural world is a revelation of God: God is within each part of creation and creation is part of God. The Guru Granth Sahib has many verses that speak of the natural world as a sign of God's power, wisdom and love for his creation.

> ❝ He is the Master who has made the world bloom; He makes the Universe blossom forth, fresh and green. He holds the water and the land in bondage. Hail to the Creator Lord! ❞
>
> *Guru Granth Sahib 24*

▲ *Does nature reveal the power of God?*

> ❝ In the bowl of the sky, the sun and moon are the lamps; the stars in the constellations are the pearls. The fragrance of sandalwood is the incense, the wind is the fan, and all the vegetation are flowers in offering to You, O Luminous Lord. What a beautiful lamp-lit worship service this is! ❞
>
> *Guru Granth Sahib 663*

Links

Remind yourself of the Design argument on pages 100–101.

> " Men, trees, sacred shrines of pilgrimage, banks of sacred rivers, clouds, fields, islands, continents, worlds, solar systems, and universes; the four sources of creation – born of eggs, born of the womb, born of the earth and born of sweat; oceans, mountains, and all beings – O Nanak, He alone knows their condition. O Nanak, having created the living beings, He cherishes them all. The Creator who created the creation, takes care of it as well. "
>
> *Guru Granth Sahib 467*

Just as a sculpture or piece of music gives an insight into the artist, so nature gives believers an insight into God. Just like Christians, when Sikhs look at the world around them, they think God is shown as creative, artistic, clever, powerful and awesome. This leads to feelings of awe and wonder at the power of God to create and to destroy.

■ Scripture as a way of understanding the divine

One of the main ways in which the divine is revealed is through the scriptures (sacred writings) of a religion. For Sikhs, the Guru Granth Sahib contains God's words revealed to the Gurus. It offers many ideas about the nature of God and describes how to become a person of truth by meditating on God's name and living a moral life. In poetry and hymns, it describes the yearning of humans for union with the divine. The scripture is considered the highest authority in Sikhism, a living Guru.

Some people, such as atheists or humanists, believe that scriptures cannot reveal anything about God because they are merely their authors' opinions. Atheists might admire scriptures as ancient historical documents, but they would not regard them as evidence for God's existence.

▲ *Can scriptures light the way to an understanding of God?*

Summary

You should now be able to discuss what is meant by a general revelation and how nature and scripture reveal the divine to some people.

Links

Remind yourself of the Sikh scriptures on pages 26–27 and 38–39.

Activities

1 Explain, giving an example, the meaning of general revelation.

2 How is a general revelation different from a special revelation?

3 Explain what nature reveals to Sikhs about God.

Research activities

1 Read the Guru Granth Sahib, page 1020, verses 16–17. What does this passage teach about the relationship between nature and God? Explain how an atheist would respond to this passage.

2 Find out Christian beliefs about how nature might reveal God to believers. How might an atheist argue against these beliefs?

Discussion activity

'Scriptures are the words of human beings, not the words of God.' With a partner or in a small group, discuss this statement. Share your ideas with the class.

Contrasting beliefs

Find out more about how Christian or non-religious beliefs about nature as general revelation differ from Sikh beliefs.

★ Study tip

It is important to be able to identify the differences between special and general revelation. Remember that scriptures can be an example of both, depending on the circumstances.

Different ideas about the divine

Religions may describe the nature of God, gods or ultimate reality in different ways. As we have already noted, it is difficult to describe the unseen, infinite God within the limits of human language. Yet there are many similarities in the way different religions understand the divine or describe God's nature.

All religions, apart from Buddhism, agree that there is only one God who is creator, controller and maintainer of the universe. God is seen as **omnipotent** (almighty), capable of doing anything, for example creating the universe. God is **omniscient** as God is aware of everything that happens, past, present and future. God is seen as **benevolent** (all-loving and all-good) in providing everything people need for survival on earth.

Sikhs believe that God is the creator, sustainer but also the destroyer of all things. God is compassionate, kind, merciful and wise, the protector of all. Only God is worthy of worship and meditation, and it is only through his will that suffering can be overcome in a person's life.

> ❝ Blessing us with His Glance of Grace, the Kind and Compassionate, All-powerful Lord comes to dwell within the mind and body. ❞
>
> *Guru Granth Sahib 49*

> ❝ The Cherisher Lord is so very merciful and wise; He is compassionate to all. ❞
>
> *Guru Granth Sahib 249*

> ❝ O Nanak, God has been kind and compassionate; He has blessed me. Removing pain and poverty, He has blended me with Himself. ❞
>
> *Guru Granth Sahib 1311*

Religious thinkers use the words immanent, transcendent, personal and impersonal to describe different ideas about God.

- An **immanent** God is present in the universe and involved with life on earth. People are able to experience God in their lives. God acts in history and influences events.
- A **transcendent** God is beyond and outside life on earth and the universe. God is not limited by the world, time or space. God existed before the universe he created so is separate from it. A transcendent God does not intervene in people's lives.
- People who believe God is **personal** think of God as having human characteristics (like 'merciful' or 'compassionate'). They believe God loves and cares about every individual and that they can have a relationship with God through prayer.

Objectives

- Investigate the different ideas about the divine that come from revelation.
- Know and understand qualities of God such as omnipotent, omniscient, benevolent, personal, impersonal, immanent and transcendent.

Key terms

- **omnipotent:** almighty, having unlimited power; a quality of God
- **omniscient:** knowing everything; a quality of God
- **benevolent:** all-loving, all-good; a quality of God
- **immanent:** the idea that God is present in and involved with life on earth and in the universe; a quality of God
- **transcendent:** the idea that God is beyond and outside life on earth and the universe; a quality of God
- **personal nature (of God):** the idea that God is an individual or person with whom people are able to have a relationship or feel close to
- **impersonal nature (of God):** the idea that God has no 'human' characteristics, is unknowable and mysterious, more like an idea or force

Links

Look back to pages 106–107 to remind yourself of why the existence of suffering and evil makes some people question these qualities of God. See also page 8 for Sikh beliefs about the nature of God.

- An **impersonal** God is the opposite – God does not have human characteristics. God is more like a force or an idea, like a prime number (a number that can only be divided by itself and 1). This God is an absolute being, who is only understood in terms of itself.

■ Can God be immanent and transcendent, personal and impersonal?

Many religious people, including Sikhs, believe they can experience God and have a personal relationship with him (immanent and personal) but also that God is the eternal, unlimited creator of the universe (transcendent and impersonal). Some religions emphasise one description more than another, but others say that all these aspects of God's nature are true even though they seem contradictory. God is a mystery, beyond human understanding.

For Sikhs, God is beyond human knowledge and understanding, omniscient and omnipotent. Sikh scripture describes God as immanent within creation, yet creation fails to contain God fully. God is also transcendent because God is truth (satnam), the changeless and timeless reality. God is referred to as brother, father, mother, friend, lover and husband, emphasising God as personal, but also as Waheguru (Wonderful Lord), which suggests the awe and joy of the worshipper who contemplates God's immense grandeur and his creation.

▲ *Sikhs believe God is present in all living things*

▲ *What does this picture suggest about God as transcendent?*

> **❝** O my True Lord and Master, You are unknowable; through the Word of the Guru's Shabad [hymn or passage of scripture], You are known. **❞**
> *Guru Granth Sahib 308*

Discussion activity

'Talking about God's nature is not as important as trying to live according to God's truth.' Discuss this statement. Try to think of different points of view.

⭐ Study tip

Use the key terms listed here in your answers to show your knowledge of technical vocabulary.

Activities

1 Explain what religious believers mean when they say God is:

   a immanent

   b personal

   c transcendent.

2 Explain why different religions have different ways of describing God.

3 'It is easier to think of God as personal rather than impersonal.' Evaluate this statement.

Summary

You should now be able to explain and discuss different ideas about the divine that come from revelation and understand some of the qualities that are used to describe what God is like.

The value of revelation and enlightenment

As we have seen, all forms of **revelation** (special or general) and **enlightenment** have great value to believers. Revelation or enlightenment can:

- provide theists with arguments to support their belief in God
- help start a religion
- enable believers to have a relationship with the divine or to understand the truth about life (enlightenment)
- help people to know what they must do to live as God wishes.

Individual revelations can have a huge impact on those who receive them, often changing not only their religion but their entire way of life.

All of these factors apply to Sikhism. God's revelation to Guru Nanak persuaded him to give up his job, give his belongings to people living in poverty, and travel far and wide to preach the word of God. He started the Sikh religion and, through his teachings, laid the foundation for his followers to live an ethical life.

▲ *Meditating on the name of God can help a Sikh to reach union with God*

Revelation – reality or illusion?

Atheists would say that God does not exist, so all revelations are illusions. Some revelations may be difficult to prove, even to religious believers, because they are subjective, cannot be tested scientifically and can be interpreted in different ways.

To determine whether a revelation is real, religious people might consider whether the revelation:

- matches the real world, e.g. the claim that people can fly is less likely to be real than the claim that water in a place can cure people and it does
- supports the beliefs of a religion or contradicts them
- has an impact, e.g. changes an atheist or agnostic into a believer, or converts someone from one religion to another. If so, it may be genuine.

Different ideas about the divine arising from these experiences

Atheists argue that religions have conflicting revelations, which shows that they cannot be true. Most Buddhists do not believe in God, and within other faiths there are different understandings of God.

There are conflicting ideas between religions about how God wants people to live, for example drinking alcohol is forbidden in the Guru Granth Sahib, but the drinking of wine forms part of Jewish festivals and Christian worship.

Even within a religion, there may be different interpretations of the meaning of particular revelations. For example, religious teachers do not always agree on the interpretation of scriptures or how these should be applied to moral issues.

Alternative explanations for the experiences

Atheists put forward other explanations for these experiences. For example, a special revelation, such as a vision, could be brought about by alcohol or drugs, or the person could be so desperate to have a revelation that it is just wishful thinking. The person may be suffering from a physical illness or mental health problem that makes them hear voices or makes their mind play tricks on them. There is also the possibility that the people who claim to have revelations are lying in order to achieve fame or money, or they are merely mistaken.

Atheists would say that general revelations depend on a person's religious beliefs in the first place, so they cannot reveal anything about God, especially to an unbeliever. For example, when an atheist and a theist look at a beautiful landscape, one just sees nature and the other sees God's creation.

> **❝** Drinking it [wine], his intelligence departs, and madness enters his mind. He cannot distinguish between his own and others' – he is struck down by his Lord and Master. **❞**
>
> *Guru Granth Sahib 554*

Activities

1 Explain why revelation is important to the Sikh community.
2 Explain three reasons why atheists reject revelations.
3 'It is impossible to prove whether or not a revelation is true.' Evaluate this statement.

⭐ **Study tip**

In this theme you may also be asked about enlightenment. Sikhs meditate on the name of God, perform selfless actions and show compassion to become enlightened.

Summary

You should now be able to explain the value of revelation and enlightenment for religious believers, and discuss the difficulties in accepting the reality of some examples of revelation.

▲ *Heat on a road can look like water, which shows that the mind can play tricks*

Philosophical arguments for and against the existence of God – summary

You should now be able to:

✔ explain and evaluate the Design and First Cause arguments, including their strengths and weaknesses

✔ explain and evaluate the argument from miracles, including its strengths and weaknesses, and describe one example of a miracle

✔ explain and evaluate the arguments against the existence of God based on science and on the problem of suffering and evil.

The nature of the divine and revelation – summary

You should now be able to:

✔ explain what is meant by special revelation and enlightenment as sources of knowledge about the divine

✔ describe one example of a vision

✔ explain what is meant by general revelation, including nature and scripture as a way of understanding the divine

✔ explain the different ideas about the divine that come from revelation

✔ explain the meaning of qualities of God such as omnipotent, omniscient, benevolent, personal, impersonal, immanent and transcendent

✔ explain the value of revelation and enlightenment as sources of knowledge about the divine

✔ explain and evaluate the difficulties in accepting some examples of revelation, and be aware of alternative explanations for the experiences

✔ explain and evaluate the problem of different ideas about the divine arising from these experiences

✔ explain contrasting perspectives in contemporary British society about all the above issues

✔ explain contrasting beliefs in contemporary British society about the three issues of miracles, visions, and nature as a source of general revelation, with reference to the main religious tradition in Britain (Christianity) and non-religious beliefs such as atheism or humanism.

Sample student answer – the 4-mark question

1. Write an answer to the following practice question:

   Explain two different beliefs in contemporary British society about nature as a source of knowledge about the divine.
   In your answer you should refer to the main religious tradition of Great Britain and non-religious beliefs. **[4 marks]**

2. Read the following sample student answer:

   "Christians believe that God designed the world because nature is so complex and suited to its purposes that there must have been a divine being who created all that there is. When a Christian looks at a beautiful natural scene, he or she may feel the presence of God. The psalm says, 'The heavens declare the glory of God; the skies proclaim the work of his hands.' This shows that Christians believe God has revealed himself through nature.

   Atheists think the world started with a big bang and humans evolved. They do not see any need for a God to have done this, so they may be impressed by nature but they do not consider it as evidence for a divine being. Nature can be quite cruel. Bigger animals eat smaller ones, so atheists think that this shows there was no loving creator behind the natural world."

3. With a partner, discuss the sample answer. Is the focus of the answer correct? Is anything missing from the answer? How do you think it could be improved?

4. What mark (out of 4) would you give this answer? Look at the mark scheme in the Introduction (AO1). What are the reasons for the mark you have given?

5. Now swap your answer with your partner's and mark each other's responses. What mark (out of 4) would you give the response? Refer to the mark scheme and give reasons for the mark you award.

Sample student answer – the 6-mark question

1. Write an answer to the following practice question:

Explain two religious beliefs about what God is like.

Refer to sacred writings or another source of religious belief and teaching in your answer. **[6 marks]**

2. Read the following sample student answer:

"Sikhs believe in the oneness of God. This belief is shown in the Mool Mantra which they say every day. They think that God alone should be worshipped and it is only through God's will that suffering can be overcome.

Sikhs also believe that God is immanent. An immanent God is one who is involved in human life and in events on earth. Sikhs think that people can experience God by praying to God and meditating on God's holy name 'Waheguru'."

3. With a partner, discuss the sample answer. It fails to do something that is important. How do you think the answer could be improved?

4. What mark (out of 6) would you give this answer? Look at the mark scheme in the Introduction (AO1). What are the reasons for the mark you have given?

5. Now swap your answer with your partner's and mark each other's responses. What mark (out of 6) would you give the response? Refer to the mark scheme and give reasons for the mark you award.

Practice questions

1 Which **one** of the following best expresses the idea that the divine (God, gods or ultimate reality) is all-knowing?

A) Omnipotent   **B)** Omniscient   **C)** Transcendent   **D)** Immanent   **[1 mark]**

2 Give a definition of 'special revelation'. **[1 mark]**

3 Explain **two** different beliefs in contemporary British society about the Design argument for God's existence.

In your answer you must refer to one or more religious traditions. You may refer to a non-religious belief. **[4 marks]**

4 Explain **two** religious beliefs about visions. Refer to sacred writings or another source of religious belief and teaching in your answer. **[6 marks]**

5 'The First Cause argument proves that God exists.'

Evaluate this statement. In your answer you:

- should give reasoned arguments to support this statement
- should give reasoned arguments to support a different point of view
- should refer to religious arguments
- may refer to non-religious arguments
- should reach a justified conclusion. **[12 marks]**
[+ 3 SPaG marks]

> **Study tip**
>
> You should aim to develop two different points of view. Different viewpoints can show differences between those who believe that God is the First Cause of the universe and those who think that the First Cause argument does not prove that God exists.

6 Religion, peace and conflict

6.1 Introduction to religion, peace and conflict

Right from the beginnings of human life, people have attempted to gain territory or settle disputes through fighting. Even today, somewhere in the world, it is likely that people will be injured, killed or displaced as a result of **war**. While all countries have laws against murder, the rules of war are different – in war, killing is considered to be acceptable.

Religions usually speak out against killing in most circumstances and their teachings do not support most wars. However, many religious people, including Sikhs, have been prepared to fight for their country or their faith. Many Sikhs fought alongside Allied troops in both world wars, during which it is estimated that over 80,000 Sikhs were killed. Sikh involvement in both world wars was acknowledged in Parliament by the politician Winston Churchill (grandson of Prime Minister Sir Winston Churchill):

> **"** British people are highly indebted and obliged to Sikhs for a long time. I know that within this century we needed their help twice and they did help us very well. As a result of their timely help, we are today able to live with honour, dignity, and independence. In the war, they fought and died for us. **"**
>
> *Winston Churchill*

In February 2015, a British Member of Parliament suggested in the House of Commons that a Sikh regiment within the British army should be formed.

There are four key concepts that you need to know to understand about attitudes towards war.

■ Peace

One definition of **peace** is the absence of war. The intention of those fighting in a war is to create peace once the war is over. But this is often difficult to achieve, because the instability and resentment left after a war often leads to fighting breaking out again.

Peace can also be thought of as a feeling of happiness, wellbeing and tranquility. This may come through religious faith, especially in prayer and meditation. Such peace brings a calmness that helps to avoid quarrels and disputes with other people. Sikhs believe that genuine peace is not possible when there is an absence of absolute forgiveness. This means that for Sikhs, peace is not necessarily just the absence of war but is also a state in which there is harmony as a result of genuine respect because of forgiveness for each other.

Objectives

- Understand war as a way of resolving differences.
- Explain the concepts of peace, justice, forgiveness and reconciliation.

Key terms

- **war:** fighting between nations to resolve issues between them
- **peace:** an absence of conflict, which leads to happiness and harmony
- **justice:** bringing about what is right and fair, according to the law, or making up for a wrong that has been committed
- **forgiveness:** showing grace and mercy and pardoning someone for what they have done wrong
- **reconciliation:** the restoring of harmony after relationships have broken down; a sacrament in the Catholic Church

▲ *This memorial near Brighton remembers Hindu and Sikh soldiers who were cremated here during the First World War*

■ Justice

Many wars are fought to achieve **justice**. Justice is often linked with equality. If different groups of people are not given the same opportunities, this may be seen as unfair (or unjust) and lead to resentment. This could lead to conflict, especially if more privileged parts of the world are seen to be the cause of the inequality. Sikhs believe in the equality of humanity and work hard to address injustice. They believe that in order to achieve true peace, justice should never be undertaken out of revenge, and should instead be built on a foundation of forgiveness.

■ Forgiveness

Forgiveness is important if people are to live peacefully. It does not necessarily mean that no action should be taken to right a wrong. But once the wrong is righted, possibly through conflict, forgiveness should follow. Action to establish peace and justice should come after the act of forgiveness, otherwise it is likely that problems will reoccur. The following quotes from the Guru Granth Sahib stress the importance of forgiveness for Sikhs:

> ❝ Where there is forgiveness, there is God Himself. ❞
> *Guru Granth Sahib 1372*

> ❝ Those who have truth as their fast, contentment as their sacred shrine of pilgrimage, spiritual wisdom and meditation as their cleansing bath, kindness as their deity, and forgiveness as their chanting beads – they are the most excellent people. ❞
> *Guru Granth Sahib 1245*

■ Reconciliation

Reconciliation follows conflict. It is more than just apologising: it involves a conscious effort to rebuild a relationship, and sometimes much work is needed to ensure there is no more conflict. If reconciliation is genuinely achieved, it makes war and conflict less likely.

▲ *Sikhs believe that getting involved in community life is important for creating a peaceful and just society*

Research activity

Read the poem *Dulce et Decorum Est*, written by Wilfred Owen towards the end of the First World War. Owen died on 4 November 1918 in northern France, a week before the end of the war. Write down your thoughts about what you have read in the poem. Find out what the final two lines mean in English.

Discussion activity

With a partner, discuss whether it is right for any person to fight. Are there any alternatives?

Activities

1 Explain the meaning of the concepts of peace, justice, forgiveness and reconciliation.

2 Can you think of any occasions when war and conflict are more important than peace and justice?

3 Should nations that are in conflict with one another work towards forgiveness and reconciliation? Explain your answer.

⭐ **Study tip**

Try to remember how peace, justice, forgiveness and reconciliation are linked to war.

Summary

You should now be aware that war is one way of resolving differences, and that the concepts of peace, justice, forgiveness and reconciliation are important after a war ends.

6.2 Violent protest

■ Protest in the UK

The right to **protest** is considered to be a fundamental democratic freedom. The law in the UK allows individuals and groups to protest in public to demonstrate their point of view. If the protest involves a procession or a march, the police must be told at least six days before it takes place. The police can request alterations to the route or even apply to a court for an order to ban the march. They may do this if they feel that the march might intimidate other people or if they predict that **violence** will be involved.

▲ *Sikh protesters carrying out a peaceful protest in London in April 2013*

Objectives

- Understand UK law regarding protest.
- Understand Sikh beliefs about protest.

Key terms

- **protest:** an expression of disapproval, often in a public group
- **violence:** using actions that threaten or harm others

Activities

1 Explain the law relating to protest in Britain.

2 Do you agree that people or groups should have the right to protest in public? Explain your reasons.

3 How important is it that police officers should always show respect towards protesters? Give reasons for your answer.

A Sikh protest in London

While the right to protest peacefully is protected in the UK, there is no right to protest violently. In October 2015, a Sikh group called Sikh Lives Matter organised a demonstration outside the Indian High Commission in London. They were protesting about the actions of Indian authorities, including the killing of two Sikhs by police in the Punjab region of India during a protest about the deliberate damaging of the Guru Granth Sahib.

Although the intention of the London protest was that it should be peaceful, some protesters caused disruption by blocking a busy road. As the police attempted to persuade protesters to clear the road, some of them turned violent. One police officer received a head injury and was sent to hospital. Twenty of the protesters were arrested. A few days after the protest, a spokesperson for the police in London apologised for the disrespectful behaviour of one police officer which contributed to the protest turning violent.

A number of the protesters were disappointed that the protest had turned violent; one of them said, 'It's not right to disturb people who are trying to go about their daily lives. We wanted to come here today and protest peacefully to raise awareness about what is happening to the Sikh community back home in India.'

■ Sikh protest against motor bike helmets

In the UK, most Sikhs are prepared to challenge what they perceive to be religious offences or an attack on religious freedom. They do not encourage a violent response but will put their point of view across forcefully if necessary. In 1972, the Road Traffic Act made it compulsory for all riders of motor bikes to wear a crash helmet. This was a problem for turban-wearing Sikhs who were faced with having to either break UK law or their religious requirements as members of the Khalsa. As their religious requirements were not likely to change, they protested against the decision of the government and in 1976, the Motor-Cycle Crash Helmets (Religious Exemption) Act was passed as an amendment to the 1972 Act. This made turban-wearing Sikhs exempt from wearing helmets although in practice, possibly for reasons of safety, not many Sikhs in Britain choose to ride motor bikes.

▲ *Turban-wearing Sikhs are exempt from wearing motor bike helmets in the UK*

Although the 1972 Road Traffic Act was not designed to be a threat to the Sikh religion, Sikhs felt they were justified in protesting. In fact, it was because they wished to obey UK law that they wanted to see a change to enable them to keep within the law while still practising their faith. There were few instances of violence in their protest but they were prepared to protest until the law was changed. Although Sikhs are required to defend threats to their faith, there are few threats to their faith in the UK, so they are able to live peacefully with people of other faiths and people of no faith.

Activities

1   Explain how most Sikhs respond to hostility towards themselves or their community.
2   Explain why Sikhs are not required to wear a helmet when riding a motor bike in the UK.

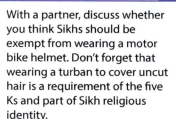

Discussion activity

With a partner, discuss whether you think Sikhs should be exempt from wearing a motor bike helmet. Don't forget that wearing a turban to cover uncut hair is a requirement of the five Ks and part of Sikh religious identity.

Contrasting beliefs

Find out what Christians believe about violence, and whether Christian attitudes to violence are similar to or different from those of Sikhs.

★ Study tip

When thinking about Sikh responses to issues that challenge them in modern life, remember that your knowledge about Sikh beliefs and practices will help you.

Summary

You should now understand UK law regarding protest. You should also understand why Sikhs may take part in peaceful protest and why most Sikhs do not support violent protest.

6.3　Reasons for war

Some people find it very difficult to understand why anyone is prepared to fight in a war or why their country wants to go to war. However, it is a fact that people are willing to fight in wars in great numbers. Whenever the UK is involved in war, both full-time and volunteer personnel are called on to fight. During the First and Second World Wars, the need for fighters was so great and casualties were so high that people in the UK were ordered to fight for their country.

■ Greed as a reason for war

Throughout history, war has been used as a way to gain more land or territory, or even to regain land lost in a previous war. **Greed** can also lead countries to invade others in order to control important resources, such as oil. In this way, rich and powerful countries can get richer and more powerful, potentially causing poverty in the defeated country when their main source of income is taken away.

In Sikhism there are considered to be five moral evils, two of which are connected to greed:

- Lobh, which means greed, is seen as a strong desire to have more than one needs or deserves. This can breed selfishness and self-centredness in a person, and take them away from their religious and moral duties.
- Moh refers to the attachment that an individual has to worldly possessions and relationships. As with lobh, it can cause a person to become self-centered and greedy, leading them away from their religious and moral duties and distracting them from focusing on God.

Using greed as a reason for war would be promoting these moral evils and cannot be supported by Sikhs. For this reason, Sikhs are forbidden to fight for anything other than religious or social equality.

■ Self-defence as a reason for war

Whenever one country attacks another, it expects to meet some resistance from the invaded country. Most people consider fighting in **self-defence** to be morally acceptable, and believe they have a right to defend the values, beliefs and ways of life that their country promotes. When considering self-defence as a valid reason for going to war, some people ask themselves what Britain would be like today had it not defended itself against the Nazi invasion during the Second World War. In their thinking, not only was it acceptable to defend the UK against invasion, but it was right to fight against the Nazi advance in mainland Europe to defeat what they saw as an evil threat to the whole of Europe.

Objectives

- Understand why wars are fought.
- Understand Sikh attitudes to reasons for war.

Key terms

- **greed:** selfish desire for something, such as wealth, goods or items of value which are not needed
- **self-defence:** acting to prevent harm to yourself or others
- **retaliation:** deliberately harming someone as a response to them harming you

Links

To read more about the five evils look back to page 17.

▲ *This First World War Sikh memorial was unveiled at the National Memorial Arboretum in Staffordshire on 1 November 2015*

In addition to defending their own country, many people believe it is acceptable to fight to defend other nations under threat. Indian Sikhs travelled thousands of miles to support those fighting to defend Europe in the Second World War, many giving their lives in the process. Sikhs believe that defending themselves and others from oppression and persecution is a religious duty, including using force if required. This duty was strengthened by the tenth Guru, Guru Gobind Singh, when he set up the Khalsa. He made the carrying of a kirpan compulsory for Sikhs as a symbol of their faith and responsibility to stand up against injustice, but not as a weapon.

■ Retaliation as a reason for war

Wars are sometimes fought in **retaliation** against a country that is seen to have done something very wrong. Retaliation means to take revenge by deliberately harming somebody who has wronged you. However, most Sikhs believe that retaliation is wrong.

Links

For more information about situations when war may be justified, see pages 126–127.

⭐ **Study tip**

Greed, self-defence and retaliation are just three causes of war. When writing about the causes of war you can also use any other causes that you can think of.

Oak Creek shooting

In August 2012, six Sikhs were shot dead by a lone shooter while they worshipped in their gurdwara in the town of Oak Creek in Wisconsin, USA. This was not a specific act of warfare. However, the shooter held strong political beliefs. He thought only white people had a right to live and practise their faith in the USA. He thought he was 'doing his bit' by fighting a personal war against the Sikhs. A few days after the tragedy, residents of Oak Creek, most of whom are not Sikhs, gathered together for a candlelit vigil in memory of those who died. Many were amazed at the Sikh community's willingness to forgive the killer, who himself was shot dead by police responding to the massacre. They appeared to have no desire to take revenge. The town's police chief, John Edwards, was quoted as saying:

'In 28 years of law enforcement, I have seen a lot of hate. I have seen a lot of revenge. I've seen a lot of anger. What I saw, particularly from the Sikh community this week, was compassion, concern, support. What I didn't see was hate. I did not see revenge. I didn't see any of that. And in law enforcement that's unusual to not see that reaction to something like this. I want you all to understand how unique that is.'

▲ *A candlelit vigil was held in Oak Creek to remember the victims of the shooting*

Activities

1 Explain how greed, self-defence and retaliation can cause war.

2 Explain which (if any) of these reasons you think is justifiable.

3 Which of these reasons (if any) do you think Sikhs would agree with? Explain why.

4 'Travelling from India to Europe to fight in a war was a great act of bravery.' Do you agree with this statement? Give reasons for your answer.

Summary

You should now understand three different causes of war and Sikh attitudes towards them.

Nuclear war and weapons of mass destruction

■ The use of nuclear weapons

▲ The Japanese city of Hiroshima shortly after an atom bomb was dropped on it on 6 August 1945

This picture was taken just after around 80,000 people in the Japanese city of Hiroshima died as a result of an atom bomb (an early form of **nuclear weapon**) being dropped on it by US forces fighting in the Second World War. The death toll rose to around 140,000 in the months that followed as many more died as a result of radiation. Three days later, a second Japanese city, Nagasaki, was also destroyed by an atom bomb. Six days after that, Japan surrendered and ceased fighting against the allied forces. This effectively marked the end of the Second World War, which for some people justified the use of these weapons.

Since the end of the Second World War, many of the wealthier countries in the world, including the UK, have researched and developed considerably more powerful nuclear weapons. Despite some countries agreeing to reduce the number of nuclear weapons they possess, there are now enough to completely destroy the world we live in several times over. Some believe that the existence of such weapons has prevented wars, arguing that nuclear weapons deter potential enemies from attacking, just in case nuclear weapons are used in retaliation against them.

There is growing concern among Sikhs and others living in India and Pakistan that as both countries possess nuclear weapons, they may use them against each other. The Punjab, a region where the majority of Sikhs live, has a border with Pakistan and so could become a target, particularly of short-range weapons. Relations between India and Pakistan are often difficult, although it is unlikely that either country would start a nuclear war. However, while each country possesses the capability to do so, there is understandable worry.

Objectives

- Understand the possible implications of using nuclear or other weapons of mass destruction.
- Consider whether the use of such weapons is justified.

Key terms

- **nuclear weapons:** weapons that work by a nuclear reaction; they devastate huge areas and kill large numbers of people
- **weapons of mass destruction:** weapons that can kill large numbers of people and/or cause great damage
- **chemical weapons:** weapons that use chemicals to harm humans and destroy the natural environment
- **biological weapons:** weapons that use living organisms to cause disease or death

Discussion activity

Do you think that dropping atom bombs on two Japanese cities, which effectively caused the Second World War to end, was justifiable?

Contrasting beliefs

Find out more about what Christians believe about weapons of mass destruction, and whether any Christian views differ from Sikh beliefs.

A number of Sikhs have tried to raise awareness of this situation and have campaigned for nuclear disarmament. The organisation United Sikhs, for example, raised its concerns at a United Nations conference in 2009. They asked governments and organisations around the world to help calm tensions between India and Pakistan, and work towards a world free of nuclear weapons.

■ Weapons of mass destruction

In addition to nuclear weapons, there are other **weapons of mass destruction** in existence.

A **chemical weapon** is a weapon containing lethal chemicals that, when released, cause numerous deaths. In 1993, the Chemical Weapons Convention (CWC) made the production, stockpiling and use of these chemicals illegal worldwide. However, since then they are believed to have been used in countries such as Iraq and Syria. **Biological weapons** introduce harmful bacteria and viruses into the atmosphere. When they enter the food chain or water supplies, they cause illness and death on a massive scale. As with chemical weapons, they are illegal but there are instances of their use and many countries still possess them.

Along with nuclear weapons, chemical and biological weapons have the capacity to kill large numbers of people including civilians. Sikhs believe that everybody has an equal right to life so using such weapons is completely unacceptable. Guru Arjan said:

> ❝ No one is my enemy, and no one is a stranger. I get along with everyone. ❞
>
> *Guru Granth Sahib 1299*

The potential use of all weapons of mass destruction is wrong to Sikhs. They cause civilian suffering on a wide scale and they damage the world that God created for humanity. This is similar to Christian belief. Speaking on behalf of four UK Christian churches, policy adviser Steve Hucklesby said:

> ❝ Faith groups in the UK are united in their conviction that any use of nuclear weapons would violate the sanctity of life and the principle of dignity core to our faith traditions. To address the security challenges that we face today, we must build relationships based on mutual cooperation rather than the threat of mutual destruction. ❞

Some Christians believe that possession of weapons of mass destruction is important because it acts as a deterrent and stops other countries from using either nuclear or conventional weapons. There are many Sikhs in the UK who share this belief; the 2016 British Sikh Report, for example, found that 57 per cent of Sikh men and 36 per cent of Sikh women want the UK to keep nuclear weapons as a deterrent.

▲ *The Punjab shares a border with Pakistan; some Sikhs worry that the region could suffer hugely if India and Pakistan targeted each other with nuclear weapons*

Activities

1. Explain the difference between nuclear weapons, chemical weapons and biological weapons.

2. Do you think it is ever right to use these weapons? Give your reasons.

3. Explain why Sikhs disagree with the use of these weapons.

Discussion activity

With a partner, discuss whether weapons of mass destruction can deter others from using weapons of war.

⭐ Study tip

Most religious people agree that it is wrong to use weapons of mass destruction. If you are looking for an alternative opinion, consider the argument about their use as a deterrent.

Summary

You should now be able to describe the effects of nuclear weapons and other weapons of mass destruction, and understand what Sikhs believe about their use.

■ The just war theory

The **just war theory** was developed by religious thinkers such as Augustine and Thomas Aquinas. It seeks to lay out the conditions under which fighting a war is justifiable, and also provides rules on how the war must be fought to ensure it is ethical. Sikhs have developed their own just war theory called **dharam yudh** ('war in defence of righteousness'). The first part of this theory is concerned with the reasons why a war is fought. Although Sikhs try to avoid fighting wars, they believe that there are sometimes circumstances that make fighting the right thing to do. However, declaring war must be a last resort, and all peaceful methods of solving the dispute must have been tried and failed. Only then can war be declared.

Dharam yudh teaches that:

- Wars must be fought for the right reason – they must be morally justifiable.
- The motive should be that the person must have their mind totally focused on what they believe God wants them to do.
- There must be no thought of personal reward such as gaining land, wealth or power, because such thoughts are motivated by greed.
- Reasons for fighting must be selfless. For example, fighting can take place to defend those unable to defend themselves, to overthrow unjust rulers, or to protect people from persecution.
- Only those who are selflessly committed to the fighting are allowed to take part. Mercenaries (people who fight for money, not a cause) must not be part of the fighting.

Objectives

- Understand the Sikh just war theory (dharam yudh).
- Apply the just war theory to a specific war.

Key term

- **just war theory:** a set of criteria that a war needs to meet before it can be justified
- **dharam yudh:** 'war in defence of righteousness'; the Sikh just war theory

Discussion activity

Without looking at the information on this page, with a partner draw up a list of conditions that you think makes fighting a war the right thing to do.

> ❝ When matters pass all other means, it is allowed to take up arms. ❞
>
> *Guru Gobind Singh*

The Sikh just war theory also sets out the rules that dictate how a war should be fought. These include the following conditions:

1. Those who are attacked must be carrying weapons and must be a threat to life.
2. Before an attack is made, enemy fighters should be challenged to see what kind of threat they pose, and to give them the chance to lay down their weapons.

▲ *Is it possible to fight a war today without harming civilians or destroying any private property?*

Fighting in the Punjab

In 1799 Ranjit Singh, a Sikh warrior, captured the city of Lahore, the capital city of the Punjab. Two years later, he declared the Punjab an independent state, with himself as the leader. He was considered to be a great leader by those living in the Punjab, even though Sikhs were in the minority. His success was partly due to the fact that he considered all his subjects to be equal, regardless of their religion. He took part in Muslim and Hindu religious celebrations, despite being a Sikh.

At that time, Britain ruled much of India but not the Punjab. In 1845, six years after the death of Ranjit Singh, Sikhs expected the British to attack, so armies from the Punjab crossed into British India. They were defeated in four battles and the British took over part of the Punjab as a result. In 1848, the Sikh army joined with rebels from Multan to fight the British. In February 1849, they were defeated and the British took control of the whole of the Punjab.

3   No private property, nor anything belonging to peaceful civilians, should be stolen or destroyed.

4   No women should be abused or raped.

5   Attempts must be made to help enemy fighters if they do not pose a threat.

6   Any treaties or agreements made between the two nations or groups who are at war must be respected.

7   If a ceasefire is declared and agreed between both sides, this must not be broken.

8   Killing that is not necessary to winning the war, such as massacres of enemy fighters or innocent civilians, must not happen.

▲ *Sikhs believe that only those who are selflessly committed to the fighting should be allowed to take part in a war*

9   Places of worship should not be damaged, regardless of what faith they belong to.

10   Those who have surrendered must not be harmed.

11   Although different strategies may be used during the fighting, these should not include lying to the enemy.

Some of these criteria were reflected in the actions of Bhai Ghanaiya, who was one of Guru Gobind Singh's followers. During a battle against the army of the Mughal emperor, Bhai Ghanaiya was seen to be tending injuries and giving water to wounded enemy soldiers, as well as to those from his own side. When questioned about this, Bhai responded that he could not distinguish between which side the injured were fighting on, because he saw the Guru's face in everyone.

Discussion activity 🗩

With a partner, discuss whether you think the Sikh wars of 1845 and 1848–9 obeyed the five Dharam yudh teachings listed on page 126. Give reasons for your decision about each of the circumstances.

⭐ Study tip

You do not need to remember all of the criteria that make a war just for Sikhs, but it would be useful to remember a few of them to use as examples.

Activities

1   Note down the five circumstances that might justify war and the eleven criteria of the just war.

2   'Any war and way of fighting should be acceptable if it leads to a better outcome.' Do you agree with this statement? Give reasons for your opinion.

Summary

You should now know the Sikh criteria for a just war, and have used the criteria to judge whether a specific war was just.

6.6 Holy war and terrorism

What is a holy war?

To many people the concept of a **holy war** seems to be a contradiction. They think that no activity that involves killing people in large numbers can possibly have any religious inspiration and justification. However, there have been a number of holy wars throughout history, such as the Crusades fought between Christians and Muslims in the eleventh to fourteenth centuries. A holy war has to be authorised by a religious leader, and the purpose of it should be to defend the faith from attack. Those who take part believe they will gain spiritual rewards.

Sikh attitudes to holy war

Sikhism was founded by Guru Nanak to be a religion of peace. However, to uphold peace in times of violent aggression, some form of defence is sometimes needed. In the history of the Sikh Gurus, there are examples of extraordinarily courageous non-violent resistance, and well as defensive military action. The term 'holy war' is not used by Sikhs. Rather, the battle to uphold what is good and right, based on values of compassion, care and responsibility, is known as 'dharam yudh'.

The fifth Guru, Guru Arjan Dev, was cruelly tortured by the Mughal authorities, leading to his martyrdom. This was after he had compiled a sacred scripture (the Guru Granth Sahib) and completed the construction of a sacred place of worship (the Harimandir Sahib in Amritsar), both of which emphasised human unity. While being made to sit on a hot plate, he is remembered for his verse about the sweet acceptance of God's will. He left instructions for the next Guru to lead with courage and resilience against tyranny.

Stressing that worldly leadership should be led by spiritual wisdom, the sixth Guru, Guru Har Gobind, built a defensive army for peace, strength and security during hostile times. He led five defensive battles, ensuring all fighting was directly against the Mughal authorities to avoid civilian bloodshed.

The ninth Guru, Guru Tegh Bahadur, was a renowned peace-builder in India, so much so that a delegation of Hindus sought his support when they suffered increasing religious persecution. Guru Tegh Bahadur made a peaceful stand, asking the Mughal emperor to protect the religious freedoms of everyone in the Mughal empire. He was publicly executed. This principle of defending the religious freedom of others means that the Sikh faith rejects the idea that violence can be used to spread a particular religion. Also, with the Sikh faith's emphasis on respecting people's faith identities, it does not have a mission to convert others.

▲ Guru Gobind Singh blessed the Sikh disciple, Bhai Kanhaiya, who gave water and aid to the wounded on both sides after a battle. His actions reflect humanitarian values in war and the Sikh teaching that, ultimately 'none is a stranger, nor an enemy'.

The tenth Guru, Guru Gobind Singh, formed the Khalsa order of committed Sikhs who lived their lives as 'saint-soldiers', combining the loving wisdom of a saint (so their primary battle is in the mind) with the courage of a solider (to protect the mistreated and downtrodden). Since the Khalsa order was established in 1699, Sikhs have actively volunteered to fight against tyranny. For example, they fought with allied forces during the First and Second World Wars.

Sikhs are keenly aware of Guru Gobind Singh's teaching that any use of the sword must be a last resort only, when all peaceful means have failed and it is necessary to protect people from injustice or harm. In one of his hymns, Guru Gobind Singh wrote:

> ❝ Cruelty, material attachment, greed and anger are the four rivers of fire. Falling into them, one is burned, O Nanak! One is saved only by holding tight to good deeds. ❞
>
> *Guru Granth Sahib 147*

> ❝ Blessed is the one who, in his mind and speech, remains ever conscious of dharam-yudh, the fight to uphold righteousness, where noble virtues conquer the ego's vices in the battlefield of the mind.
>
> Fully conscious of his mortality, he contemplates on Divine praise, to ascend the Guru's boat to safely navigate life's perilous ocean.
>
> Forging deep patience, he makes his body the abode of forbearance. He illuminates his mind with the lamp of Divine wisdom. Sweeping up ignorance, he brushes away the dross and dregs of cowardice. ❞
>
> *Dasam Granth Sahib 551*

■ Terrorism

Terrorism is one way that religion and belief may be seen to be a cause of war and violence in the contemporary world. This is where an individual, or a group who share certain beliefs, use terror as part of their campaign to further their cause. Their violence is often committed against innocent civilians and takes place in public. Suicide bombers, car bombs, and gunmen shooting into crowds of people are all tactics of terrorism. Terrorists believe that by killing people in this way, the rest of society will become more aware of their cause, will be scared of them and will force the authorities into giving way to their demands.

Most Sikhs consider acts of violence (including terrorism) to be wrong, especially as the victims are usually innocent people going about their daily business. Sikhs believe in the equality and freedom of all human beings, and pray for the whole of humanity each day. Their view is that all people should be able to live in peace and harmony and be tolerant of the beliefs of others.

⭐ Study tip

Using an example is helpful to provide evidence to support a point you are making.

Summary

You should now know the features of a holy war. You should have considered whether religion is a cause of war and violence and understand Sikh attitudes to terrorism, war and the use of violence.

Activities

1. Explain what Sikhs believe about using violence to defend their faith.
2. How far do you think Sikhs should go to defend their faith?
3. Do you believe that violence should ever be used to defeat terrorism? Explain your reasons.

6.7 Pacifism and peacemaking

■ What is pacifism?

A pacifist is a person who, religious or not, believes that war and violence can rarely or never be justified, and that conflicts should be settled in a peaceful way. Few Sikhs are pacifists because they believe that war and conflict is justified in defence of their faith, or if fighting to combat oppression or a lack of human rights. Sikhs aim to build harmony between faiths and nations, but most would accept war as a means of achieving this as a last resort.

▲ *Sikhs in the British Indian army*

Sikhism requires each Sikh to become a saint-soldier (Sant Siphahi): someone who prays and works for peace like a saint, but has the courage and ability to fight for justice and peace if all other means fail, like a soldier. The concepts of Miri and Piri are linked to the concept of saint-soldiers because Miri symbolises the need to defend the faith and Piri is a reminder of spiritual authority. Sikhs need to balance the development of their physical skills with the promotion of spiritual growth.

Guru Nanak stressed the importance of working to transform people who were harming others, and preached that all are equal regardless of their faith. He was keen to emphasise that this applied to Hindus and Muslims who were opposed to the new faith of Sikhism.

When trying to bring reconciliation to warring groups, Guru Nanak tried to identify the root causes of the conflict, and show a better, more harmonious way of life that accepted and respected differences between people. However, he realised that this was not an easy task, and that it would take great courage to make genuine peace on earth a reality. He suggested that those who follow the Sikh religion of peace and love should be prepared to make great sacrifices.

Objectives

- Consider **pacifism** as an alternative to conflict.
- Understand why only some Sikhs are pacifists.
- Understand the work of **peacemakers**.

Key terms

- **pacifism:** the belief of people who refuse to take part in war and any other form of violence
- **peacemaker:** a person who works to establish peace in the world or in a certain part of it

Links

To learn more about when Sikhs may fight, read about the just war theory on pages 126–127.

Contrasting beliefs

Find out more about what Christians believe about pacifism, and whether any Christian views differ from Sikh beliefs.

Today Sikhs continue to strongly believe that it is best to work at preventing war from becoming a possibility. They believe, as Guru Nanak did, that promoting justice and human rights is an important part of this. If people are not denied basic freedoms and rights, they are less likely to engage in conflict. Peace is not just an absence of war; it is a sense of wellbeing and security that comes through religious faith, supported by prayer and meditation. Being at peace with oneself helps people to avoid conflict with others.

Religions for Peace

Religions for Peace is a worldwide organisation with thriving groups in Britain. Members come from across all faiths, including Sikhism, to promote peaceful alternatives to war. They claim to be the largest international coalition of representatives from the world's great religions dedicated to promoting peace.

Their mission statement includes the following paragraph:

'Founded in 1970, Religions for Peace enables [religious] communities to unleash their enormous potential for common action. Some of Religions for Peace's recent successes include building a new climate of reconciliation in Iraq; mediating dialogue among warring factions in Sierra Leone; [and] organizing an international network of religious women's organisations.'

In February 2016, they issued a call for young people to be involved in peace activities as part of the European Interfaith Youth Network (EIYN).

■ A different Christian view about pacifism

Although many Christians agree with fighting war, especially if it follows the Christian just war theory – which provides criteria that make fighting an acceptable thing to do – there are some who completely disagree with war under any circumstances. The Religious Society of Friends (Quakers) is a group within Christianity for whom total pacifism is important. They disagree with any war for any reason, although if efforts to prevent war fail, and war happens, they will work to help the victims of the fighting, and try to find a peaceful solution.

Many Christian pacifists take their inspiration from the teaching of Jesus:

> 66 'Blessed are the peacemakers for they shall be called sons of God.' 99
>
> *Matthew 5:9 [NIV]*

Activities

1 Explain why few Sikhs are pacifists.
2 'Pacifists believe that peace and justice should be brought about through non-violent means.' Explain how you think this could be achieved.

Discussion activity

'Sikhs believe that the best way to establish peace is to promote justice and human rights for all.' With a partner, discuss whether you agree with this statement and give reasons for your opinions.

Research activity

Find out more about the European Interfaith Youth Network (EIYN) and the work that it does.

⭐ **Study tip**

When discussing an alternative Christian view to Sikh beliefs about pacifism, you could use the example of the Quakers, supported by the quote from the Gospel of Matthew.

Summary

You should now be able to explain the idea of pacifism. You should understand why few Sikhs are pacifists but many wish to be peacemakers. You should have also considered a different belief on pacifism from Christianity.

Religious responses to victims of war

■ Providing help to victims of war

Casualties are an unavoidable part of war. In addition to the harm that is caused to those directly involved in the fighting, harm is also caused to their families and friends. For example, if the main wage earner dies in a war, their family may struggle financially without them. If a place of work is destroyed in a war, nobody can earn a wage there. If crops are destroyed or water supplies polluted, starvation could follow for those who live in the surrounding area.

Objectives

- Understand what can be done to help victims of war.
- Understand the work of a present-day Sikh organisation that helps victims of war.

▲ In 2014, Khalsa Aid set up a bakery to provide fresh bread to Syrian refugees

In the UK this is not such a problem because if a member of the military is killed or injured, financial systems are in place to look after those left behind. Injured military personnel receive free health care with some specialised care being provided by charities such as Help for Heroes. However, injury or death still have devastating effects on friends and families and can cause long-term emotional wounds.

There are many organisations that offer help and care for victims of war, wherever they live and whichever side of the war they or their family member was fighting for. They believe that the life and welfare of human beings is all that matters.

■ Khalsa Aid

Khalsa Aid is a British Sikh charity that helps those in need throughout the world, including in war zones. It was founded on the Sikh principles of selfless service and universal love, inspired by the teaching of Guru Gobind Singh.

Khalsa Aid provides a range of help that is necessary in war zones, including assisting refugees made homeless by the fighting, for example:

Research activity

Find out more about how Sikh organisations and individuals help refugees that have had to flee their homes because of war.

❝ Someone is Hindu and someone a Muslim, then someone is Shia, and someone a Sunni, but all the human beings, as a species, are recognised as one and the same. ❞

Guru Gobind Singh

- In 2011, Khalsa Aid delivered 25,000 litres of drinking water to the Choucha Refugee camp in Libya, and pledged to provide more until a water filtration system had been installed at the camp to make the water safe to drink.

- In 2014, Khalsa Aid set up a bakery in Iraq, 10 kilometres from the Syrian border. They paid for the machinery that was needed and employed four members of staff, three of whom were from a refugee camp. The cost of the machines and a commitment to provide fresh bread for 16,000 people every day for at least six months was around £40,000, which came from charitable donations.

▲ In 2015, Khalsa Aid worked with Mona Relief to provide basic food supplies for victims of the Yemen civil war

- In 2015, Khalsa Aid partnered with Mona Relief to provide over 250,000 meals to citizens of Yemen who had fled from their homes because of civil war. Khalsa Aid provided food parcels consisting of 25kg of wheat, 5kg of rice, 5kg of sugar and 2 litres of cooking oil per family.

- In 2016, Khalsa Aid assisted many people who became refugees as a result of the invasion of part of their countries by ISIS. They delivered supplies to over 150 refugee families in Iraq, and to Syrians who had fled to Lebanon to protect themselves from violence and oppression.

A Sikh response to terrorist attacks in Paris

On 13 November 2015, a minority group of Muslims with extreme views launched deadly attacks at several locations in Paris, killing around 130 people. The city was in a state of panic because nobody knew when or where the next attack would be. Rohan Singh Kalsi, a Sikh from Coventry, used the website Twitter to let people know, 'Anybody who's stranded in Paris and needs shelter and somewhere safe, any Sikh Gurdwara (temple) will be happy to accommodate'.

His tweet was retweeted over 13,000 times and received 10,000 'likes' on Twitter. One person referred to him as 'a bright light on a very very dark night' to which he responded, 'I am no bright light … Sikhs are here to serve humanity at all times.' He followed this by saying, 'Just to be clear though, this isn't about me … I was just doing what our beautiful Gurus taught us to do, be good people, help humanity and treat everybody with love and respect. I'm glad I was able to show the beauty of Sikhism to everyone and just hope my tweet helped some people in Paris last night.'

Rohan's response was typical of the reaction of Sikhs to violence, and their desire to offer help to victims or those who are under serious threat. This is the message Guru Nanak emphasised when founding the Sikh faith.

Activities

1 Explain in detail how war can have a negative effect on people.

2 Write a paragraph to show how Khalsa Aid helps victims of war. Try to find more recent examples of their work with victims of war.

3 'Refugees should be helped before help is given to those who fight.' Write down your thoughts about this quote and give your reasons for your opinion.

4 Explain how Rohan Singh Khalsi demonstrated the teaching of his faith.

⭐ Study tip

Case studies are useful because they provide real-life evidence of how people respond to issues.

Summary

You should now know about and understand the support that Sikhs give to victims of war, including the work of Khalsa Aid.

Religion, violence, terrorism and war – summary

You should now be able to:

✔ explain beliefs and teachings about the meaning and significance of peace, justice, forgiveness and reconciliation

✔ explain beliefs and teachings about violence, including violent protest

✔ explain beliefs and teachings about holy war and terrorism

✔ explain beliefs and teachings about reasons for war, including greed, self-defence and retaliation

✔ explain beliefs and teachings about the just war theory, including the criteria for a just war

✔ explain beliefs and teachings about pacifism.

Religion and belief in twenty-first century conflict – summary

You should now be able to:

✔ explain attitudes to the use of nuclear weapons and weapons of mass destruction, including Sikh beliefs

✔ consider religion and belief as a cause of war and violence in the contemporary world

✔ explain beliefs and teachings about pacifism and peacemaking

✔ explain Sikh responses to victims of war

✔ explain contemporary British attitudes (both religious and non-religious) about all of the above issues

✔ explain contrasting beliefs in contemporary British society about the three issues of violence, weapons of mass destruction and pacifism, with reference to the main religious tradition in Britain (Christianity) and one or more other religious traditions.

Sample student answer – the 12-mark question

1. Write an answer to the following practice question:

   'The best way to bring about world peace is for more individuals to become pacifists.' Evaluate this statement.

   In your answer you:
   • should give reasoned arguments to support this statement
   • should give reasoned arguments to support a different point of view
   • should refer to religious arguments
   • may refer to non-religious arguments
   • should reach a justified conclusion.

   [12 marks]
   [+ 3 SPaG marks]

2. Read the following sample student answer:

   "I can see why people may feel that this is true. If everybody was a pacifist then there would be no fighting, although it would only take one person not to be a pacifist for this to not work. It is an ideal and most ideals don't work out too well when people get involved with them.

   Guru Nanak was a peace maker. He is quoted as saying: 'No one is my enemy, no one is a foreigner. I am at peace with all.' These words make it seem as though Guru Nanak would have agreed with the statement although obviously he didn't know much about world peace, just what it was like in part of India.

   However, Guru Gobind Singh seems to have disagreed with Guru Nanak (they didn't live at the same time). As Sikhs faced persecution, if they had been pacifists, they would all have been killed and there would be no Sikhism today. The fact that Sikhs shouldn't be pacifists is shown by their symbol which contains two swords and a type of dagger. They have to carry a sword as one of the 5 Ks but shouldn't use it even in self defence. Sikhs should fight in self defence or to protect others from oppression though. An example of this is that lots of Sikhs came from India to fight in Europe in World War 2.

I do think that pacifism is an ideal and is unlikely to work because someone will always be violent so as people have a right to defend themselves and others, pacifism wouldn't work. Guru Gobind Singh would agree with me."

3. With a partner, discuss the sample answer. Is the focus of the answer correct? Is anything missing from the answer? How do you think it could be improved?

4. What mark (out of 12) would you give this answer? Look at the mark scheme in the Introduction (AO2). What are the reasons for the mark you have given?

5. Now swap your answer with your partner's and mark each other's responses. What mark (out of 12) would you give the response? Refer to the mark scheme and give reasons for the mark you award.

Practice questions

1 Which **one** of the following most accurately suggests a violent protest?

A) Demonstration   **B)** Riot   **C)** Campaign   **D)** March   **[1 mark]**

2 Give **one** reason for war.   **[1 mark]**

3 Explain **two** different beliefs in contemporary British society about whether countries should possess weapons of mass destruction.

In your answer you must refer to one or more religious traditions.   **[4 marks]**

4 Explain **two** reasons why religious believers should help victims of war.

Refer to sacred writings or another source of religious belief and teaching in your answer.

        [6 marks]

> **Study tip**
>
> The information on Khalsa Aid in this chapter refers to help given to refugees. Refugees are victims of war even though they do not fight.

5 'The just war theory is the best religious response to whether it is right to fight.'

Evaluate this statement. In your answer you:
- should give reasoned arguments to support this statement
- should give reasoned arguments to support a different point of view
- should refer to religious arguments
- may refer to non-religious arguments
- should reach a justified conclusion.   **[12 marks]**
        [+ 3 SPaG marks]

> **Study tip**
>
> The Sikh just war theory is different from the theory in Christianity. If you have also studied Christianity you can refer to the Christian theory as a different point of view, provided you focus upon differences.

7 Religion, crime and punishment

7.1 Introduction to religion, crime and punishment

■ What are crime and punishment?

A **crime** is any action which is against the law that has been put in place by the proper rulers of any state. In the UK, this is the government, who must get the approval of Parliament before any new crimes are written into law. Police arrest people who are suspected of having broken the law by committing crimes. If after questioning the police and Crown Prosecution Service (CPS) have evidence to prove their suspicions, they charge the person with having committed the offence.

When a suspected offender is charged with a crime, they face a hearing in a Magistrates' Court. If the crime is serious, they will then have to appear in a Crown Court before a judge and a jury of twelve people, selected at random. For some minor crimes, the police can give the offender a caution if they admit they are guilty.

▲ Police exist to protect the public from crime and to apprehend those who break the law

Offenders who are found guilty by a court face a legal **punishment**. Most serious offences such as murder and rape carry a life sentence in prison, although this rarely means they spend the rest of their life in prison. Less serious offences are punished by a shorter prison sentence, or with non-custodial sentences such as community service or paying a fine. If a court decides that the person has committed no crime, they are released without any punishment. In the UK, the law does not permit a sentence which causes physical harm (corporal punishment) or death (capital punishment). In India, the death penalty is used as a punishment for certain extremely serious crimes but it is rarely used.

An individual victim of a crime is not allowed to punish the offender afterwards. This is against the law.

Civil law is different from criminal law. Civil law concerns disputes between private individuals or groups. This includes such matters as the settlement of a divorce, disputes between landlords and tenants, and disputed wills.

■ Good and evil actions

Many people would say that any action that obeys the law is a good action. While this is true, good actions also include actions that are generous, helpful and loving, even if they are not actually specified in the law. There is no law that says whether you have to support charities or not, but offering support, whether financial or by actively doing things to help people, is usually considered to be a good action. Sikhs have a duty, called sewa, to carry out good deeds in society. Society usually considers actions that are encouraged or required by genuine religious faith to be good when they benefit other people.

▲ *Sikh men packing sacks full of grain for charity as part of their religious duty to do good*

Evil actions are actions that may be violent or result in violence, and which sometimes involve the suffering of innocent people. The suffering may include injury and death. Such actions can include mass murder, serial killing, causing a terrorist explosion, multiple rape or repeated serious child abuse. These are the types of crimes that can result in life imprisonment with no chance of early release.

While many religions have a belief in a personal force of evil in the form of the devil, Sikhism does not. All people are believed to be born good, and with a strong spirit that helps them to overcome difficulties. Sikhism teaches that the root cause of evil or suffering is the human ego, which has become distracted by the five vices of anger, lust, greed, worldy attachment and pride. These vices lead to evil but are not linked to any idea of a personal force of evil.

When people speak about evil criminal actions, they usually mean that the offence is profoundly immoral and wicked as a result of people allowing themselves to give into temptation. Thus evil actions are always against the will of God.

■ Good and evil intentions – a Sikh response

Sikhs believe that there is no such thing as an evil person. Although they are born good, human beings are not perfect and make mistakes. Some do evil things, but this is because they have not resisted temptation. It is not because they are evil in themselves, or because their intention was necessarily evil. Sikhs believe in reincarnation, so they believe in punishment after death. However, they know they must face punishment on Earth for wrongdoings, too. Sikhs believe that having good intentions, such as obeying the law and protecting the public by punishing lawbreakers, helps Sikhs to build good karma.

Discussion activity

In a small group, discuss whether there is such a thing as an evil action.

> **❝** The self-willed manmukh [self-centred person] receives only more punishment. **❞**
> *Guru Granth Sahib 361*

⭐ Study tip

Remember that Sikhs believe that God wants everyone to live together in peace and harmony, and they believe it is important to support law and order.

Summary

You should now know more about the meaning of crime and punishment, understand why intentions and actions are described as good and evil, and understand Sikh attitudes to these issues.

■ Reasons why some people commit crime

While most people believe that all crime is wrong, sometimes how wrong it is may depend on why it was committed. Crimes may be due to selfishness, or there may be circumstances that make some crimes more understandable. Sikhs believe that committing crime is never right because they have a duty to treat people fairly, and committing crime goes against this. A justice system based on the teachings of the Gurus brings God's justice into the world.

However, because God gave humans free will, at times their imperfections lead them to commit crimes.

▲ *Reasons why people commit crime*

Poverty

In the UK, some people live in **poverty** and cannot afford the necessities of life. Work or welfare payments for those who cannot work or those who earn low wages should cover living expenses, but sometimes they do not. This can lead some people to steal food because they do not have enough money to buy it. Even though this may seem to be a good reason, stealing is against the law and thus wrong.

Poverty offends Sikh ideas about fairness and oppression. Sikhs work hard to create situations where there is no poverty. Their belief in sewa means that they have a duty to serve the community, especially those who are living in poverty. The langar in a gurdwara serves food to any in the community who are in need, and so helps people not to steal to get food.

Upbringing

Growing up in a household or community where crime is a way of life may influence a young person so they follow the example of others and drift into crime themselves. Once they have been drawn into a life of crime it is difficult for them to change, even though they know that what they are doing is wrong. Sikhs emphasise a strong family structure, where the wisdom and experience of the elderly is respected. This should ensure that Sikh children grow up to respect the law by following the good examples they are set.

Mental health problems

Mental health problems do not often lead to crime. People with mental health problems are more likely to be victims of violent crime, rather than perpetrators.

Objectives

- Know and understand reasons why some people commit crime.
- Know and understand Sikh responses to reasons why some people commit crime.

Key terms

- **poverty:** being without money, food or other basic needs of life
- **mental health problem:** a medical condition that affects a person's behaviour, thoughts, feelings or emotions, and sometimes their ability to relate to others
- **addiction:** a physical or mental dependency on a substance or activity that is very difficult to overcome
- **greed:** selfish desire for something, such as wealth, goods or items of value which are not needed

❝ One may run away from the courts of other men, but where can one go to escape the Lord's Kingdom? ❞

Guru Granth Sahib 591

Activities

1. Write a sentence to explain each of the reasons for crime described on these pages.

2. Are there any reasons for crime that you could add to the list? Note them down and explain why.

3. Sikhs believe it is wrong to take anything that may cause an addiction. Do you think they are correct? Give reasons why.

However, there is a link between some mental health problems and crime. For example, antisocial personality disorder affects how a person thinks and relates to others. This can range in severity from occasional bad behaviour to repeated lawbreaking.

Addiction

Addiction to drugs means that the human body cannot cope without them. Addicts face the choice of not taking drugs, an action that they know will make their life physically and mentally very hard, or spending money on buying their next 'fix'. If they do not have the money, the only way they may be able to get it is to steal.

The drug that causes more crime than any other is alcohol. People who have drunk too much alcohol lose some of their decision-making ability, to the extent that they may get into fights and commit acts of violence. If they drive while under the influence of alcohol, they are more likely to cause an accident than somebody who is sober.

Sikh teachings forbid the taking of intoxicants, including illegal drugs and alcohol. They believe that they are a temptation which leads people to do wrong and so should be resisted.

Greed

In a country where personal possessions and wealth are seen as signs of status, some people who cannot afford them feel they have the right to obtain them illegally. **Greed** for items that people living in poverty cannot afford, or for items that further increase the wealth of wealthy people, can lead to crime, especially theft or fraud. In Sikh belief, greed is one of the five evils, and is seen as unnecessary and destructive:

> ❝ Crying out, "Mine, mine!" he spends his life [...] in ignorance. The Messenger of Death watches over him every moment, every instant; night and day, his life is wasting away. ❞
>
> *Guru Granth Sahib 1049*

Hate

Hatred is a negative feeling or reaction that can lead to prejudice and violence against someone the offender hates. Sikhs believe that every human is created by God and has a divine spark, so hating anyone would be wrong and acting against God's will.

Opposition to an unjust law

According to lawmakers, breaking the law is always wrong. However, throughout the twentieth and twenty-first centuries people have broken laws they believed to be unjust and brought about change to laws that were based on racial or gender prejudice. Some people believe it is acceptable to break laws in order to protest to try to change an unjust law. Sikhs have protested against laws they felt to be unjust or laws that prevented them from fulfilling their religious duties, such as the law concerning motor bike helmets (see page 121).

▲ *Addicts may commit crimes in order to fuel their addictions, or because their addictions cause them to lose their decision-making ability*

> ❝ Drinking it, his intelligence departs, and madness enters his mind. He cannot distinguish between his own and others' – he is struck down by his Lord and Master. Drinking it, he forgets his Lord and Master, and he is punished in the Court of the Lord. Don't drink the false wine at all, if it is in your power. ❞
>
> *Guru Granth Sahib 554*

Discussion activity

With a partner, discuss which of these reasons for committing crime can be avoided, and which cannot. Explain your choices and compare them with those of another group.

⭐ Study tip

Although these reasons for crime are the ones listed in the examination specification, you can write about any others you can think of.

Summary

You should now know and understand some reasons why people may commit crimes and have considered Sikh responses to some of them.

7.3 Sikh attitudes to lawbreakers and different types of crime

■ Sikh attitudes to lawbreakers

Sikhs are against people committing crime. They believe that God requires them to promote justice and equality, both of which are damaged by crime. There is no doubt that UK law is there to protect the rights and security of all citizens, although there may be laws that some Sikhs are uneasy with. They recognise that without laws, society would descend into disorder and chaos, justice and equality would be threatened, and oppression of the vulnerable would increase.

The law also governs how offenders are dealt with. All suspected offenders are presumed to be innocent until they are proved guilty, and the courts exist to decide whether there is any doubt as to whether somebody is guilty. If there is any reasonable doubt, they are found innocent and allowed to resume their life without any punishment.

There are many different attitudes to lawbreakers. Some believe the punishment should reflect the fact that the lawbreaker's actions are unacceptable. Sikhs believe that serious offenders should be put in prison in order to protect others in society. They also believe that while in prison the offender should not be mistreated and their rights should be protected.

Sikhs also believe offenders should be helped and educated not to offend again. Their punishment should reflect the fact that they are capable of change, and this change should be encouraged. While the crime may be hated, the person who committed it is not.

▲ Sir Mota Singh – Britain's first Sikh judge. Judges consider the crime and the offender in each case, before deciding on a suitable punishment.

Objectives

- Understand Sikh attitudes to lawbreakers and different types of crime.
- Consider Sikh attitudes to lawbreakers and types of crimes.

Key term

- **hate crimes:** crimes, often including violence, that are usually targeted at a person because of their race, religion, sexuality, disability or gender identity

Activities

1 What rights do you think an offender should have? Give reasons for your opinion.
2 Do you think it is right to hate a crime but not the person who commits it? Explain your opinion.
3 Note down what Sikhs believe about lawbreakers.

Discussion activity

'Severe punishment helps offenders.' Discuss with a partner whether you believe this is true.

■ Different types of crime: hate crime, theft and murder

There are many different types of crimes, some more serious than others. More severe punishments are reserved for the more serious crimes. Sikhs condemn all crime that has a bad effect on others.

Some crimes are considered to be **hate crimes**. These are crimes, often including violence, that are usually targeted at a person because of their race, religion, sexuality, disability or gender identity, for example because they identify as transgender (someone whose gender is not the same as, or does not sit comfortably with, the sex they were assigned at birth). These are considered to be serious crimes.

Hate crimes make the Sikh ideal of a society without prejudice or discrimination impossible to achieve. The Mool Mantra describes God as being without hate and Sikhs believe that in this they should be like God.

Theft causes great upset to the person whose property is stolen, but the crime is usually more about the property and not about the victim, who is often unknown to the offender. Even if a person steals due to poverty, theft is still wrong. Sikhs may be sympathetic towards people committing theft out of need rather than greed. However, they believe that the community should care for the needy, so that they are less likely to commit crimes.

▲ Sikhs may be more sympathetic to those stealing out of need rather than greed, but they believe that theft is always wrong

In many people's opinion, the most serious crime, which may also be a hate crime, is murder. Murder means to unlawfully and deliberately kill a fellow human being. Some types of murder are worse than others, and the amount of violence employed and suffering caused may vary, but the end result is the same – a person dies. Sikhs are strongly opposed to murder because it leads to a great deal of pain for those left behind, and because only God has the right to give and take life at a time of his choosing. Taking this choice from God is seen as the offender trying to make him or herself equal to God. Murder is strictly forbidden in the Sikh Code of Conduct, the Rehat Maryada.

Activities

1 Explain the meaning of hate crimes, theft and murder.

2 Explain why Sikhs are opposed to hate crimes, theft and murder.

3 Is theft always wrong? Explain your answer.

Extension activity

'There is no worse crime than one committed out of hate and prejudice.' Give and explain arguments for and against this statement.

Research activity

Use the internet to find out about the attack on Sandeep Singh, an American Sikh, in New York in 2014.

You could also find out about the response of the Sikh community to this attack.

 Study tip

If you write about hate crimes, you can use any crime that is targeted at a person out of prejudice. This may include theft and murder.

Summary

You should now understand Sikh attitudes to lawbreakers and different types of crime, and have analysed these attitudes.

Sikh attitudes to suffering

■ Sikh attitudes to suffering

For many people, suffering is an unfortunate part of living. There are commonly thought to be two types of suffering.

Natural suffering is suffering that has natural causes, such as earthquakes and floods, which humanity cannot control. They are sometimes referred to as acts of God, but Sikhs do not believe this to be literally true because they do not believe God causes suffering. Nobody can be blamed for causing these natural events, and the effects can be devastating, but they do provide an opportunity for others to show compassion by helping the victims.

Human-made suffering refers to the suffering people cause to others. This may be the result of such things as crime or war and the suffering caused by inequality or oppression. Again, Sikhs do not believe that God causes this suffering. It is thought to be caused by humans using their **free will** badly by making choices harmful to themselves and others. Those who commit crimes which cause suffering are legally punished if proven guilty.

On occasions, people accidentally cause others to suffer. For example, if a person drives a car after drinking alcohol, there is an increased risk that they will harm themselves or others because the alcohol affects their reactions and judgements. Sikhs prevent the possibility of such suffering by not allowing believers to drink alcohol or to take other intoxicants.

Sikhs believe that although God does not cause suffering, he permits it to happen as a test of faith and courage, and ultimately of understanding and being content with God's will. This is potentially a big step for a Sikh. When a Sikh becomes more content with God's will, they do not judge events so much as 'good' or 'bad' but as part of the normal rollercoaster of life.

Sikhs believe that bad actions have negative consequences for spiritual development, and can potentially lead to greater suffering and moving further away from God. However, if people respond positively to the will of God by using their free will in the way he wishes, there will be less suffering.

People who are suffering can bring out great qualities in others through their responses to suffering. This includes acting with compassion by helping people to deal with suffering and to reduce its effects on their life.

> ❝ Knowing their Lord and Master, people show compassion; then, they become immortal, and attain the state of eternal dignity. ❞
>
> *Guru Granth Sahib 340*

Objectives

- Know and understand Sikh attitudes to suffering.
- Evaluate whether it is ever right to cause people to suffer.
- Know and understand good and evil intentions and actions.

Key term

- **free will:** belief that God gives people the opportunity to make decisions for themselves

▲ *Drinking alcohol increases the risk of car accidents. Sikhism forbids such intoxicants.*

> ❝ Why do you slander the Lord? You are ignorant and deluded. Pain and pleasure are the result of your own actions. ❞
>
> *Guru Granth Sahib 695*

The only way that a person is released from suffering completely is when the divine spark, which is the part of God in everyone, is reabsorbed into God, and the person is released from the cycle of birth and death.

■ Causing suffering to others

Sikhs believe that they should have sufficient compassion and a strong sense of right and wrong, which means they should not cause suffering to others. Their belief in karma means that if they cause others to suffer, the consequences may be that they will suffer either later in this life or in the next. However, it can be argued that punishing offenders is deliberately inflicting suffering on others. Sikhs believe that punishment can be a valuable experience for offenders provided it is aimed at changing the offender's behaviour in the future, and focuses on active support and education.

■ Good and evil intentions and actions

Most people believe evil actions to be actions that are unspeakably awful, and are intended to be so. Human evil, sometimes called moral evil, is caused by deliberately making wrong choices for several possible reasons, all of which are selfish or negative. Sikhs believe that evil and suffering are caused when a person's ego or sense of self is controlled by the five vices (anger, lust, greed, worldy attachment and pride). Murder, rape and terrorism are all examples of evil actions resulting from evil intentions. Sikhs also include exploitation, tyranny and oppression as examples of evil actions because they show no compassion or empathy and are rooted in self-centredness. Throughout history, many Sikhs have worked to oppose oppression and have given their lives in doing so.

Evil actions can be made more bearable by other people making selfless sacrifices to comfort the victims of evil actions. This is what Sikhs are taught to do.

▲ *A representation of karma*

Discussion activity

'Suffering is the medicine, and pleasure the disease, because where there is pleasure, there is no desire for God' (Guru Granth Sahib 469). With a partner, discuss what this quotation means. Do you agree with it? Explain your reasons.

⭐ **Study tip**

You can use simple representations of important concepts (such as karma) to remember what they mean.

Summary

You should now have increased your knowledge and understanding of Sikh attitudes to suffering, why Sikhs should not cause suffering to others, and why evil intentions and actions are wrong.

Activities

1 Explain, giving examples, the two different types of suffering.
2 How do Sikhs explain God's role in suffering?
3 How do Sikhs see suffering in a positive way?
4 Explain why Sikhs do not cause others to suffer.
5 Explain why punishing others may be a positive action.
6 What do you think makes intentions and actions evil?

When a court imposes a punishment, the judge has to consider what purpose the punishment will serve. In the UK, no matter how severe the punishment, it is intended as a positive action: to protect society, to assist the offender, to stop others from making the same mistakes, or a combination of these. It should not cause intentional harm to the offender. In the past, this has not always been the case, and in some countries it still isn't. Sikhism stresses that punishments should follow the principle of equality. Wealthy people should be punished in the same way as people living in poverty, and men in the same way as women. Equality is emphasised in the Guru Granth Sahib, and whatever punishment is given to offenders, it should be compassionate because even offenders have a divine spark that is part of God:

> 66 The entire universe is made of the same clay. The Potter has shaped it into all sorts of vessels. The five elements join together, to make up the form of the human body. Who can say which is less, and which is more? 99
>
> *Guru Granth Sahib 1128*

Three main aims of punishment are: retribution, deterrence, reformation.

■ Retribution

For an offender, **retribution** is the least positive of the aims of punishment. It means to get your own back. In other words, retribution means that society is getting its own back on the offender. It follows that killers should be killed, and those who steal should lose their property. This is often referred to as revenge. However, none of this is supported by Sikh beliefs and teachings. Taking revenge is regarded as a crime in itself because it comes from anger, one of the five evils. This is not what God wills and it is not compassionate.

> 66 Do not be angry with anyone else; look within your own self instead. Be humble in this world, O Nanak, and by His Grace you shall be carried across. 99
>
> *Guru Granth Sahib 259*

■ Deterrence

Many believe that if offenders receive a punishment for wrongdoing, and in some cases a severe punishment, it will put them off committing the same crime again, and also put off others from committing the crime too. This is called **deterrence**. While this may be effective in controlling some people's behaviour, many doubt whether people have been persuaded not to commit murder by the likelihood of spending

Objectives

- Know and understand three aims of punishment.
- Understand religious attitudes to three aims of punishment.

Key terms

- **retribution:** an aim of punishment – to get your own back; 'an eye for an eye'
- **deterrence:** an aim of punishment – to put people off committing crimes
- **reformation:** an aim of punishment – to change someone's behaviour for the better

Activities

1 Explain the three aims of punishment.
2 Explain carefully why many Sikhs agree with reformation and deterrence but not retribution.
3 Explain what you think the quotation from Guru Granth Sahib 1128 means.

many years in prison. Reasons why people commit serious crimes may be more complex than a simple fear of punishment. However, people considering committing less serious offences may be influenced by possible punishment.

Some Sikhs favour deterrence because it teaches that bad actions bring bad consequences, which is the basis of the belief of karma.

■ Reformation

The UK punishment system emphasises the importance of **reformation**. It is hoped that punishment will encourage offenders to change their attitude and become responsible, law-abiding members of the community. In order for this to work, offenders need to realise that their behaviour is wrong before they can hope to be reformed. This may involve group therapy sessions, individual counselling and treatment (if required), meeting their victims so they realise the harm they may have caused, or working in the community (community service).

Sikhs believe that reformation is the best aim of punishment. It recognises that offenders have the potential to change. This change may include the desire to listen to and follow the word of God. The Rehat Maryada addresses what should happen when Sikhs break their religious vows. It states that they should repent, change their ways and perform a service to the community as punishment. The community should help them to make their change of behaviour effective. This is exactly how many Sikhs believe offenders should be treated, because it follows Sikh principles of compassion, forgiveness and equality.

▲ Prison is thought to deter people from committing crimes

Research activity 🔍

Find out more about other aims of punishment, especially protection, vindication and reparation.

Discussion activity 💬

Discuss with a partner which of the three aims of punishment you think is the most effective.

⭐ **Study tip**

When discussing the *aims* of punishment, make sure you do not mix them up with *types* of punishment, such as prison and community service.

Summary

You should now know and understand three main aims of punishment and what Sikhs think about them.

▲ A building course is contributing to prisoners' reformation by giving them skills they can use once they are released from prison

■ Treatment of criminals in the UK

In UK law, there are many ways that criminals can be legally punished, and several ways that they cannot. Someone who commits murder can expect a long term in **prison**. In the most serious cases, or if the murderer would be a danger to the

▲ In the UK, most offenders are tried in a Magistrates' Court

public if released, this may be for life. Less serious crimes are punished less severely. Payment of a fine is one form of punishment. A specified number of hours of **community service** is another option, if the judge considers it to be the best way of punishing a particular individual.

In UK law, those punished must be treated with dignity. Even though offenders have been found guilty of a crime, this does not justify ill treatment. This is reinforced by human rights legislation that the UK supports. Part of this is that punishment should not cause physical harm to the person who is being punished. Reformation is considered to be the most important aim used in deciding punishment, because if through punishment a criminal is changed, both the individual and society benefit. All offenders are treated equally and all face the same range of punishments, dependent on the crime they have committed. The British legal system is based on equality, and offenders have the same rights, regardless of their race, wealth or gender. Sikhs agree with the way this legal system operates, and with the principles on which it is based.

■ Prison

Prison is reserved for those who have committed a serious crime. Those considered a serious threat to society when released, or to themselves or other prisoners, are kept in a high security prison. Conditions in some UK prisons have been criticised by official inspectors, because the punishment a prison should impose is loss of liberty, not poor living conditions, and the conditions in some UK prisons are not considered adequate. Having no choice to live as ordinary people do, being locked in a cell for much of the day, being fed at certain set times, and having to do manual work for little money are part of the loss of freedom that prison imposes.

Sikhs agree with the use of prison, but only if the prison experience is aimed at reforming the criminal, and if it treats them with respect

Links

For more about the aims of punishment, see pages 144–145.

and compassion. Prisons also serve as a deterrent, and protect society because they ensure the prisoner cannot reoffend while in prison. In this way, they follow Sikh principles of creating a safe society based on compassion and equality.

■ Corporal punishment

Corporal punishment means to punish an offender by causing them physical pain. This could be by whipping them, hitting them repeatedly with a cane, or by other methods. Many believe this to be a breach of human rights. It is illegal in the UK, but exists in some other parts of the world, where it can be carried out in public and is believed to deter people from committing crime.

Sikhs do not support corporal punishment because it is believed to be against Sikh principles and teaching. It is harmful, lacks compassion, and makes no effort to reform the offender.

Sikh opposition to corporal punishment is similar to the beliefs of Christianity, the main religious tradition in Britain.

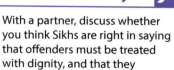

Discussion activity

With a partner, discuss whether you think Sikhs are right in saying that offenders must be treated with dignity, and that they should have rights.

Contrasting beliefs

Find out more about what Christians believe about corporal punishment, and whether any Christian views differ from Sikh beliefs.

■ Community service

Some crimes are punishable by community service. This may include offences such as vandalism, benefit fraud or minor assaults. Community service offers the offender a chance to make up for what they have done, and to receive help in reforming their behaviour. The aim of community service is positive and offers the chance to give something back to society. This reflects Sikh principles and reinforces sewa, the duty to serve the community. This way, God is honoured and good karma is earned and set against the bad karma generated by the crime itself. Sikh teaching suggests that reformation occurs through service and prayer, and the soul can evolve into a higher spiritual being as a result.

▲ *Community service may include picking up litter*

Activities

1 Explain why Sikhs agree with the way the British legal system operates.
2 Think about and explain how a nation's justice system can help to bring equality into society.
3 Explain how different forms of punishment may affect offenders and the community.
4 Which of the three punishments do Sikhs agree and disagree with? Explain why.
5 'Prisoners should be treated badly as part of their punishment.' Explain reasons that can be given for and against this statement.

⭐ **Study tip**

It would be helpful to learn the reasons why Sikhs support prison and community service as punishments.

Summary

You should now know and understand three forms of punishment and the responses of Sikhs to each.

Forgiveness is a fundamental principle in Sikhism, closely linked to the Sikh belief in equality. Once Sikhs have learned that wrong actions are the result of weaknesses which all humans share, they are able to follow the example of the Gurus and show compassion for others. The offence can be condemned but not the offender. Forgiveness is often a more powerful response to wrongdoing than many other responses. It sends a message that, despite the offender's wrongdoing, they must be respected and valued, even if they themselves have not respected and valued other people.

The Guru Granth Sahib emphasises the importance of forgiveness:

> 66 Where there is falsehood, there is sin. Where there is greed, there is death. **Where there is forgiveness, there is God Himself.** 99
>
> *Guru Granth Sahib 1372*

However, forgiveness is not a replacement for punishment. Nor does it allow for wrong actions to be completely forgotten, because this may mean the offender repeats them and is no better off. Humane punishment is part of a Sikh response to prevent further harm occurring.

For Sikhs, the action of forgiving is linked to selfless giving. To forgive means to let go of, and not hold on to, past grudges or pain. It is not the same as burying these feelings. Forgiveness is a very difficult and profound spiritual process of courageously accepting and moving past an injustice, for one's own good and the wider good. This is supported by a Sikh teaching that explains that, when a person is able to forgive, they come closest to a state of oneness with God, and of living in God's image.

> 66 Those who have truth as their fast, contentment as their sacred shrine of pilgrimage, spiritual wisdom and meditation as their cleansing bath, kindness as their deity, and forgiveness as their chanting beads — they are the most excellent people. 99
>
> *Guru Granth Sahib 245*

Objectives

- Understand Sikh beliefs, teachings and attitudes about forgiveness.
- Consider a real-life case study related to forgiveness.

Key term

- **forgiveness:** showing grace and mercy and pardoning someone for what they have done wrong

⭐ Study tip

When learning quotations, try to remember the most important bit. For example, from the Guru Granth Sahib 1372 quotation it would be helpful to learn: 'Where there is forgiveness, there is God Himself.'

> 66 To practise forgiveness is the true fast, good conduct and contentment. 99
>
> *Guru Granth Sahib 223*

Contrasting beliefs

Find out what Christianity teaches about forgiveness. How does it differ from Sikh teachings?

Activities

1. Explain what Sikhs believe about forgiveness.
2. Is forgiveness a powerful response to wrongdoing? Explain the reasons for your answer.

Pardeep Kaleka

In August 2012, Wade Michael Page killed six and wounded four others in a mass shooting at a gurdwara in Oak Creek, Wisconsin, USA. One of those killed was the father of Pardeep Kaleka. Pardeep wrote about his beliefs and feelings following the event:

'One of our immediate responses to the atrocity was to ask how it could have happened. Perhaps because people weren't familiar with Sikhism. Perhaps we weren't open enough to the rest of the community of Oak Creek. We knew it was important to educate our youth, but what about the others? We decided we needed to reach out and get to know our neighbours, making contributions to our community and learning together.

▲ *Sikhs attended worship in memory of the victims of the shooting*

I decided to respond to this tragedy with compassion. There is a saying in Sikhism, *Charhdi Kala*, which means 'we move in relentless optimism'. *Charhdi Kala* and compassion go hand in hand. Some people think of compassion as offering forgiveness and all is forgiven, but I think of it as a process, in other words I attach a purpose to what's happening in life and appreciate the good things when they come. On 5 August, there was a purpose to what happened. With *Charhdi Kala* the purpose of our response is to reach out, to include the other and say this will not happen again.

I've learnt more about my journey of forgiveness from my friend and colleague, Arno Michaelis. After the shooting I felt grief and frustration and couldn't understand why Wade Michael Page had pulled

the trigger. Arno was able to help me understand the behaviour and fears of Page. He spoke about the self-destructive nature of hate. Through the organisation we've created together, Serve 2 Unite, children of all ethnicities, from the inner city to the suburbs, are coming together to cherish each other as human beings and to assume the identity of peacemakers in their schools and communities.

Choosing forgiveness is making a decision and embarking on a process. Some days will be good and others more difficult. I try to enjoy the time with my family, friends and community and experience life to the fullest. Sometimes my daughter and my son say that I hug them too long. Perhaps I do. I value each day more than someone who hasn't gone through this, but I wouldn't wish it upon anyone.'

Discussion activities

With a partner, discuss the case study of Pardeep Kaleka.

1   Discuss how his reaction to his father's death shows compassion and forgiveness.
2   'Choosing forgiveness is making a decision and embarking on a process.' What does this sentence mean?

Summary

You should now understand more about Sikh attitudes to forgiveness, and have considered a case study related to forgiveness.

Sikh attitudes to the death penalty

■ The death penalty

The **death penalty** was abolished in the UK in 1965 as a five-year experiment and permanently abolished in 1969. The European Community has since made it illegal in all member countries. Several campaigns have been carried out in the UK to try to have it reintroduced but all have failed.

▲ Hanging as a punishment for murder was abolished in the UK in 1965, and replaced with life imprisonment

Since its abolition, three people executed in the early 1950s have been pardoned because new evidence emerged after they were put to death that showed they were innocent. In addition, there have been several instances, since abolition, where it has been discovered that people were wrongly convicted of murder and so released from prison. If the death penalty had still been legal in the UK, it is likely that they would have been executed for crimes they did not commit. The chance of killing an innocent person is one of the arguments against bringing back the death penalty in the UK.

■ Sikh attitudes to the death penalty

Sikh teaching is against the death penalty. Sikhs believe that only God has the right to take a life, unless all other ways of stopping injustice have failed. This does not include executing offenders. In addition, they believe that the death penalty is based on retribution and revenge, and these can never be justified. Also, it does not allow offenders to change.

The death penalty may deter others from committing crimes and protect others in society from the effects of crime. It might be justified using the principle of utility, which states that an action is good if it produces happiness for the majority. For Sikhs, however, it does not overrule Sikh teaching about taking life. Imprisonment also aims to protect and deter but, in addition, gives the opportunity for reformation and compassion, which the death penalty does not.

> ❝ He alone has the Power in His Hands. He watches over all. ❞
> *Guru Granth Sahib 7*

In addition, Sikhs believe that everyone has a part of God within them. So the sanctity of life is an important principle for Sikhs.

Stories from Sikh tradition

Sajjan

Sajjan to all appearances was a good man. He welcomed Hindus and Muslims into his guesthouse, provided travellers with food and shelter, and built a temple and mosque for them. However, over time he became a thief and a murderer. If travellers who stayed with him were wealthy, he told his servants to kill them as they slept and steal their money and possessions. The bodies were hidden.

While travelling through the area where Sajjan lived, Guru Nanak and his companions were invited to stay with Sajjan. When they went to their room for the night, Sajjan waited outside the door to check when they were asleep. However, rather than sleeping, Nanak and his companions spent much of the night singing hymns and praising God. Sajjan waited and listened and became transformed by God's word which was coming from Nanak's room. He eventually burst into

▲ *Sajjan confessing his sins to Guru Nanak*

the room and confessed to ordering the death of wealthy travellers, before promising to spend the rest of his life making up for his sins. He gave away all his wealth and spent the rest of his life serving God.

Even those who commit the most serious offences are part of God, and capable of being transformed by the word of God. One person who was transformed was Sajjan, a thief and murderer who lived at the same time as Guru Nanak (see Stories from Sikh tradition).

Killing an offender implies that they are unworthy of being allowed to live. However, in most societies, and certainly in Sikh thought, the right to life is a basic right. In Sikh teachings, every soul has a divine spark. The death penalty also implies that there are some crimes that are so bad that they cannot be forgiven. This is also contrary to Sikh beliefs and teachings.

Links

You may find it helpful to read about forgiveness again on pages 148–149.

■ Beliefs about the death penalty in Christianity

Christian beliefs about the death penalty are similar to Sikh beliefs. They also believe that God is the giver and taker of life, and that humans have no right to kill even the worst offenders. However, some Christians emphasise deterrence as an aim of punishment that would justify the use of the death penalty in some circumstances.

⭐ Study tip

If comparing and contrasting Sikh and Christian beliefs about the death penalty, it would be helpful to include the idea that some Christians believe it is justified as a deterrent in some situations.

Activities

1   Explain the legal situation regarding the death penalty in the UK.
2   For what reasons do you think people might be in favour of the death penalty?
3   Carefully explain Sikh attitudes to the death penalty.
4   Do you agree that the death penalty should never be used? Explain your reasons.
5   Do you agree with Sikhs that there are no crimes that cannot be forgiven? Explain your opinion.

Summary

You should now have greater knowledge and understanding of the death penalty, and should understand Sikh attitudes to the death penalty.

Religion, crime and the causes of crime – summary

You should now be able to:

✔ explain beliefs and teachings about good and evil intentions and actions, including whether it can ever be good to cause suffering

✔ explain different reasons for crime, including poverty and upbringing, mental health problems and addiction, greed and hate, and opposition to an unjust law

✔ explain views about people who break the law for these reasons

✔ explain views about different types of crime, including hate crimes, theft and murder.

Religion and punishment – summary

✔ explain beliefs and teachings about the aims of punishment, including retribution, deterrence and reformation

✔ explain beliefs and teachings about the treatment of criminals, including prison, corporal punishment and community service

✔ explain beliefs and teachings about forgiveness

✔ explain beliefs and teachings about the death penalty

✔ explain ethical arguments related to the death penalty, including those based on the principle of utility and the sanctity of life.

Sample student answer – the 4-mark question

1. Write an answer to the following practice question:

   Explain **two** different beliefs in contemporary British society about corporal punishment.
   In your answer you should refer to the main religious tradition of Great Britain and one or more other religious traditions. **[4 marks]**

2. Read the following sample student answer:

   "Sikhs are not allowed to use corporal punishment because it is not respectful to the offender and seems to be based on retribution. In contemporary British society, corporal punishment is not used. It is not a loving action because it harms people, some of whom may be innocent and doesn't reform them. Christians believe God did not give people the right to harm each other in this way."

3. With a partner, discuss the sample answer. Can you identify two different points? Is there reference to the main religious tradition in Great Britain (Christianity) and at least one other religious tradition? Can it be improved? If so, how?

4. What mark (out of 4) would you give this answer? Look at the mark scheme in the Introduction (AO1). What are the reasons for the mark you have given?

5. Now swap your answer with your partner's and mark each other's responses. What mark (out of 4) would you give the response? Refer to the mark scheme and give reasons for the mark you award.

Sample student answer – the 6-mark question

1. Write an answer to the following practice question:

   Explain two religious beliefs about reasons why some people commit crimes.
   Refer to sacred writings or another source of religious belief and teaching in your answer.

   [6 marks]

2. Read the following student sample answer:

   "Some people commit crimes because they have a mental health problem. As it is an illness, they should be treated and helped but punished as well. Sikhs believe help and punishment go together. Others may commit crimes because they are greedy and want things that don't belong to them. Sikhs condemn greed because it is unnecessary and destructive."

3. With a partner, discuss the student answer. Can you identify two religious beliefs about reasons why people commit crimes? Are the beliefs detailed and is the teaching relevant, accurate, and applied to the question? Can it be improved? If so, how?

4. What mark (out of 6) would you give this answer? Look at the mark scheme in the Introduction (AO1). What are the reasons for the mark you have given?

5. Now swap your answer with your partner's and mark each other's responses. What mark (out of 6) would you give the response? Refer to the mark scheme and give reasons for the mark you award.

Practice questions

1. Which **one** of the following is an aim of punishment?

   A) Prison   **B)** Deterrence   **C)** Forgiveness   **D)** Murder   **[1 mark]**

2. Give **one** cause of crime.   **[1 mark]**

    Study tip

   A cause of crime is a reason why people commit crimes, not an example of a crime.

3. Explain **two** different beliefs in contemporary British society about whether the death penalty should exist in the UK.

   In your answer you must refer to one or more religious traditions.   **[4 marks]**

    **Study tip**

   You do not have to choose beliefs simply for and against the death penalty, although of course you could do so if you wish. You could choose to explain one belief against the death penalty and one in favour of the death penalty but only for murder, for example.

4. Explain **two** reasons why religious believers believe reformation is the best aim of punishment.

   Refer to sacred writings or another source of religious belief and teaching in your answer.   **[6 marks]**

5. 'It is right to forgive all offenders whoever they are and whatever they have done.'

   Evaluate this statement. In your answer you:
   - should give reasoned arguments to support this statement
   - should give reasoned arguments to support a different point of view
   - should refer to religious arguments
   - may refer to non-religious arguments
   - should reach a justified conclusion.   **[12 marks]**
   [+ 3 SPaG marks]

8 Religion, human rights and social justice

8.1 Human rights

■ What are human rights?

Many people in the world are treated unfairly. The organisation Amnesty International reports that in many countries torture still exists, many people face unfair trials, many are denied the freedom to express their opinions, and some people are enslaved. Although progress has been made in the past hundred years, millions of people still suffer from a lack of **human rights**. In some cases, this is a result of governments suppressing opposition or communities not wishing people to have freedom of expression or religion. People are still bullied, exploited or treated as second-class citizens. This might happen because of ethnicity, religion, age, class, sex or because they have a disability. In the worst cases it can result in death. For example, the Nazis murdered millions of people during the Second World War including Jewish people, Roma and Sinti people (often referred to as 'Gypsies'), people who are attracted to people of the same sex, and disabled people.

■ The Universal Declaration of Human Rights

In 1948, the United Nations sought to address some of the concerns about the lack of human rights in some countries by passing the Universal Declaration of Human Rights. In its Preamble, it says:

> ❝ … disregard and contempt for human rights have resulted in barbarous acts which have outraged the conscience of mankind, and the advent of a world in which human beings shall enjoy freedom of speech and belief and freedom from fear and want has been proclaimed as the highest aspiration of the common people. ❞
>
> *Universal Declaration of Human Rights*

Thirty articles in the Universal Declaration of Human Rights outline what should be every person's human rights. For example:

> ❝ All human beings are born free and equal in dignity and rights. They are endowed with reason and conscience and should act towards one another in a spirit of brotherhood. ❞
>
> *Universal Declaration of Human Rights, article 1*

> Everyone has the right to freedom of thought, conscience and religion … ❞
>
> *Universal Declaration of Human Rights, article 18*

Objectives

- Understand the need for laws to protect human rights.
- Understand Sikh teachings, beliefs and attitudes about human rights, and explore the responsibilities that come with human rights.

Key terms

- **human rights:** the basic rights and freedoms to which all human beings should be entitled
- **responsibility:** a duty to care for, or having control over, something or someone

Activities

1 Give some examples of where human rights are being abused in the world.
2 Explain why the Universal Declaration of Human Rights was made.
3 Explain Sikh attitudes to human rights.
4 Explain why Sikhs believe that everyone has the responsibility not to abuse their human rights.

Research activity

Use the internet or library to find out more about the Sikh Human Rights Group.

Sikhism and human rights

Sikhism is founded on the principles of working towards the common good of all. For Sikhs, this means reaching out to serve all humanity and creation as an expression of devotion to God, who created all things. Sikhs believe in promoting respect for all life, and encouraging everyone to consider others and protect human rights. In protecting or seeking to spread their own religious beliefs or their own traditions or culture, people sometimes attack the beliefs and ways of others. Sikhs recognise this danger, and encourage everyone to care for their neighbour and protect their human rights, even if they belong to another faith. Guru Tegh Bahadur set an example when he supported the Kashmiri Hindus to protect their way of life. Lord Indarjit Singh of Wimbledon, in response to an attack on Sikhs, said in the House of Lords in February 2016 that 'Human rights abuses against anyone are the responsibility of us all.'

Speech

Education

Religion

Marriage

Human rights

Security

Rest

Freedom

Privacy

▲ *Some of the freedoms that human rights laws seek to protect*

Sikh Human Rights Group

The Sikh Human Rights Group was formed in 1984 in response to the deteriorating human rights situation in North West India. It consists of volunteers and professionals who campaign to protect and promote human rights, and resolve conflicts in a peaceful way. They support minority rights, diversity and sustainable development, and take an active role in conferences and writing reports. Its approach and aims are based on Sikh principles of promoting equality, religious rights and freedom of thought and speech. The organisation works with the United Nations and other groups that share its aims to support human rights.

Responsibilities

Along with having human rights comes the **responsibility** to respect the rights of others. It would be wrong to abuse the right of freedom of speech by preaching hatred and stirring up prejudice and violence. Instead of deliberately offending people, there is the responsibility to listen to the views of others, even if they are different from our own. If children have the right to be protected from exploitation and neglect, they also have a responsibility not to bully or harm each other. This principle applies to all the human rights. It would be hypocritical for a person to insist on having human rights if they abuse them themselves and deny others the same rights. These ideas have been brought together in a Universal Declaration of Human Responsibilities proposed by the InterAction Council, which has been endorsed by secular and religious leaders from around the world.

▲ *Peaceful protest is one way to demand human rights for everyone*

⭐ Study tip

It would be helpful to know some specific examples of rights given by the Universal Declaration of Human Rights and be able to explain their importance.

Summary

You should now be able to explain the need for laws to protect people's rights, and Sikh attitudes towards human rights.

■ Sikhism and equality

Sikhism teaches that, in the eyes of God, all people are of equal value regardless of caste, colour, class, gender, religion or wealth.

> 66 Recognise the Lord's Light within all, and do not consider social class or status; there are no classes or castes in the world hereafter. 99
>
> *Guru Granth Sahib 349*

When Sikhism began, the caste system was very important in Hinduism and India. People of a high class would have nothing to do with a person from a lower caste. Food was served to servants and workers who sat on the floor, while those of a higher caste sat on chairs and tables. Sikhism rejected the caste system, and the first Guru, Guru Nanak, started the first langar, a free community kitchen. Each gurdwara has a langar where everyone is treated as equals, irrespective of their religion or background. The Sikh congregation and their guests sit together on the floor and no one is regarded as superior or inferior. Guru Gobind Singh gave all Sikh men the last name 'Singh' and all Sikh women the last name 'Kaur', so that no one could identify anyone's caste. Guru Nanak said, 'There is neither Hindu nor Muslim' because everyone is equal in Sikhism. All people have been created by God:

> 66 All beings and creatures are His; He belongs to all. 99
>
> *Guru Granth Sahib 425*

■ What is social justice?

Social justice is about making sure that no one is exploited and everyone enjoys equal treatment. It means everyone receives a fair allocation of community resources and their human rights are protected. Where there is injustice, it is challenged, and care is taken of the least advantaged members of society. In some countries this is not the situation. Sometimes this is because of a breakdown of law and order or because the government does not treat everyone fairly, or because of a vast difference between wealthy people and people living in poverty. Those who wish to see social justice support fairer treatment for everyone and equal opportunities for everyone, irrespective of their age, disability, gender, politics, race, religion or sexuality.

Objectives

- Understand what is meant by social justice.
- Understand Sikh beliefs about **equality** and social justice.

Key terms

- **equality:** the state of being equal, especially in status, rights and opportunities
- **social justice:** the promotion of fairness in the distribution of wealth, opportunities and privileges in society
- **justice:** bringing about what is right and fair according to the law, or making up for a wrong that has been committed

▲ *An international day promoting social justice and encouraging those working to alleviate poverty and inequality is held on 20 February every year*

■ Sikhs and social justice

Sikhs believe that it is important to earn an honest living, to share with those in need, to give selfless service to the community and to pray. The practice of these principles helps towards achieving social justice. Work is seen as worship and, through earning a wage, the basic necessities of life, food, shelter and warmth can be provided. Supporting good charities and causes also helps those in need. For example, the sharing of food at the langar helps members of society who are struggling financially. Sikhs are expected to do voluntary work and to serve the community without expecting any reward or recognition. They also have a duty to pray and spend time contemplating the name of God.

▲ Sikhs in the UK protesting against the caste system in India, which creates inequality

Sikhs are concerned that there is disease, exploitation, hunger, poverty and injustice in many parts of the world. This situation cries out for people to consider the purpose of life and to understand God's creation. Sikhism calls for a world society of people who recognise that God and spiritual things are important. God-conscious (gurmukh) people are motivated by an intense desire to do good, transforming their surroundings and bringing about social justice. Sikhs are required to stand up for the rights of the weak, and to fight for **justice** and fairness for all. Guru Gobind Singh set up the Khalsa, whose members have stood up for the rights of the oppressed and spoken out against anyone who has threatened the dignity of human beings. Khalsa members believe that everyone should enjoy the fruits of God's wonderful creation.

> **"** **God does not ask about social class or birth;** you must find your true home. That is your social class and that is your status – the karma of what you have done. **"**
>
> *Guru Granth Sahib 1330*

Discussion activity

With a small group or in pairs, discuss the following statement:

'It's a dream to think that there will be social justice in every country in the world. It will never happen, so what is the point in trying to bring it about?'

★ Study tip

When studying other parts of this chapter, consider how they relate to social justice, for example the responsibilities and uses of wealth (see pages 164–165).

Summary

You should now be able to explain Sikh beliefs about equality and social justice.

Activities

1 What does Sikhism teach about equality?
2 Give examples of how Sikhs have to put their beliefs about equality into action.
3 What is meant by the term social justice?
4 Explain how Sikhs support the idea of social justice.
5 'It's the duty of everyone to stand up for the oppressed.' Do you agree? Give reasons for your opinion.

Religious freedom in the UK

The main religious tradition in Britain is Christianity, but people of other faiths are free to worship in the way they choose. This has not always been the case. During times in the past when Roman Catholics and Protestants were hostile towards each other, certain kinds of worship were forbidden. Nowadays, the Human Rights Act 1998 and the Universal Declaration of Human Rights give protection to the individual regarding **freedom of religion**. The law allows people to obey their conscience, and promotes tolerance and respect for those who hold different beliefs. People in Britain are allowed **freedom of religious expression**, providing it does not stir up hatred against others of different beliefs. Individuals may choose to belong to any religion or have no religion at all. This means that religious believers, such as Buddhists, Christians, Hindus, Jews, Muslims and Sikhs, can have places of worship and openly follow their faith without fear of persecution. UK groups like the Inter Faith Network promote good relations, understanding and cooperation between people of the different faiths.

Sikhs and religious freedom

Sikhs believe that there is only one God, and that he is the same God for all religions and for everyone in the world. However, Sikhs do not claim to have a monopoly on the truth or to be the only path to God. Most Sikhs are not just tolerant of other faiths, but genuinely respect the devotion of those faiths.

> **❝** Do not say that the Vedas, the Bible and the Koran are false. Those who do not contemplate them are false. **❞**
>
> *Guru Granth Sahib 1350*

The Adi Granth contains hymns from Hindu and Muslim writers as well as the Sikh Gurus. The Gurus taught that the faith into which someone is born is the faith that they should try to excel in. Sikhs are more concerned about the moral behaviour of a person rather than the religion they follow.

For example, one of Guru Nanak's closest friends was Bhai Mardana, a Muslim, who travelled with him on many of his journeys. The fact that they were of different faiths did not matter. Guru Tegh Bahadur was prepared to risk his life to help to protect Kashmiri Hindus, because he believed that they should have the right to freely follow the faith of their choice. So Sikhs believe that everyone should have the freedom to follow their own religion and express their faith in their own way.

Objective

- Explore issues of freedom of religion and belief, including religious expression.

Key terms

- **freedom of religion:** the right to believe or practise whatever religion one chooses
- **freedom of religious expression:** the right to worship, preach and practise one's faith in whatever way one chooses, provided it is within the law

▲ *Sikhs are allowed to carry a kirpan in public in the UK if it is for religious reasons; other blades are banned*

In the UK, Sikhs can worship in their own gurdwaras and have the freedom to express their religion as they wish. Sikh men and women are allowed to wear the five Ks in Britain. These are five symbols of their faith. These are kachhehra, cotton shorts; kangha, a wooden comb; kara, a steel bracelet; kesh, uncut hair; and kirpan, a ceremonial dagger. The uncut hair is worn underneath a turban, and special laws have been passed enabling Sikhs to wear their turbans when other citizens have to wear protective headgear. For example, the British Parliament passed a law in 1976 that 'exempts any follower of the Sikh religion while he is wearing a turban' from having to wear a crash helmet when riding a motorbike. Similarly, Sikhs are allowed to wear turbans at work, although there were problems at construction sites where employers were concerned about their employees' safety. In some countries, the wearing of a real kirpan is banned in public for safety reasons, and so many Sikhs wear a small symbolic one. Although these items make a Sikh stand out from the rest of society, the laws in Britain give them the freedom to express their religion in this way.

▲ *In Britain, Sikhs are allowed to wear a turban at work*

Discussion activity

With a partner, in a small group or as a class, discuss whether you agree with the following: 'People should not be pressured into joining any religion.'

Contrasting beliefs

Use the internet to find out more about Christian beliefs about freedom of religious expression, and inter-faith organisations, such as the Inter Faith Network for the UK.

Links

Read more about the five Ks on page 21.

Read about the 1976 Motor-Cycle Crash Helmets (Religious Exemption) Act on page 121.

⭐ Study tip

If you are asked to express an opinion about religious freedom and freedom of religious expression, include your own personal view and the reasons why you have arrived at your conclusion.

Summary

You should now be able to explain Sikh views concerning freedom of religion and freedom of religious expression.

Activities

1 What laws have been adopted in the UK that give people freedom of choice regarding religious belief and religious expression?

2 Explain what Sikhs mean when they say that they do not have the monopoly on truth.

3 Give two examples of how the Gurus showed respect for people of other faiths.

4 Explain ways that show how Sikhs are free to express their religion in the UK in the way that they choose.

5 'All people everywhere should be free to express their religious beliefs in any way they choose.' Do you agree? Give reasons for your answer.

■ Prejudice and discrimination

Prejudice is judging or thinking of a person in a biased way, for example thinking less or more of them because of their age, colour, race, religion or sex. Prejudice is not illegal because an attitude or thought cannot be illegal. However, a prejudiced attitude can lead to illegal **discrimination**, such as refusing a person a job because of their race or religion. In the UK, several Acts of Parliament have been passed to make discrimination illegal, including the Race Relations Act of 1976, the Race Relations (Amendment) Act 2000 and the Equality Act 2010.

Positive discrimination is not illegal because it is designed to help a person or minority group. For example, wheelchair users may be given front seats at a football stadium so they can see the football match. Sometimes positive discrimination is used to help those who have not been given equal opportunities in the past. This might include employing more women in senior roles, or employing people from minority ethnic groups.

■ Sikh attitudes towards prejudice and discrimination

Sikhism teaches that God (Waheguru) created every person and is in everyone, so Sikhs should not show prejudice against anyone. Guru Nanak said that there is no Hindu and no Muslim, meaning that everyone is the same in God's eyes, and so should be treated with respect, fairness and justice. Article 2 in the United Nations Universal Declaration of Human Rights reflects Sikh teaching:

▲ A Sikh at an inter-faith rally in Birmingham

> 66 Everyone is entitled to all the rights and freedoms set forth in this Declaration, without distinction of any kind, such as race, colour, sex, language, religion, political or other opinion, national or social origin, property, birth or other status. 99
>
> *Universal Declaration of Human Rights*

Objectives

- Understand the difference between prejudice and discrimination.
- Investigate Sikh beliefs about same-sex sexual relationships, racial prejudice and discrimination.

Key terms

- **prejudice:** unfairly judging someone before the facts are known; holding biased opinions about an individual or group
- **discrimination:** actions or behaviour that result from prejudice
- **positive discrimination:** treating people more favourably because they have been discriminated against in the past
- **racism:** showing prejudice against someone because of their ethnic group or nationality

Discussion activities

In small groups or in pairs discuss the following statements:

1 'It is impossible to stop prejudice and discrimination. Neither laws nor religion will prevent it.'

2 'No Sikh should be opposed to same-sex sexual relationships.'

The Sikh Gurus taught that **racism** is wrong.

> ❝ The clay is the same, but the Fashioner has fashioned it in various ways. There is nothing wrong with the pot of clay – there is nothing wrong with the Potter. ❞
>
> *Guru Granth Sahib 1350*

This means that everyone, whatever their race, has been created by God and so is of equal value. Sikhs, for example, welcome people of all races to join them in eating together in the langar. No distinction is made concerning a person's colour, race or religion.

Guru Nanak and the subsequent Gurus opposed the caste system, which was very important in Hindu society when Sikhism began. Sikhs do not regard anyone as second-class citizens. The Gurus taught social and religious equality, and encouraged people to worship together, whatever their background. Sikhs welcome people to worship with them because they are taught that prejudice and discrimination are wrong.

▲ *People of all races and religions are welcome to eat in a Sikh langar*

■ Same-sex sexual relationships

The Guru Granth Sahib and Sikh Gurus did not mention same-sex sexual relationships, but did encourage opposite-sex marriage and the life of a householder (family life). Most Sikhs believe that same-sex sexual relationships are not acceptable. They are not mentioned in the scriptures and are not part of the lifestyle taught by the Gurus. Some point to the Sikh Code of Conduct, and say that since lust is one of the five evils, it suggests that same-sex sexual relationships are wrong because people are lusting after members of their own sex. Others say that the teaching about lust applies equally to opposite-sex sexual relationships, and does not indicate that same-sex sexual relationships themselves are wrong. Some argue that the soul does not have a gender, so same-sex sexual relationships should be permitted. The goal of a Sikh is to feel no hatred towards any person, regardless of their caste, gender, race, religion or sexuality. Most Sikhs do not treat same-sex sexual relationships as a matter of importance. Sikhs are more interested in attaining enlightenment and becoming one with God, than concerning themselves with a person's sexuality.

> ❝ God does not ask about social class or birth … ❞
>
> *Guru Granth Sahib 1330*

⭐ Study tip

When discussing issues like prejudice and discrimination, it is important to know teachings from the Guru Granth Sahib or the example of actions taken by the Gurus.

Summary

You should now know the difference between prejudice and discrimination, and be able to explain Sikh attitudes to same-sex sexual relationships and racism.

Activities

1 Explain the difference between prejudice and discrimination.
2 What is positive discrimination?
3 Explain Sikh attitudes to racism.
4 Why did Sikhs oppose the caste system in India?
5 Explain Sikh attitudes to same-sex sexual relationships.

■ Treatment of women

In the past, in some societies, women have been treated as though their opinions are not as important as men's. Their **role** in many communities was seen as limited to having children, bringing up the family and looking after the home. In many ways, women were treated as inferior, and denied independent thought and **status**. This was true of Indian society at the time that Sikhism began. The function of a woman was seen to be to serve male members of society. The practice of sati was common in Hindu society. This meant that if the husband died, the wife was encouraged to be cremated alive with her husband's body. Guru Amar Das denounced sati, and condemned all practices in which women were not equal to men.

■ The status of women in Sikhism

The Guru Granth Sahib stresses the importance of women in bringing about the existence of the whole human race. There is no suggestion that women are in any way inferior to men, or should be treated as if they are less important:

> ❝ From woman, man is born; within woman, man is conceived; to woman he is engaged and married. Woman becomes his friend; through woman, the future generations come. When his woman dies, he seeks another woman; to woman he is bound. So why call her bad? From her, kings are born. From woman, woman is born; without woman, there would be no one at all. ❞
>
> *Guru Granth Sahib 473*

■ Role in leadership

In many religions, only men are allowed leadership roles. For example, in some Christian denominations like Roman Catholicism, the priests are men. In Islam, the imams are male and in Orthodox Judaism the rabbis are all men. This is not the case in Sikhism. The position of men and women are equal in both secular and religious areas of life.

The Gurus taught that God is in every person:

> ❝ The Beloved Himself enjoys every heart; **He is contained within every woman and man.** ❞
>
> *Guru Granth Sahib 605*

▲ *Women are allowed to lead worship in Sikhism*

Objective

● Explore beliefs about the status, role and treatment of women within Sikhism.

Key terms

● **role:** the actions a person performs; what they do
● **status:** how important a person's role makes them in other people's estimation

Discussion activity

In pairs or small groups, discuss the following statement:
'Any gender prejudice and discrimination within society or religion is wrong.'

There is no difference between the soul of a man or a woman, so both should have the same opportunities. Guru Nanak welcomed women into the sangat (congregation) as equal to men with no restrictions. He believed that the message about God was as much for women as for men, and therefore there should be no gender distinctions. The Gurus encouraged freedom of speech and full participation in worship for women and men alike. In Sikhism, women take part in all religious activities, including reading the Guru Granth Sahib to the congregation, and so have equal status to men. Women may serve as the granthi and lead prayers and worship, participate in the Akhand Path (the continuous reading of the Guru Granth Sahib), perform kirtan (congregational singing of hymns) and take part in all activities in the gurdwara. Women as well as men help to spread the faith. For example, Guru Amar Ras sent out fifty-two women as missionaries. No role is kept solely for men.

▲ *The Gurus encouraged freedom of speech for women and men alike*

■ Sikh beliefs

Guru Angad encouraged women as well as men to get a good education. A good education for all is seen as extremely important in Sikhism. The Rehat Maryada (Sikh Code of Conduct) places no restrictions on women, except that wearing clothes which expose the body could breed lustful thoughts, and so is considered dishonourable for both men and women.

Guru Amar Das condemned the practice of women wearing the veil, and he also forbade female infanticide (the killing of female new born babies). Guru Gobind Singh made the initiation ceremony into the Khalsa available for both genders. During the amrit ceremony, men are given the name Singh, which means lion, and women are given the name Kaur, which means princess. A woman keeps this name for the rest of her life and does not have to take her husband's name. Both men and women keep the five Ks. Sikhism does not allow polygamy, and strongly supports marriage as a partnership between a man and a woman. It is seen as important to bring up the family together.

> ❝ O Baba, the pleasures of other clothes are false. Wearing them, the body is ruined, and wickedness and corruption enter into the mind. ❞
>
> *Guru Granth Sahib 16*

Contrasting beliefs

Use the internet or books to find out about the status of women in Christianity. Compare Roman Catholicism with, for example, a Church of England or Methodist view.

⭐ Study tip

It would be helpful to be able to compare and contrast the status of women in religion between Sikhism and Christianity.

Summary

You should now be able to explain Sikh beliefs about the status, role and treatment of women within Sikhism.

Activities

1 Give examples of how, in the past, women were treated as inferior to men.
2 Explain what the Guru Granth Sahib says about the status of women.
3 Explain how Sikh women are treated as equals in Sikh worship.
4 Give examples of how the Sikh Gurus encouraged gender equality.
5 Do you think that it is a good idea for all Sikh men to be called 'Singh' and all Sikh women to have the name 'Kaur'? Give reasons for your answer.

■ Uses of wealth

Sikhs believe that they have a responsibility to try to make the world a better, more equal place for everyone. The value of money is in the good that it can do, rather than what it is.

Wealth is seen as a blessing if it is used to help others or redistribute riches so that there is more equality in the world. There are many people in the world who suffer from poverty while others live in luxury.

Many people in low-income countries have a very low standard of living. These people have limited access to a good education, modern medical care and technology. Sikhs are concerned about social justice, and believe everyone should have a right to enjoy the wealth God has provided. So Sikhs are encouraged to give **dasvandh**, at least one tenth of their income, to help with community projects. It is seen as very important to show kindness and do righteous acts to help the community and those in need.

■ The right attitude to wealth

The Sikh Gurus taught that people should earn an honest living while remembering God. The Guru Granth Sahib reminds Sikhs that wealth is not permanent. It cannot be taken on to a new reincarnation.

 India, where the majority of Sikhs live, is a low-income country where many people live in poverty

> ❝ O mortal, why are you so proud of small things? With a few pounds of grain and a few coins in your pocket, you are totally puffed up with pride. With great pomp and ceremony, you control a hundred villages, with an income of hundreds of thousands of pounds. The power you exert will last for only a few days, like the green leaves of the forest. **No one has brought this wealth with him, and no one will take it with him when he goes.** Emperors, even greater than Raawan, passed away in an instant. ❞
>
> *Guru Granth Sahib 1251*

However, being poor is not seen as a virtue and essential for goodness. What needs to be avoided is the evil of greed.

> ❝ The greedy mind is enticed by greed. Forgetting the Lord, it regrets and repents in the end. ❞
>
> *Guru Granth Sahib 1172*

Key terms

● **dasvandh:** giving one tenth of annual produce or earnings to help the community

● **illusion:** everything in the world which seems real, but is not; in Sikhism, called maya

Discussion activities

In small groups or in pairs discuss the following statements:

1 'Greed makes people forget about God.'

2 'Wealth is only useful for the good that it can do.'

The Gurus warned that becoming attached to possessions and being greedy for wealth is foolish and wrong. Guru Nanak said that the accumulation of wealth is not possible without sins, and Guru Amar Das suggested that the worshipper of maya (**illusion**) is utterly lost.

> ❝ Maya is a serpent, clinging to the world. Whoever serves her, she ultimately devours. ❞
>
> *Guru Granth Sahib 510*

Sikhs are taught that nothing should distract them from becoming God-centred (gurmukh):

> ❝ You shall have to abandon the straw which you have collected. These entanglements shall be of no use to you. ❞
>
> *Guru Granth Sahib 676*

▲ *Sikhs believe they should use their wealth to help those in the community, for example donating to charities that provide children with education*

Contrasting beliefs

Use the internet or a library to find out about Christian beliefs about the uses of money. Do any differ from Sikh beliefs?

Stories from Sikh tradition

Guru Nanak meets Duni Chand

In Sikh tradition there is a story about Guru Nanak meeting a rich man called Duni Chand. Duni Chand was very proud of his wealth, and had the ambition to become the richest man in Lahore. Consequently, he devoted himself to gaining riches and ignored the plight of those living in poverty. When Guru Nanak visited his country (present day Pakistan), he gave him a needle and asked him to look after it and return it to him after the next reincarnation. At first, Duni Chand felt honoured, but later realised that it was impossible to take it to the next world because no one can take anything with them into the next incarnation. So he gave it back to Guru Nanak, saying that there was no way of taking it to the next world. The Guru then pointed out that Duni Chand would not be able to take his millions with him either. Instead of hoarding his riches, it would be much more sensible to share his money in the name of God with those who were struggling because of poverty. As a result, he would gain good karma which would go with him to the next world. It is said that Duni Chand listened to the advice and began sharing his wealth with people who needed it.

Activities

1 According to Sikhs, what is the value of money?

2 Why do Sikhs believe that having money isn't something that is permanent?

3 What does the Guru Granth Sahib say about greed?

4 What did Guru Amar Das mean when he said that 'maya is a serpent'?

5 Explain what Duni Chand learned from his meeting with Guru Nanak.

Summary

You should now be able to explain Sikh beliefs about wealth and its uses.

 Study tip

You should aim to be able to compare and contrast Sikh beliefs about money and its use with those of Christianity.

■ Poverty

Poverty is a major problem in the world. More than 1.3 billion people live in extreme poverty surviving on less than £1 a day. Hunger causes more deaths and disease than anything else in the world. UNICEF estimates that around 22,000 children die each day due to the effects of poverty. The charity Oxfam estimates that it would cost around £40 billion annually to end extreme worldwide poverty. That is less than a quarter of the income of the top 100 richest billionaires. Sikhs believe that this is wrong, and they work towards a redistribution of wealth so that there is more fairness in society. Sikh teaching emphasises the importance of sharing and of service (sewa).

A major factor in causing poverty is unreliable or extreme climate conditions. For example, droughts may result in insufficient water for drinking, to support livestock and to grow crops. Diseases can also cause problems, for example HIV/AIDS and malaria. Corruption, **exploitation**, war and population growth are all causes of poverty. Governments in low-income countries are unable to provide sufficient health care, and productivity is low as a result. Often they have borrowed large amounts of money and, in order to pay the interest on the loans, crops are sold to other countries rather than used to feed the local people. Sikhs oppose excessive interest rates on loans because they support the idea of social justice. Individuals may also borrow money at very high rates of interest, and then find it extremely difficult to make the repayments. Sikhs are encouraged to work, share, and remember God. They would not want to get themselves into situations where they are paying excessive interest on loans to unscrupulous lenders.

■ Work and fair pay

Guru Nanak taught that it is important for Sikhs to make sure they do honest work. Sikhism teaches that those who are poor have a responsibility to try and get themselves out of poverty, rather than just beg others to help them. Not working is regarded as being lazy and selfish if jobs are available. Whether it is manual, skilled or professional work does not matter. However, some jobs, such as sex work and the production of harmful intoxicants

▲ *Poverty is a major problem around the world, and one that many Sikhs are trying to help solve*

and drugs, are regarded as unacceptable. Gambling is not encouraged because it is not regarded as earning a living honestly. Sikh employers have a duty to give employees good working conditions and fair wages. In return, employees should work honestly and earn their reward. In some countries, workers suffer from exploitation at the hands of employers. Forcing children and adults to work extremely long hours in poor conditions for little pay is seen as unjust. Most Sikhs support the introduction of the minimum wage and the national **living wage** in the UK because it helps to prevent workers from being exploited.

▲ *Harjit Singh Sajjan; a Sikh earning an honest living by setting an example of truthful leadership Sajjan is the Former Canadian Minister of National Defence*

■ People-trafficking

People-trafficking is an international problem which is opposed by Sikhs. Millions of people are trafficked worldwide, and because it is a criminal business it is very difficult to wipe out. The vast majority of victims are women and children. Many victims of people-trafficking are exploited for labour, such as domestic work, construction or agriculture. Others are victims of forced marriage or forced sexual exploitation.

In August 2014, the Essex police found a group of thirty-five men, women and children inside a shipping container. People-smugglers had been paid to illegally transport this group, who originally came from Afghanistan. They were discovered when screaming and banging was heard from inside the container. When they were let out one man was already dead and the rest were suffering from severe dehydration and hypothermia. This is not a unique story, and those who survive are often exploited by criminal people-trafficking gangs because they do not have the papers to work lawfully.

> ### Discussion activity
>
> In small groups or in pairs, discuss the following statement: 'It is impossible to stop the exploitation of people.'

Study tip

It is useful to write some summaries of the main points on poverty, fair pay and people-trafficking.

Activities

1 Record three facts about those who are suffering from poverty.
2 What are the main causes of poverty?
3 According to Sikhs, what responsibilities do those in poverty have?
4 Explain why Sikhs support the idea of a fair wage for a fair day's work.
5 How are humans exploited by people-trafficking?

> **Summary**
>
> You should now be able to discuss issues surrounding poverty, the exploitation of people living in poverty, excessive interest on loans and the problem of people-trafficking.

■ Giving aid

Sometimes aid is needed immediately following an emergency. This may be after a natural disaster, such as an earthquake, tsunami, flood or drought. The destruction caused may leave people homeless and unable to look after themselves or their families. Food, drinking water, shelter and medical care are required as quickly as possible for the survivors. Immediate help is known as **emergency aid**. In addition, the infrastructure of the area needs to be repaired. This may take years to complete and requires a lot of investment. Money given to help with the reconstruction is known as **long-term aid**. Long-term aid may also assist with projects that will enable people to become more self-sufficient, for example by providing education and training for farmers in better agricultural methods, or the provision of irrigation projects. Sikhs see it as their duty to be involved with both emergency and long-term aid.

Guru Amar Das started the practice among Sikhs of giving a tenth of their surplus wealth to the service of the community. This religious obligation of regular giving is known as dasvandh, and the gifts are often used for projects such as building hospitals or schools or maintaining the gurdwaras. Dasvandh is a similar idea to tithing in Christianity. Sewa or service to the community (sadh sangat) is an important part of Sikhism.

Guru Nanak set up the langar in the gurdwara so that the community could eat together. A free meal is provided for everyone, whatever their race or religion, so no one is hungry. Sikhs regard it as a privilege and a duty to share in the tasks of preparation, providing the food, cooking, serving and cleaning.

Objective

● Understand how Sikhs assist those in poverty, including the work of Sikh charities.

Key terms

● **emergency aid:** also known as short-term aid; help given to communities in a time of disaster or crisis, e.g. food during a famine, shelter after an earthquake

● **long-term aid:** assistance given to a low-income country over a long period of time that has a lasting effect

▲ Long-term aid, such as training and equipment for farmers, helps people to become more self-sufficient

Sikh Aid International

The belief in equality and compassion encourages Sikhs to share their wealth by supporting good causes and charities. One such charity is Sikh Aid International, which is based in Birmingham. Run by volunteers, it is committed to helping those in need, regardless of their race, religion or gender, and it works with other organisations with similar aims. The founder, Dr Manjit Singh Bhogal, originally began by treating people with homeopathic medicine, and inspired others to join him in voluntary sewa. Now, Sikh Aid helps those suffering in many parts of the world. Its work includes providing eye and dental clinics in poor areas of India with the aim of curing eye ailments and giving dental treatment. The charity seeks to serve humanity by providing education, help for victims of disaster, and by showing love and compassion.

> ❝ In the midst of this world, do sewa, and you shall be given a place of honour in the Court of the Lord. ❞
>
> *Guru Granth Sahib 26*

Khalsa Aid

Khalsa Aid began in 1999, and is founded on the Sikh principles of selfless service and love. Those who work for the charity are volunteers, and it is mainly funded by Sikhs based in Britain. The organisation also has voluntary workers in Asia and North America who are involved in fundraising or Khalsa Aid projects. Since its formation, it has given assistance to those affected by natural disasters and wars in many countries of the world.

Khalsa Aid's first project was to provide food and shelter to thousands of refugees on the Albania/Yugoslavia border. The following year, help was given to the victims of a cyclone which hit the state of Orissa on the eastern side of India, and in 2001 medical aid was provided after an earthquake in Turkey. Since then the organisation has provided emergency aid in many countries, including the Democratic Republic of Congo, Somalia, Pakistan, Bangladesh and Haiti. An extension of the charity, Langar Aid, has been active in the Middle East in response to the violence in Iraq and Syria. It has made free bread and water available for refugees and those fleeing the fighting.

▲ *In 1999, Khalsa Aid provided help to the victims of the cyclone in Orissa, mainly by providing educational materials for over 6000 children*

Activities

1   What is the difference between emergency aid and long-term aid?
2   Give two reasons why some people may need assistance.
3   What is meant by dasvandh?
4   Explain what Sikh Aid International and Khalsa Aid do to help those in need.
5   Explain how these charities reflect the Sikh principles of selfless service and love.

Discussion activity

In small groups or pairs discuss the following statement: 'Everyone should give a tenth of their income to help those in need.'

Research activity

Use the internet to find out about current projects being carried out by Sikh charities.

> ❝ All men are the same though they appear different. The bright and the dark, the ugly and the beautiful, The Hindus and the Muslims have developed in accordance with their different surroundings; All human beings have the same eyes, the same ears … All human beings are the reflection of one and the same Lord. Recognise ye the whole human race as one. ❞
>
> *Guru Gobind Singh*

⭐ Study tip

It is important to be able to explain the work that Sikh charities do. Knowing up-to-date examples of current or recent projects is useful. Remember that it is the faith of Sikhs which inspires them to help people in need.

Summary

You should now know how Sikhs assist those in need, including the work of two Sikh charities.

Human rights – summary

You should now be able to:

- ✔ explain prejudice and discrimination in religion and belief, including the status and treatment within Sikhism of women and people who are attracted to people of the same sex
- ✔ explain issues of equality, freedom of religion and belief, including freedom of religious expression
- ✔ explain what is meant by human rights and the responsibilities that come with rights, including the responsibility to respect the rights of others
- ✔ explain Sikh views about social justice
- ✔ explain Sikh attitudes to racial prejudice and discrimination.

Wealth and poverty – summary

You should now be able to:

- ✔ explain Sikh teachings about wealth, including the right attitude to wealth and the uses of wealth

- ✔ explain the responsibilities of having wealth, including the duty to tackle poverty and its causes
- ✔ describe and explain the problem of exploitation of people living in poverty, including issues relating to fair pay, excessive interest on loans and people-trafficking
- ✔ explain the responsibilities of those living in poverty to help themselves overcome the difficulties they face
- ✔ explain what Sikhism teaches about charity, including issues related to giving money to people living in poverty
- ✔ explain contrasting perspectives in contemporary British society about all the above issues
- ✔ explain contrasting beliefs in contemporary British society about the three issues of the status of women in religion, the uses of wealth, and freedom of religious expression, with reference to the main religious tradition in Britain (Christianity) and non-religious beliefs such as atheism or humanism.

Sample student answer – the 12-mark question

1. Write an answer to the following practice question:

   'Racism is the worst form of prejudice.'

   Evaluate this statement.
   In your answer you:
   - should give reasoned arguments to support this statement
   - should give reasoned arguments to support a different point of view
   - should refer to religious arguments
   - may refer to non-religious arguments
   - should reach a justified conclusion.

   [12 marks]
   [+ 3 SPaG marks]

2. Read the following student sample answer:

   "Many would argue that all prejudice is wrong, whether it is racial, religious, caste, disability or gender. Racism is a particularly nasty form of prejudice if it develops into discrimination. It can lead to such hatred that people kill each other. Examples of this include the Nazis sending millions of Jewish people to death camps and the genocide that took place in Rwanda between different ethnic groups. If one race of people have suffered at the hands of a different race during a war, then I could understand why they might feel prejudice. But Sikhs discourage this because they believe in equality. Others may say that when it comes to sport, then there is nothing wrong in being prejudiced in favour of your own national team so racism in that sense isn't bad.

   At the time of Guru Nanak, the caste system was very strong in India. People were very prejudiced against people lowest on the hierarchy ('untouchables') and treated them as second-class citizens. Sikhs believe that class prejudice is very wrong and that everyone should be treated equally and with respect. Many would argue that it is just as bad as racial prejudice. The practice of sati, the result of gender prejudice, is also something which has been opposed by Sikhs. Men and women should be thought of as equals and prejudice against either is wrong.

Personally I believe that all negative prejudice is wrong as it leads to discrimination, which may have a devastating effect on people. Racism is particularly bad if it leads to hatred and violence. So many people have been killed because of racism."

3. With a partner, discuss the sample answer. Is the focus of the answer correct? Is anything missing from the answer? How do you think it could be improved?

4. What mark (out of 12) would you give this answer? Look at the mark scheme in the Introduction (AO2). What are the reasons for the mark you have given?

5. Now swap your answer with your partner's and mark each other's responses. What mark (out of 12) would you give the response? Refer to the mark scheme and give reasons for the mark you award.

Practice questions

1 Which **one** of the following is the main religious tradition in Great Britain?

A) Buddhism   **B)** Christianity   **C)** Islam   **D)** Sikhism   **[1 mark]**

2 Give **one** cause of poverty.   **[1 mark]**

3 Explain **two** different beliefs in contemporary British society about what role women should be allowed in worship.

In your answer you should refer to the main religious tradition of Great Britain and one or more other religious traditions.   **[4 marks]**

> **Study tip**
>
> Make sure you develop the points you are making. This may be done by giving detailed information, such as referring to examples. Include different beliefs in your answer. This can be done by referring to a Christian belief and a different view from another religion such as Sikhism.

4 Explain **two** religious beliefs about social justice.

Refer to sacred writings or another source of religious belief and teaching in your answer.   **[6 marks]**

5 'All religious believers must give to charities that help people living in poverty.'

Evaluate this statement.

In your answer you:

- should give reasoned arguments to support this statement
- should give reasoned arguments to support a different point of view
- should refer to religious arguments
- may refer to non-religious arguments
- should reach a justified conclusion.   **[12 marks]**
    [+ 3 SPaG marks]

> **Study tip**
>
> Note that the question says 'all' religious believers, not some or most. The statement suggests that it should be compulsory for religious believers to give money to charities that support people living in poverty. Give arguments for and against this idea and include religious teachings. Include examples of the work of specific religious charities in the development of your arguments. Include a final concluding paragraph with justified reasons for your opinion.

Glossary

A

abortion: the removal of a foetus from the womb to end a pregnancy, usually before the foetus is 24 weeks old

abuse: misuse; of the world and the environment

adaptation: a process of change, in which an organism or species becomes better suited to its environment

addiction: a physical or mental dependency on a substance or activity that is very difficult to overcome

adultery: voluntary sexual intercourse between a married person and a person who is not their husband or wife

agnostic: someone who thinks there is not enough evidence for belief in God

amrit: a mixture of water and sugar crystals prepared by the Panj Piare, used in the ceremony of initiation and sometimes in a birth ceremony

Amrit Sanskar: the Sikh initiation ceremony

amritdhari: a Sikh who has been initiated into the Khalsa; sometimes known as a 'Khalsa Sikh'

Ardas: the prayer with which Sikhs begin and complete worship

atheist: a person who believes that there is no God

awe: a feeling of respect, mixed feelings of fear and wonder

B

benevolent: all-loving, all-good; a quality of God

Big Bang: a massive expansion of space which set in motion the creation of the universe

bigamy: the offence in the UK of marrying someone while already married to another person

biological weapons: weapons that use living organisms to cause disease or death

C

chauri (chaur sahib): a fan that is waved over the Guru Granth Sahib as a sign of respect

chemical weapons: weapons that use chemicals to harm humans and destroy the natural environment

civil partnership: legal union of same-sex couples

cohabitation: a couple living together and having a sexual relationship without being married to one another

community service: a way of punishing offenders, often by making them do unpaid work in the community

contraception: the methods used to prevent a pregnancy from taking place

corporal punishment: punishment of an offender by causing them physical pain – now illegal in the UK

creation: the act by which God brought the universe into being

Creator: the one who makes things and brings things about

crime: an offence which is punishable by law, for example stealing or murder

D

dasvandh: giving one tenth of annual produce or earnings to help the community

death penalty: capital punishment; form of punishment in which a prisoner is put to death for crimes committed

deforestation: the cutting down of large amounts of forest, usually for business needs

Design argument: the argument that God designed the universe because everything is so intricately made in its detail that it could not have happened by chance

deterrence: an aim of punishment – to put people off committing crimes

dharam yudh: war in defence of righteousness'; the Sikh just war theory

discrimination: actions or behaviour that result from prejudice

Divali: a festival remembering Guru Hargobind; sometimes written as Diwali

divorce: legal ending of a marriage

diwan: originally a royal court; means 'in the court of the Guru'; refers to an act of worship of the Sikh community in a gurdwara

dominion: dominance or power over something; having charge of something or ruling over it

E

educating children in a faith: bringing up children according to the religious beliefs of the parents

effort (saram khand): the third stage of liberation; the limit of development by human effort

emergency aid: also known as short-term aid; help given to communities in a time of disaster or crisis, e.g. food during a famine, shelter after an earthquake

enlightenment: the gaining of true knowledge about God, self or the nature of reality, usually through meditation and self-discipline; in Buddhist, Hindu

and Sikh traditions, gaining freedom from the cycle of rebirth

equality: the state of being equal, especially in status, rights, and opportunities

equality of all: the state of all humans being equal, especially in status, rights and opportunities

eternal: without beginning or end

euthanasia: killing someone painlessly and with compassion, to end their suffering

evil: the opposite of good; a force or the personification of a negative power that is seen in many traditions as destructive and against God

evolution: the process by which living organisms are thought to have developed and diversified from earlier forms of life during the history of the Earth

exploitation: misuse of power or money to get others to do things for little or unfair reward

extended family: a family which extends beyond the nuclear family to include grandparents and other relatives as well

F

faith: a commitment to something that goes beyond proof and knowledge, especially used about God and religion

family: a group of people who are related by blood, marriage or adoption

family planning: the practice of controlling how many children couples have and when they have them

First Cause argument: also known as the cosmological argument; an argument that all things in nature depend on something else for their existence and so must have been started by an independent being, such as God

forgiveness: showing grace and mercy and pardoning someone for what they have done wrong

free will: belief that God gives people the opportunity to make decisions for themselves

freedom of religion: the right to believe or practise whatever religion one chooses

freedom of religious expression: the right to worship, preach and practise one's faith in whatever way one chooses, provided it is within the law

G

gender discrimination: to act against someone on the basis of their gender; discrimination is usually seen as wrong and may be against the law

gender equality: the idea that people should be given the same rights and opportunities regardless of their gender identity

gender prejudice: unfairly judging someone before the facts are known; holding biased opinions about an individual or group based on their gender

general revelation: God making himself known through ordinary, common human experiences

grace (karam khand): the fourth stage of liberation; spiritual blessing given by God

granthi: a person who reads the Guru Granth Sahib and officiates at ceremonies in the gurdwara

greed: selfish desire for something, such as wealth, goods or items of value which are not needed

gurdwara: a Sikh place of worship; it literally means 'the door of the Guru'

gurmukh: God-centred; wisdom-centred

gurpurb: 'festival of a Guru'; festivals which celebrate the anniversary of the birth or death of a Guru

Guru: a spiritual teacher of wisdom; there are ten Gurus in Sikh history, followed by the Guru Granth Sahib, 'the living Guru'

Guru Granth Sahib: the holy scriptures of the Sikh faith, regarded as the ultimate authority

gutka: a prayer book which contains some of the daily or regular prayers from the Guru Granth Sahib

H

Harimandir Sahib: the Golden Temple, the temple of God

hate crimes: crimes, often including violence, that are usually targeted at a person because of their race, religion, sexuality, disability or gender identity

haumai: pride or self (ego); relying only on oneself, not God

heterosexual: sexually attracted to members of the opposite sex

holy war: fighting for a religious cause or God, probably controlled by a religious leader

hukam: the act of opening the Guru Granth Sahib at random and reading a verse

human rights: the basic rights and freedoms to which all human beings should be entitled

human sexuality: how people express themselves as sexual beings

I

illusion: everything in the world which seems real, but is not; in Sikhism called maya

immanent: the idea that God is present in and involved with life on earth and in the universe; a quality of God

impersonal nature (of God): the idea that God has no 'human' characteristics, is unknowable and mysterious, more like an idea or force

J

Japji: a Sikh prayer

just war theory: a set of criteria that a war needs to meet before it can be justified

justice: bringing about what is right and fair, according to the law, or making up for a wrong that has been committed

K

karma: destiny; consequences of one's actions

Khalsa: the community of the 'pure ones'; the body of committed Sikhs

khand: a stage or a part of human spiritual development

kirtan: devotional singing of the hymns from the Guru Granth Sahib

knowledge (gian khand): the second stage of liberation; knowing God through experiencing him

L

langar: 1. Guru's kitchen or the free kitchen within each gurdwara; 2. the food that is served in the kitchen

liberation: freedom from the cycle of life, death and rebirth

living wage: a wage that is high enough to maintain the basic cost of living

long-term aid: assistance given to a low-income country over a long period of time that has a lasting effect

M

manmukh: self-centred; ego-centred

marriage: a legal union between a man and a woman (or in some countries, including the UK, two people of the same sex) as partners in a relationship

mental health problem: a medical condition that affects a person's behaviour, thoughts, feelings or emotions, and sometimes their ability to relate to others

miracle: a seemingly impossible event, usually good, that cannot be explained by natural or scientific laws, and is thought to be the action of God

monotheistic: believing in only one God

Mool Mantra: the 'root chant', a statement of all the core beliefs at the beginning of the Guru Granth Sahib

mukti: the ultimate goal of human life; liberation from the cycle of birth, death and rebirth

mutatin: the changing of the structure of a gene or chromosome which gives the life form a different feature from that of the parents; this difference may be transmitted to following generations

N

nam japna: meditating on the name of God

natural resources: materials found in nature – such as oil and trees – that can be used by people

nature: the physical world including plants, animals and landscape; the environment or natural world

non-renewable resources: raw materials which cannot be replaced when they are used up

nuclear family: a couple and their dependent children regarded as a basic social unit

nuclear weapons: weapons that work by a nuclear reaction; they devastate huge areas and kill large numbers of people

O

omnipotent: almighty, having unlimited power; a quality of God

omniscient: knowing everything; a quality of God

oneness of humanity: the belief that since all humans were created by God, they all have within them the divine spark which unites them

P

pacifism: the belief of people who refuse to take part in war and any other form of violence

palki: a canopy which is placed above the raised platform, above the Guru Granth Sahib

peace: an absence of conflict, which leads to happiness and harmony

peacemaker: a person who works to establish peace in the world or in a certain part of it

people-trafficking: the illegal movement of people, typically for the purposes of forced labour or commercial sexual exploitation

personal nature (of God): the idea that God is an individual or person with whom people are able to have a relationship or feel close to

piety (dharam khand): the first stage of liberation; the opportunity for devotion to God

polygamy: the practice or custom of having more than one wife at the same time

positive discrimination: treating people more favourably because they have been discriminated against in the past

poverty: being without money, food or other basic needs of life (being poor)

prejudice: unfairly judging someone before the facts are known; holding biased opinions about an individual or group

prison: a secure building where offenders are kept for a period of time set by a judge

procreation: bringing babies into the world; producing offspring

proof: evidence that supports the truth of something

protection of children: keeping children safe from harm

protest : an expression of disapproval, often in a public group

punishment: something legally done to somebody as a result of being found guilty of breaking the law

Q

quality of life: the general wellbeing of a person, in relation to their health and happiness; also, the theory that the value of life depends on how good or how satisfying it is

R

racism: showing prejudice against someone because of their ethnic group or nationality

rebirth: the return of the soul, born into a new body

reconciliation: the restoring of harmony after relationships have broken down; a sacrament in the Catholic Church

recycling: reusing old products to make new ones

reformation: an aim of punishment – to change someone's behaviour for the better

reincarnation: being born again into a new body

remarriage: when someone marries again, after a previous marriage or marriages have come to an end

responsibility: a duty to care for, or having control over, something or someone

retaliation: deliberately harming someone as a response to them harming you

retribution: an aim of punishment – to get your own back; 'an eye for an eye'

revelation: God showing himself to believers; this is the only way anybody can really know anything about God

role: the actions a person performs; what they do

rumalla: a highly decorated, rich cloth used to cover the Guru Granth Sahib

S

sahajdhari: a Sikh who is not born into a Sikh family; he or she believes in the Ten Gurus and the Guru Granth Sahib but has not been initiated into the Khalsa

same-sex marriage: marriage between partners of the same sex

same-sex parents: people of the same sex who are raising children together

samsara: the cycle of birth, death and rebirth

sanctity of life: the theory that life is holy and given by God, therefore only God can take it away

sangat: the company of Sikhs meeting in the presence of the Guru Granth Sahib; Sat Sangat means the 'True Congregation'

scriptures: the sacred writings of a religion

self-defence: acting to prevent harm to yourself or others

sewa: selfless service

sex before marriage: sex between two unmarried people

sex outside marriage: sex between two people where at least one of them is married to someone else; adultery; having an affair

sexual stereotyping: having a fixed general idea or image of how men and women will behave

Sikh: a learner or a disciple; a believer in the religion of Sikhism

social justice: the promotion of fairness in the distribution of wealth, opportunities, and privileges in society

special revelation: God making himself known through direct personal experience or an unusual specific event

stability: safety and security; a stable society is one in which people's rights are protected and they are able to live peaceful, productive lives without continuous and rapid change

status: how important a person's role makes them in other people's estimation

stewardship: the idea that believers have a duty to look after the environment on behalf of God

suffering: when people have to face and live with unpleasant events or conditions

sustainable development: building and progress that tries to reduce the impact on the natural world for future generations

T

takht: 'throne'; the raised platform and the structure inside on which the Guru Granth Sahib rests

terrorism: the unlawful use of violence, usually against innocent civilians, to achieve a political goal

the divine: God, gods or ultimate reality

theist: a person who believes in God

transcendent: the idea that God is beyond and outside life on earth and the universe; a quality of God

truth (sach khand): the fifth stage of liberation; the realisation of God

truthful living: following God, who is Truth, in the way in which life is led; it includes spreading the truth, and honesty and fairness in dealings with others

U

ultimate reality: an eternal, unchanging truth that governs the universe; theists believe the ultimate reality to be God or gods

universe: all there is in space, including planets, galaxies and stars; it encompasses all matter

V

Vaisakhi: the most important of the Sikh festivals; also written as Baisakhi

vegan: a person who does not eat animals or food produced by animals (such as eggs); a vegan tries not to use any products that have caused harm to animals (such as leather)

vegetarian: a person who does not eat meat or fish

violence: using actions that threaten or harm others

vision: seeing something especially in a dream or trance, that shows something about the nature of God or the afterlife

W

war: fighting between nations to resolve issues between them

weapons of mass destruction: weapons that can kill large numbers of people and/or cause great damage

wonder: marvelling at the complexity and beauty of something

Index